Freda Clough.

VI. β.

1934-5.

KING

HENRY THE EIGHTH

EDITED BY

D. NICHOL SMITH, M.A.

Reader in English, Oxford University; Editor
of the *Warwick* edition of "King Lear"

BLACKIE & SON LIMITED
LONDON AND GLASGOW

BLACKIE & SON LIMITED
50 Old Bailey, London
17 Stanhope Street, Glasgow

BLACKIE & SON (INDIA) LIMITED
Warwick House, Fort Street, Bombay

BLACKIE & SON (CANADA) LIMITED
1118 Bay Street, Toronto

Printed in Great Britain by Blackie & Son, Ltd., Glasgow

GENERAL PREFACE

In this edition of SHAKESPEARE an attempt is made to present the greater plays of the dramatist in their literary aspect, and not merely as material for the study of philology or grammar. Criticism purely verbal and textual has only been included to such an extent as may serve to help the student in the appreciation of the essential poetry. Questions of date and literary history have been fully dealt with in the Introductions, but the larger space has been devoted to the interpretative rather than the matter-of-fact order of scholarship. Aesthetic judgments are never final, but the Editors have attempted to suggest points of view from which the analysis of dramatic motive and dramatic character may be profitably undertaken. In the Notes likewise, while it is hoped that all unfamiliar expressions and allusions have been adequately explained, yet it has been thought even more important to consider the dramatic value of each scene, and the part which it plays in relation to the whole. These general principles are common to the whole series; in detail each Editor is alone responsible for the play intrusted to him.

Every volume of the series has been provided with a Glossary, an Essay upon Metre, and an Index; and Appendices have been added upon points of special interest, which could not conveniently be treated in the Introduction or the Notes. The text is based by the several Editors on that of the *Globe* edition: the only omissions made are those that are unavoidable in an edition likely to be used by young students.

By the systematic arrangement of the introductory matter, and by close attention to typographical details, every effort has been made to provide an edition that will prove convenient in use.

NOTE

THE WARWICK SHAKESPEARE has been prepared under the general editorship of Professor C. H. HERFORD, Litt.D., F.B.A., and contains the following volumes:

CONTENTS

ADDENDUM: SHAKESPEARE'S STAGE IN ITS BEARING UPON HIS DRAMA, by Prof. C. H. HERFORD, Litt. D.

INTRODUCTION.

1. DATE AND HISTORY OF THE PLAY.

The Famous History of the Life of King Henry the Eighth, the last in historical order of Shakespeare's Histories, and probably the last in date of composition, was not published separately in quarto form. It is one of the twenty plays which first appeared in the collected edition of his works issued in 1623 by his fellow-actors John Heminge and Henry Condell, and now known as the *First Folio*. The text there given is comparatively free from corruptions. The variations in the Second, Third, and Fourth Folios (1632, 1663–64, and 1685) are not always an improvement, while the emendations of modern critics are for the most part of little moment.

The Folio Text.

The date of the first performance of *Henry VIII.* is a matter of controversy. There is indisputable evidence that a play dealing with the reign of Henry VIII. was being acted on 29th June, 1613, when the Globe Theatre was destroyed by fire. There are at least three contemporary statements of this :—

Date of the First Performance.

(1) The Rev. Thomas Lorkin, writing to Sir Thomas Puckering on 30th June, 1613, says that "no longer since then yesterday, while Bourbage his companie were acting at the Globe the play of *Henry VIII.*, and there shooting of certayne chambers in way of triumph, the fire catch'd and fastened upon the thatch of the house and there burned so furiously as it consumed the whole house and all in lesse then two houres".[1]

---

[1] Quoted from Dr. Aldis Wright's *Henry VIII.* (Clarendon Press), p. vi., in which the passage was first printed fully.

(2) Sir Henry Wotton, in a letter to his nephew on 2nd July, 1613, writes: "Now, to let matters of State sleep, I will entertain you at the present with what hath happened this week at the Banks side. The Kings Players had a new Play, called *All is True*,[1] representing some principal pieces of the Raign of *Henry* 8, which was set forth with many extra-ordinary circumstances of Pomp and Majesty, even to the matting of the Stage; the Knights of the Order, with their Georges and Garter, the Guards with their embroidered Coats, and the like: sufficient in truth within a while to make greatness very familiar, if not ridiculous. Now, King *Henry* making a Masque at the Cardinal *Wolsey's* House, and certain Canons being shot off at his entry, some of the Paper, or other stuff, wherewith one of them was stopped, did light on the Thatch, where being thought at first but an idle smoak, and their eyes more attentive to the show, it kindled inwardly, and ran round like a train, consuming within less than an hour the whole House to the very grounds."[2]

(3) Edmond Howes, in his continuation of Stow's *Chronicle*, states that the burning of the Globe was due to the "negli-gent discharging of a peale of ordinance...the house being filled with people to behold the play, viz. of Henry the 8".[3]

Is the play of *Henry VIII.* here referred to that which we now have? Everything goes to prove the identity. There is nothing irrelevant in the above descriptions. The pageant-ry is excessive and sometimes interferes with the more legi-timate dramatic effects; and in the fourth scene of the first act, in which 'King Henry [is] making a masque at the Car-

---

[1] This was apparently an alternative title of *Henry VIII*. There seems to be reference to it in the Prologue (see notes). A ballad "upon the pittifull burneing of the Globe Play-House in London", has the refrain:

O sorrow, pittifull sorrow, and yet all this is true;

but its authenticity is doubtful. See Collier, *Annals of the Stage* (1879), i. pp. 371-3.

[2] *Reliquiae Wottonianae*, third edition, 1672, pp. 425, 426.

[3] *The Annales, or Generall Chronicle of England, begun first by Maister Iohn Stow, continued unto the ende of this presente yeere 1614 by Edmond Howes*, 1615, p. 926, col. 2.

dinal Wolsey's house', there is the special stage-direction
'chambers discharged'.[1] To escape the conclusion that the
existing play of *Henry VIII.* is substantially the same as that
which brought about the burning of the Globe Theatre, it is
necessary to hold, as some do, that there was another play
of the same title and nature, and identical in some of its
incidents; but there are no facts to justify this view. The
only known contemporary play dealing with Henry VIII. is
Samuel Rowley's *When you see me you know me,* and it does
not tally at any point with the above descriptions.

But was *Henry VIII.* a new play in 1613? The only
external evidence that bears directly on this question is the
statement of Wotton, who says expressly that the Globe
was burnt down during the performance of *a new play.*
The internal evidence of metre and style would likewise
point to a date towards the end of Shakespeare's career, but
the probability of a joint authorship (see section iii.) affects
its value. There remains, however, the internal evidence of
allusion to historical events. The closing scene contains a
panegyric on James I., and probably a reference to the first
settlement of Virginia in 1607, or, according to Malone, to
the state lottery granted expressly for the establishment of
English colonies in Virginia in 1612. There would thus seem
to be every reason for accepting without demur the direct
testimony of Wotton that *Henry VIII.* was 'a new play' in
1613. As it so happens, Malone is one of those[2] who hold
that the passage dealing with James I. is an interpolation,
and that the play was originally written during the lifetime
of Elizabeth. It need only be said that if there are no facts
to confute this theory there are none to support it; but it
may well be doubted, as Professor Ward[3] points out, whether

---

[1] The origin of the fire is further confirmed by a letter, dated 8th July 1613,
from John Chamberlaine to Sir Ralph Winwood: "But the burning of *the Globe*
or *Playhouse* on the Bankside on St. Peter's Day cannot escape you; which fell
out by a Peale of *Chambers* (that I know not upon what Occasion were to be
used in the Play)".—Winwood's *Memorials,* 1725, iii. 469.

[2] Most of the older Shakespearian critics, *e.g.* Theobald, Johnson, Steevens,
Collier, as well as Schlegel, Kreyssig, and Elze.

[3] *History of English Dramatic Literature* (1899), ii. 203.

Queen Elizabeth would have relished the entire picture of her father's and mother's love-making, and the contrast in which it stands to the treatment of the character of Katharine. Others again hold that *Henry VIII.* was written immediately after the accession of James I., and that the closing scene was intended to show the respect in which Elizabeth's memory was held and the anticipations entertained of her successor.[1] There is less to be said against this view, for the allusion to the events of 1607 or 1612 is at the best conjectural; but any theory that urges a date earlier than 1613 for the first performance, if not made expressly to suit preconceived notions, is not supported by any evidence. Whatever arguments may be urged against the year for which we have Wotton's testimony, it must be remembered that the trial in *Henry VIII.* is a companion picture to the trial in the *Winter's Tale*, that internal evidence would seem to show that they were written about the same time, and that the *Winter's Tale* cannot be assigned to an earlier date than 1610.

There is every indication that the play was popular at the beginning of the seventeenth century. It was revived in

Stage History.   1663, without undergoing the extensive 'adaptations' which Shakespearian plays usually met with at the hands of the Restoration dramatists. Langbaine, in his *Account of the English Dramatic Poets*, says that 'this play frequently appears on the present stage',[2] and Pepys refers to it as 'the so much cried-up play of Henry the Eighth'.[3] It appears to have won much of its popularity from its pageantry. Its coronation ceremony ensured its success in 1727, the year of the coronation of George II.[4] Dr. Johnson, writing in 1755, says that 'the play of Henry

---

[1] Hunter, *New Illustrations of Shakespeare*, ii. 101.

[2] Langbaine, p. 457 (ed. 1691).

[3] *Diary*, 1st January, 1663–64. On 27th January he speaks of a play 'which for show, they say, exceeds Henry the Eighth'.

[4] See Genest, *English Stage*, iii. pp. 197–209. Professor Ward appears to be wrong in stating (*Eng. Dram. Literature*, ii. p. 209) that *Henry VIII.* was then 'represented forty times in succession'. The coronation ceremony, which ultimately separated from *Henry VIII.* and tacked on to other plays, alone had this long run.

the Eighth is one of those which still keeps possession of the
stage by the splendour of its pageantry.   The coronation
about forty years ago drew the people together in multitudes
for a great part of the winter.   Yet pomp is not the only
merit of this play.'   At the beginning of this century it was
performed by Kemble, with his sister Mrs. Siddons in the
part of Katharine; and a few years ago it was revived by
Sir Henry Irving.   It is interesting to note that, while the
title-rôle used formerly to be played by the leading actor,
Kemble and Irving each took the part of Wolsey.   We learn
from Boswell that Mrs. Siddons considered Katharine 'the
most natural' character in Shakespeare, and that Dr. Johnson
agreed with her.

2. THE SOURCE OF THE INCIDENTS.

The chief source of the materials for *Henry VIII.*, as
for the other Histories, is the second edition of Raphael
Holinshed's *Chronicle* (1587).   It is often said   Holinshed,
that certain passages were directly suggested   Hall, and Foxe.
by Cavendish's *Life of Wolsey*, which, though not published
till 1641, was widely circulated in MS. during Shakespeare's
lifetime; but it is probable that the dramatist (or dramatists)
was indebted only to the passages from this biography added
in Holinshed's second edition.   It may be safely said that
there is no detail apparently due to the *Life of Wolsey* which
might not as well have been taken from the *Chronicle*,
and there is certainly one instance in which a divergence,
dramatically unnecessary, from facts expressly stated by
Cavendish, is best explained by an inaccuracy in Holinshed's
transcript.[1]   (See note on i. 4. 50.)   Edward Hall's *Chronicle*,
more correctly called *The Union of the Two Noble and
Illustre Famelies of Lancastre and Yorke* (1548), supplies an

---

[1] Holinshed, however, was not indebted to Cavendish directly.   He incorporated
the transcription made by John Stow in the *Annals or General Chronicle* (1580).
'Here it is necessary', says Holinshed, 'to add that notable discourse, which I
find in Iohn Stow, concerning the state of the cardinall, both in the yeares of his
youth and in his settled age' (p. 917).   Stow acknowledges his indebtedness to
Cavendish (ed. 1615, p. 500).

occasional detail. As this is another book from which
Holinshed borrowed largely, it would appear at first sight
that it need not have been consulted directly; but there are
certain points in the drama which remove any doubt on
this score. (See note on v. 3. 10–15.) Foxe's *Actes and
Monumentes of the Churche* (first edition, 1563) affords most
of the material of the fifth act: there is no question here of
Holinshed being an intermediary, for the collaborators in
the second edition of the all-absorbing *Chronicle* did not
place Foxe under contribution.

Holinshed, Hall, and Foxe are probably the only books
which were consulted in the composition of the drama; at
least they are alone sufficient to have supplied all its historical
details. A certain divergence was necessary to bring the
material into a dramatic setting, and the large number of
events dealt with in *Henry VIII.—e.g.* the fall of Buckingham, the divorce of Katharine, the fall of Wolsey, the rise
and marriage of Anne Bullen, the birth of Elizabeth, the rise
of Cranmer, &c.—has made this divergence greater than in
some of the other Histories. In none, however, is there a
larger debt in the matter of phraseology than in *Henry VIII.*
Certain passages, as may be judged from the Appendix, are
little more than a versified form of Holinshed's prose, and
occasionally the meaning of a difficult phrase can be definitely
settled only by reference to the statement on which it was
modelled (*e.g.* see note on i. 1. 86, 87). The divergences from
the historical authorities may best be treated under four
heads: (1) Changes in Time and Place; (2) Invention of Incidents; (3) Changes affecting Character; (4) New Characters.

(1) The play covers a period of twenty-four years—from
the Field of the Cloth of Gold (1520) to Cranmer's appearance before the council (1544). The events
Changes in
Time and Place. are represented as happening on a few days—
seven, according to Daniel—with intervals. The chronolo-
gical sequence of events is not followed strictly, and perhaps
none of the Histories contains more anachronisms than
Henry VIII. But in most of the rearrangements of the
historical events—the chief of which are pointed out in the

notes—there is an evident dramatic purpose. Another form of historical inaccuracy consists in the compression of several events into one great action, the order in which they actually happened being preserved. An excellent example is afforded by the second scene of the third act. When Wolsey enters he is still at the summit of his power, and when the curtain falls he has uttered his last words; but historically there was an interval of more than a year between his disgrace and his death, and during that time he had been pardoned and restored to some of his offices. (See notes on *Dramatis Personæ*.) This compression is the very essential of dramatic representation. It produces a unity of effect and heightens the intensity by dealing only with what is salient, and, though false to the facts of history, is true to the spirit.[1] It is for a similar reason that the scenes are laid only at London, Westminster, and Kimbolton, though the preliminary examination of Buckingham's servants (i. 2), and the christening of Elizabeth (v. 5), actually occurred at Greenwich, and Wolsey uttered his last words in Leicester Abbey.

(2) The divergence from Holinshed consists mostly in the rearrangement of details. Of the incidents which have been specially invented, the most noticeable are the meeting of Henry and Anne Bullen in the New Incidents. masque at York-place, and Wolsey's inadvertent delivery to the king of an inventory of his own private wealth. Both are in perfect keeping: the former emphasizes the fact that it was hardly on conscientious grounds that Henry desired Katharine's divorce, while the latter makes Wolsey the victim of the very mistake whereby in actual life he had procured the ruin of a rival. (See note on iii. 2. 124.) Of the great scenes in the drama, those least indebted to Holinshed deal with Katharine; the description of her death is in the main purely imaginative.

(3) There is little to be noted under the third head. The characters of *Henry VIII.* are largely dramatic adaptations from Holinshed. That Wolsey appears as the incarnation of

1 Hence Froude declared that 'the most perfect English history which exists is to be found in the historical plays of Shakespeare' (*Short Studies*, ii. p. 596).

pride and self-seeking ambition, and that his great states-
Changes affect-
ing Character. manship is not even suggested, is to be accounted
for by the prejudiced picture which is given by
the chronicler; and this is the only reason why, on the other
hand, Buckingham, of whom the modern estimate is not high,
figures as a courageous and high-souled patriot. Dramatic
representation tends to make a character either typically good
or typically bad, by throwing the outstanding qualities into
stronger relief. Katharine, for instance, is invested with a
nobility which she hardly has in Holinshed. But such
changes are necessary in a drama for the sake of clearness
and distinction; and they cannot be said to make a character
untrue. The chief departure from Holinshed is in the treatment of Norfolk and the Earl of Surrey (see notes on *Dramatis
Personæ*); but it is doubtful if it was deliberate, and, as it
does not materially affect the character of the two nobles, it
may more properly be considered simply an anachronism.

(4) The *Porter*, the *Old Lady*, and *Patience* are new
characters. The first recalls the more famous porter in
New Charac-
ters. *Macbeth*, and the second has a certain similarity
to the nurse in *Romeo and Juliet*. Perhaps
Brandon should be included, though his introduction seems
to be due merely to confusion with another character. (See
note i. 1. 198.)

Mention has been made above of Samuel Rowley's *When
you see me you know me*,[1] as a contemporary play dealing
Rowley's *When
you see me you
know me*. with much the same subject. If *Henry VIII.*
is indebted to Holinshed for the outline of the
story, it seems to owe to this play several of its
minor details. Many of the similarities of the two plays are
to be explained by their material being derived from a common source, but certain coincidences point to the direct influence of the one on the other. Attention was drawn to this
by Professor Karl Elze, who, in the introduction to his edition
of Rowley's play, notes the following points of resemblance.

---

[1] The full title is *When you see me you know me, or the famous Chronicle
Historie of King Henry the Eight, with the birth and vertuous life of Edward
Prince of Wales*. It was first printed in 1605.

"King Henry...with both poets makes frequent use of his favourite ejaculation Ha!;...by both poets he is exhibited leaning on the shoulder of some one of his intimate courtiers, by both walking in the gallery as was his 'custom always of the afternoon'. Both poets show the king's angry impatience when interrupted in his privacy; the only difference is that with Rowley it is Wolsey who provokes the king's rage by his impertinence, whereas with Shakespeare the dukes of Suffolk and Norfolk have to 'endure the storm' on such an occasion. The unceremonious intrusion of an overhasty messenger into the king's presence and his angry repulsion by the latter have been transferred by Shakespeare to the dying-scene of Queen Katharine...The incident of the king's sending his ring to Cranmer is also common to both poets... The fatal influence which the cardinal exercises over the king is by both poets ascribed to his wonderful eloquence... Both poets derive the cardinal's downfall almost in the self-same words from the same causes: from his extorting large sums from the people and heaping up immense treasures with which to attain the last object of his ambition, the papal throne; from the arrogant formula '*Ego et Rex meus*', which Wolsey did not scruple to employ in his correspondence with the pope and foreign princes; and lastly, from his impudence in stamping the cardinal's hat on the king's coin...Some critics may be inclined to explain these coincidences by the circumstance that both poets borrowed most of their materials from Holinshed, who indeed enumerates the above facts among the charges raised against the cardinal...This was certainly the common source of both poets, but why did they select from among the long list of charges the very same items for introduction into their plays? And what common source can be found out for those scenes, where the births of the Prince of Wales and Princess Elizabeth are looked forward to and announced? Rowley makes the king say:

> Ladies, attend her! (viz. the queen); Countess of Salisbury!
>   Sister Mary!
> Who first brings word that Henry hath a son
> Shall be rewarded well.

To which the fool adds: 'Ay, I'll be his surety: but do you hear, wenches, she that brings the first tidings, howsoever it fall out, let her be sure to say the child's like his father, or else she shall have nothing'. In strict accordance with this artful precept the old lady in Shakespeare, who bears the message of the queen's delivery, proclaims the likeness in the strongest terms:

> 'T is like you
> As cherry is to cherry—

The amount of the recompense is not mentioned by Rowley. ...Shakespeare's old lady receives a hundred marks."

Professor Elze's list is by no means exhaustive. Other points of similarity are mentioned in the notes. The allusion in v. 3. 30 is explained at once by reference to Rowley:

> Much bloodshed there is now in Germany
> About this difference in religion,
> With Lutherans, Arians, and Anabaptists,
> As half the province of Helvetia
> Is with their tumults almost quite destroyed (pp. 56, 57).

The letter to the chamberlain (ii. 2. 1–8) may have been suggested by

> Another citizen there is, complains
> Of one belonging to the cardinal,
> That in his master's name hath taken up
> Commodities (pp. 33, 34).

Most interesting of all is Wolsey's criticism of Katharine Parr:

> Holy Saint Peter shield his majesty,
> She is the hope of Luther's heresy:
> If she be queen, the protestants will swell,
> And Cranmer, tutor to the Prince of Wales,
> Will boldly speak 'gainst Rome's religion.
> But, bishops, we'll to court immediately
> To plot the downfall of these Lutherans...
> I do suspect that Latimer and Ridley,
> Chief teachers of the fair Elizabeth,
> Are not sound catholics. (p. 39.)

In *Henry VIII.* this is Wolsey's criticism of Anne Bullen
(see note iii. 2. 99); while the remarks on Latimer and Ridley
correspond with Gardiner's taunt at Cranmer and Cromwell
(v. 3. 80, &c.).

3. THE AUTHORSHIP OF THE PLAY.

By far the most difficult question presented by *Henry VIII.*
is that concerning its authorship.   What may be called the
orthodox view nowadays is that it is the joint- *Three Main*
work of Shakespeare and Fletcher, and perhaps *Theories.*
of even another dramatist; but a strong number still maintain the old opinion that it is wholly Shakespeare's, while
a third party do not consider it to be Shakespeare's at all.
The question is entirely one of internal evidence.   As early
as 1758, Roderick pointed out[1] three peculiarities in the
versification of *Henry VIII.*: (1) the uncommonly frequent
redundant syllable; (2) the remarkable character of the
cæsura; and (3) the clashing of the emphasis with the
cadence of the metre; but he confessed himself unable to
draw any conclusion from them.   The matter received only
passing attention till 1850, when the late Mr. Spedding investigated it in a paper entitled "Who wrote Shakespeare's
Henry VIII.?"[2]   The weak and disappointing 1. *Joint Author-*
effect of the play as a whole, the want of unity *ship of Shake-*
in both spirit and action, and the metrical pecu- *speare and
Fletcher—*
liarities, led him to undertake the examination, *Spedding's*
to which he was further prompted by a casual *Argument.*
remark of the late Lord Tennyson, that 'many passages in
Henry VIII. were very much in the manner of Fletcher'.
He first criticised the play on æsthetic grounds, 'with an
eye open to notice the larger differences of effect, but without staying to examine small points', and he then verified
his results by metrical tests.   As his method has been the

[1] In Thomas Edwards's *Canons of Criticism*, sixth edition, 1758.
[2] First published in the *Gentleman's Magazine* of August, 1850; reprinted in
the *New Shakspere Society's Transactions*, 1874.

pioneer and model of further investigations on the authenticity of other plays usually ascribed to Shakespeare,[1] the
following lengthy quotation may not be out of place.

"The opening of the play,—the conversation between
Buckingham, Norfolk, and Abergavenny,—seemed to have
the full stamp of Shakespeare, in his latest manner: the same
close-packed expression; the same life, and reality, and
freshness; the same rapid and abrupt turnings of thought,
so quick that language can hardly follow fast enough; the
same impatient activity of intellect and fancy, which having
once disclosed an idea cannot wait to work it orderly out;
the same daring confidence in the resources of language,
which plunges headlong into a sentence without knowing
how it is to come forth; the same careless metre which
disdains to produce its harmonious effects by the ordinary
devices, yet is evidently subject to a master of harmony;
the same entire freedom from book-language and common-
place; all the qualities, in short, which distinguish the
magical hand which has never yet been successfully imi-
tated.

"In the scene in the council-chamber which follows (Act i.
Sc. 2), where the characters of Katharine and Wolsey are
brought out, I found the same characteristics equally strong.

"But the instant I entered upon the third scene, in which
the Lord Chamberlain, Lord Sands, and Lord Lovel con-
verse, I was conscious of a total change. I felt as if I had
passed suddenly out of the language of nature into the
language of the stage, or of some conventional mode of
conversation. The structure of the verse was quite different
and full of mannerism. The expression became suddenly
diffuse and languid. The wit wanted mirth and character.
And all this was equally true of the supper scene which
closes the first Act.

"The second Act brought me back to the tragic vein, but
it was not the tragic vein of Shakespeare. When I compared
the eager, impetuous, and fiery language of Buckingham in
the first Act with the languid and measured cadences of his

[1] So says Dr. Furnivall, *N.S.S. Trans.*, 1874, p. 242.

farewell speech, I felt that the difference was too great to be accounted for by the mere change of situation, without supposing also a change of writers. The presence of death produces great changes in men, but no such change as we have here.

"When in like manner I compared the Henry and Wolsey of the scene which follows (Act ii. Sc. 2) with the Henry and Wolsey of the council-chamber (Act i. Sc. 2), I perceived a difference scarcely less striking. The dialogue, through the whole scene, sounded still slow and artificial.

"The next scene brought another sudden change. And, as in passing from the second to the third scene of the first Act I had seemed to be passing all at once out of the language of nature into that of convention, so in passing from the second to the third scene of the second Act (in which Anne Bullen appears, I may say for the first time, for in the supper scene she was merely a conventional court lady without any character at all), I seemed to pass not less suddenly from convention back again into nature. And when I considered that this short and otherwise insignificant passage contains all that we ever see of Anne (for it is necessary to forget her former appearance) and yet how clearly the character comes out, how very a woman she is, and yet how distinguishable from any other individual woman, I had no difficulty in acknowledging that the sketch came from the same hand which drew Perdita.

"Next follows the famous trial scene. And here I could as little doubt that I recognized the same hand to which we owe the trial of Hermione. When I compared the language of Henry and of Wolsey throughout this scene to the end of the Act, with their language in the council-chamber (Act i. Sc. 2), I found that it corresponded in all essential features: when I compared it with their language in the second scene of the second Act, I perceived that it was altogether different. Katharine also, as she appears in this scene, was exactly the same person as she was in the council-chamber; but when I went on to the first scene of the third Act, which represents her interview with Wolsey and Campeius, I found her as much changed as Buckingham was after his sentence, though without any alteration of circumstances to account for an alteration of temper. Indeed the whole of this scene seemed to have all the peculiarities of Fletcher, both in conception, language, and versification, without a single feature that reminded me of Shakespeare; and, since in both passages the true narrative of Cavendish is followed minutely and carefully, and both are therefore copies from the same original and in the same style of art, it was the more easy to compare them with each other.

"In the next scene (Act iii. Sc. 2) I seemed again to get out of Fletcher into Shakespeare; though probably not into Shakespeare pure; a scene by another hand perhaps which Shakespeare had only remodelled, or a scene by Shakespeare which another hand had worked upon to make it fit the place. The speeches interchanged between Henry and Wolsey seemed to be entirely Shakespeare's; but in the altercation between Wolsey and the lords which follows, I could recognize little or nothing of his peculiar manner, while many passages were strongly marked with the favourite Fletcherian cadence;[1] and as for the famous 'Farewell, a long farewell', etc., though associated by means of Enfield's Speaker with my earliest notions of Shakespeare, it appeared (now that my mind was opened to entertain the doubt) to belong entirely and unquestionably to Fletcher.

"Of the 4th Act I did not so well know what to think. For the most part it seemed to bear evidence of a more vigorous hand than Fletcher's, with less mannerism, especially in the description of the coronation, and the character of Wolsey; and yet it had not to my mind the freshness and originality of Shakespeare. It was pathetic and graceful, but one could see how it was done. Katharine's last speeches, however, smacked strongly again of Fletcher. And altogether it seemed to me that if this Act had occurred in one of the plays written by Beaumont and Fletcher in conjunction, it would probably have been thought that both of them had had a hand in it.

---

[1] Spedding quotes in a foot-note, iii. 2. 238–244.

"The first scene of the 5th Act, and the opening of the second, I should again have confidently ascribed to Shakespeare, were it not that the whole passage seemed so strangely out of place. I could only suppose (what may indeed be supposed well enough if my conjecture with regard to the authorship of the several parts be correct), that the task of putting the whole together had been left to an inferior hand; in which case I should consider this to be a genuine piece of Shakespeare's work, spoiled by being introduced where it has no business. In the execution of the christening scene, on the other hand (in spite again of the earliest and strongest associations), I could see no evidence of Shakespeare's hand at all; while in point of *design* it seemed inconceivable that a judgment like his could have been content with a conclusion so little in harmony with the prevailing spirit and purpose of the piece."

Mr. Spedding then proceeded to examine the style of the play, and concluded that in certain passages it bore absolutely no resemblance to that of Shakespeare at any stage of its development. He cites as an example Buckingham's farewell speech (ii. 1. 55–78). In Shakespeare's earlier plays, he says, "when his versification was regular and his language comparatively diffuse, there is none of the studied variety of cadence which we find here; and by the time his versification had acquired more variety, the current of his thought had become more gushing, rapid, and full of eddies; not to add that at no period whatever in the development of his style was the proportion of thought and fancy to words and images so small as it appears in this speech of Buckingham's".

Lastly he applied the metrical test. The redundant syllable, on which Roderick had remarked, he found to be disproportionately common only in those scenes which, on æsthetic grounds, he had already assigned to Fletcher. In those parts which he considered to be Shakespeare's, it was no more frequent than in other late plays, such as *Cymbeline* and the *Winter's Tale*. He tabulated his results as follows:—

Act.	Scene.	Lines.	Red. Syll.	Prop'n.	Author.
I.	1.	225	63	1 to 3·5	[Shakespeare.
	2.	215	74	— 2·9	,,
	3 and 4.	172	100	— 1·7	Fletcher.
II.	1.	164	97	— 1·6	,,
	2.	129	77	— 1·6	,,
	3.	107	41	— 2·6	Shakespeare.
	4.	230	72	— 3·1	,,
III.	1.	166	119	— 1·3	Fletcher.
	2.[1]	193	62	— 3	Shakespeare.
	3.	257	152	— 1·6	Fletcher.
IV.	1.	116	57	— 2	,,
	2.	80	51	— 1·5	,,
	3.	93	51	— 1·8	,,
V.	1.	176	68	— 2·5	Shakespeare (altered).
	2.	217	115	— 1·8	Fletcher.
	3.	Almost all prose.			,,
	4.	73	44	— 1·6	,,]

He could find nothing in the subject or character of the
several scenes to account for these metrical differences.
"The light and loose conversation at the end of the first
Act, the plaintive and laboured oration in the second, the
querulous and passionate altercation in the third, the pathetic
sorrows of Wolsey, the tragic death of Katharine, the high
poetic prophecy of Cranmer, are equally distinguished by
this peculiarity. A distinction so broad and so uniform,
running through so large a proportion of the same piece,
cannot have been accidental; and the more closely it is
examined the more clearly will it appear that the metre in
these two sets of scenes is managed upon entirely different
principles, and bears evidence of different workmen…
The general difference may easily be made evident by
placing any undoubted specimen of Shakespeare's later
workmanship by the side of the one, and of Fletcher's
middle workmanship by the side of the other; the identity
in both cases will be felt at once."

Mr. Spedding's views were no sooner published than it was
found that another Shakespearian scholar, Mr. Samuel Hick-

---

[1] As far as the exit of King Henry.

son, had already investigated the matter independently, and
had arrived at identical results, except that he   Other Metrical
did not detect a third hand in Act v., scene i.   Tests.
The strong presumption of a joint authorship afforded by
this coincidence has been strengthened by other verse tests
(*e.g.* rhymes, double-endings, unstopped lines,[1] &c.) applied
by Mr. Fleay, Dr. Furnivall,[2] and others. Dr. Abbott says
emphatically that "the fact that in *Henry VIII.*, and in no
other play of Shakespeare's, *constant exceptions are found
to this rule* (that the extra syllable is rarely a monosyllable),
seems to me a sufficient proof that Shakespeare did not
write that play". Certainly the verse tests are as decisive
as they can be against Shakespeare's sole authorship.[3]

There are others, however, who refuse to depart from the
old view that the play is entirely Shakespeare's. Their case
has been stated most cogently by Mr. Swin-   2. Shakespeare's
burne in his *Study of Shakespeare*. Admirer of   Sole
Fletcher as he is, he cannot believe that he   Authorship—
could have risen to the poetical heights attained   Defence.
in the passages ascribed to him. He admits that "much of
the play is externally as like the usual style of Fletcher as it
is unlike the usual style of Shakespeare"; but he contends
that the question is "whether we can find one scene, one
speech, one passage, which in spirit, in scope, in purpose,
bears the same or any comparable resemblance to the work
of Fletcher". The farewell speech of Buckingham, for
instance, is at first sight like the finest speeches of the kind
in Fletcher, but a closer examination of it, or of the farewell
speech of Wolsey, will show a "loftier self-control and
severer self-command" than Fletcher has ever shown elsewhere. "And yet, if this were all," he continues, "we might
be content to believe that the dignity of the subject and the
high example of his present associate had for once lifted the
natural genius of Fletcher above itself. But the fine and
subtle criticism of Mr. Spedding has in the main, I think,

---

[1] See Appendix B.   [2] See *N.S.S. Trans.*, 1874, p. 23[*], 24[*].
[3] Prof. Dowden holds that Mr. Spedding's argument is conclusive (*Primer*,
p. 153).

successfully and clearly indicated the lines of demarcation undeniably discernible in this play between the severer style of certain scenes or speeches and the laxer and more fluid style of others; between the graver, solider, more condensed parts of the apparently composite work, and those which are clearer, thinner, more diffused and diluted in expression. If under the latter head we had to class such passages only as the dying speech of Buckingham and the christening speech of Cranmer, it might after all be almost impossible to resist the internal evidence of Fletcher's handiwork. Certainly we hear the same soft continuous note of easy eloquence, level and limpid as a stream of crystalline transparence, in the plaintive adieu of the condemned statesman and the panegyrical prophecy of the favoured prelate. If this, I say, were all, we might admit that there is nothing —I have already admitted it—in either passage beyond the poetic reach of Fletcher. But on the hypothesis so ably maintained by the editor of Bacon there hangs no less a consequence than this: that we must assign to the same hand the crowning glory of the whole poem, the death-scene of Katharine. Now, if Fletcher could have written that scene—a scene on which the only criticism ever passed, the only commendation ever bestowed, by the verdict of successive centuries, has been that of tears and silence—if Fletcher could have written a scene so far beyond our applause, so far above our acclamation, then the memory of no great poet has ever been so grossly wronged, so shamefully defrauded of its highest claim to honour. But, with all reverence for that memory, I must confess that I cannot bring myself to believe it. Any explanation appears to me more probable than this. Considering with what care every relic of his work was once and again collected by his posthumous editors—even to the attribution, not merely of plays in which he can have taken only the slightest part, but of plays in which we know that he had no share at all—I cannot believe that his friends would have let by far the brightest jewel in his crown rest unreclaimed in the then less popular treasure-house of Shakespeare." Mr. Swinburne recognizes the plausibility of Mr. Spedding's hypothesis, but he contends that the evidence of style is not alone sufficient to attribute to Fletcher passages which, to judge from his accredited work, are far outside his poetic range. "We admit, then," he continues, "that this play offers us in some not unimportant passages the single instance of a style not elsewhere precisely or altogether traceable in Shakespeare; that no exact parallel to it can be found among his other plays; and that if not the partial work it may certainly be taken as the general model of Fletcher in his tragic poetry. On the other hand, we contend that its exceptional quality might perhaps be explicable as a tentative essay in a new line by one who tried so many styles before settling into his latest; and that, without far stronger, clearer, and completer proof than has yet been or can ever be advanced, the question is not solved but merely evaded by the assumption of a double authorship." Whatever the value of this suggested solution of the peculiarities in style, Mr. Swinburne has at least shown that Fletcher's co-operation is not to be accepted hastily.[1]

A third party fails to discover any trace whatever of Shakespeare in *Henry VIII*. The theory has been advanced by Mr. Robert Boyle[2] that the play "was not written by Fletcher and Shakespeare, but by Fletcher and Massinger, to supply the place of the lost Shakespeare play, *All is True*, destroyed in the Globe fire of 1613". He assigns the same scenes to Fletcher as Mr. Spedding had done, with the exception of the coronation scene (iv. 1); this and the rest of the play he claims for Massinger, largely on linguistic considerations.

3. Non-Shake-
spearian
Authorship—
Boyle and
Wright.

---

[1] Among those who do not believe in the divided authorship are Singer, Knight, Ulrici, Elze, and Halliwell-Phillipps. Professor Ward has gone over to the Spedding party in the new edition of his *Eng. Dram. Literature*. He had held that the metrical peculiarities might be regarded as "after all, only extreme developments of tendencies which indisputably become stronger in Shakespeare's versification with the progress of time"; but he now admits that "such an explanation cannot in the present instance be held to be sufficient", and says definitely that "the assumption of a co-operation on Fletcher's part in *Henry VIII.*, as we possess it, may be regarded as removed beyond reasonable doubt". (ii., pp. 206, 207.)

[2] *N.S.S. Transactions*, 1880–5.

Dr. Aldis Wright[1] likewise fails to recognize the hand of Shakespeare anywhere, and draws attention to the large number of 'un-Shakespearian' words and phrases; but he does not offer any suggestion as to the real author or authors. So far this party has few declared adherents.

It may safely be said that it is impossible to arrive at a satisfactory solution. There is no external evidence of any value. The play was included in the First Folio; but this collection also contained *Titus Andronicus*, in which there is every reason to believe that Shakespeare had little share. The contemporary references to the burning of the Globe Theatre state merely that it was 'the play of *Henry VIII.*' which was being acted at the time, and give no hint as to who wrote it. The verse tests, whatever their value may be, point decisively to a joint authorship. And in many passages the style is not what we associate with Shakespeare. There is no 'thinking from metaphor to metaphor', no crowding in of thought upon thought. The images are worked out steadily to their conclusion, and, far from blending with one another, are usually separated by a plain and direct statement. But the highest test is the consideration of the play as a whole. The most striking feature is the absolute lack of unity. The beginning has little connection with the middle, and neither has any connection with the end. This fact alone makes it impossible for us to believe that the play we now have was written by Shakespeare entirely at one period. There is the alternative that he hurriedly worked up an earlier draft of the play; but this explanation implies, no less than the other, the failing of his artistic sense. The faulty construction is undoubtedly the most convincing argument against Shakespeare's sole authorship. But if another hand can be traced in *Henry VIII.*, is it Fletcher's? Both metre and style point to him. Yet the passages with which he is credited are the finest in the play,[2]

Recapitulation.

Preface to Clarendon Press edition of *Henry VIII.*

[2] Dr. Johnson, for instance, considered the death scene of Katharine (iv. 2) "above any other part of Shakespeare's tragedies, and perhaps above any scene of any other poet".

and nowhere in his undoubted work does he attain to their height. An explanation of this superiority is that Fletcher may have been employed to replace those parts of a play by Shakespeare which were burnt, presumably, in the Globe fire of 1613, and that he worked up what he recollected of the original play.[1] On the other hand, it has been suggested that, in such a passage as Wolsey's farewell to Cromwell, Shakespeare may have given 'proof of his versatility by echoing in a glorified key the habitual strain of Fletcher, his colleague and virtual successor'.[2] Both conjectures are plausible. Unfortunately there is not one item of positive information to bear out either.

4. CRITICAL APPRECIATION.

It remains for us to consider the play as it stands, without regard either to the source of its incidents or the circumstances of its composition.

When Pepys described *Henry VIII.* as 'made up of a great many patches', he passed one criticism on the Elizabethan drama with which we are not inclined to quarrel. In every well-constructed play there *Unity of Action.* must be a central incident, evolved directly out of the previous events and in itself beginning the denouement; otherwise the play will be only a collection of episodes. Without a climax there can be no dramatic unity. There is no such central incident in *Henry VIII.* The numerous episodes are whimsically pieced together, and some of them seem to be introduced only for their own sake. The action and characters are at first grouped round Wolsey; but his part is ended by the third act, and his disappearance has absolutely no bearing on what follows. The fourth act is taken up with the coronation of Anne Bullen, who remains in the background throughout the whole play, and with the death of Katharine, who has hitherto divided with Wolsey all the

[1] F. G. Fleay, *Shakespeare Manual*, p. 171. After Mr. Boyle's paper, Mr. Fleay declared in favour of a triple authorship,—Shakespeare, Fletcher, and Massinger—only I. 2, II. 3 and 4 being assigned to Shakespeare.

[2] Sidney Lee, *Life of Shakespeare*, p. 262. He, however, also favours triple authorship, assigning to Shakespeare I. 1, II. 3 and 4, III. 2. 1–203, and V. 1.

interest of the drama. In the fifth act the leading part is taken by Cranmer, who now appears for the first time. The long episode of his appearance before the council, whatever are its merits in itself, is merely an unnecessary preliminary to the christening of Elizabeth, though it happens to bring out some of the better qualities in Henry. And, in the earlier part of the play, the prominence given to Buckingham is, if Wolsey is not the real hero, out of all proportion. Mere episodes are treated with as much importance as the main facts of the story, and the consequent confusion is so great that it is difficult to discover the dramatic motive. There is no play of Shakespeare chargeable with a like disregard of the unity of action. His comedies sometimes contain as many as four or five distinct threads, but he weaves these together with such skill that the total effect is complete. And in the histories, where he has not the same liberty of manipulating the plot, he contrives to give dramatic intensity by centring the action in the historical crisis. In *Richard II.*, for instance, the story begins when the faults of Richard's character are shaping to his fall and Bolingbroke's rise. But in *Henry VIII.* we have merely a succession of incidents; and the dramatic motive which should unite them is so obscure that it has been possible for a critic of Elze's standing to suggest that it is a glorification of the downfall of Catholicism and the approaching dawn of Protestantism. Coleridge implied a severe criticism on the structure of the play in classifying it by itself as ‘a sort of historical masque or show-play’. Hertzberg has gone further in calling it ‘a chronicle-history with three and a half catastrophes, varied by a marriage and a coronation pageant, ending abruptly with the baptism of a child,...and all this loosely connected by the nominal hero’. Drastic as this criticism is, it is impossible to deny its justice.

But there is an even graver defect, of which a like example is not to be found in Shakespeare, and which is the strongest of all arguments against his sole authorship. *Unity of Spirit.* There is no unity of thought or spirit. “The strongest sympathies which have been awakened in us”, says Mr. Spedding in a striking passage, "run opposite to the course of the action. Our sympathy is for the grief and goodness of Queen Katharine, while the course of the action requires us to entertain as a theme of joy and compensatory satisfaction the coronation of Anne Bullen and the birth of her daughter; which are in fact a part of Katharine's injury, and amount to little less than the ultimate triumph of wrong. For throughout the play the king's cause is not only felt by us, but represented to us, as a bad one. We *hear*, indeed, of conscientious scruples as to the legality of his first marriage; but we are not made, nor indeed asked, to believe that they are sincere, or to recognize in his new marriage either the hand of Providence, or the consummation of any worthy object, or the victory of any of those more common frailties of humanity with which we can sympathize. The mere caprice of passion drives the king into the commission of what seems a great iniquity; our compassion for the victim of it is elaborately excited; no attempt is made to awaken any counter-sympathy for *him*: yet his passion has its way, and is crowned with all felicity, present and to come. The effect is much like that which would have been produced by the *Winter's Tale* if Hermione had died in the fourth act in consequence of the jealous tyranny of Leontes, and the play had ended with the coronation of a new queen and the christening of a new heir, no period of remorse intervening. It is as if Nathan's rebuke to David had ended, not with the doom of death to the child just born, but with a prophetic promise of the felicities of Solomon...I know no other play in Shakespeare which is chargeable with a fault like this, none in which the moral sympathy of the spectator is not carried along with the main current of action to the end. In all the historical tragedies a providence may be seen presiding over the development of events, as just and relentless as the fate in a Greek tragedy. Even in *Henry IV.*, where the comic element predominates, we are never allowed to exult in the success of the wrong-doer, or to forget the penalties which are due to guilt. And if it be true that in the romantic comedies our moral sense does sometimes suffer a passing shock, it is never owing to an error in the general design, but always to some incongruous circumstance in the original story which has lain in the way and not been entirely got rid of, and which after all offends us rather as an incident improbable in itself than as one for which our sympathy is unjustly demanded. The singularity of *Henry VIII.* is that while four-fifths of the play are occupied in matters which are to make us incapable of mirth,—Be sad as we would make you, &c.,—the remaining fifth is devoted to joy and triumph, and ends with universal festivity." It may be urged that *Henry VIII.*, in its lack of poetical justice, is untrue even to the facts of history, for the birth of Elizabeth did not make an end of the troubles of the reign. If retribution has no place in the drama, it certainly figured prominently in the real life.

Henry is the central figure only in so far as he keeps the stage throughout the play and is connected directly or
The Leading
Characters. indirectly with all its incidents. In the first four acts he is subservient to Katharine and Wolsey, and even in the fifth he arouses less interest than Cranmer. We know that he must control the events of the drama, but we do not feel that he does so. Unlike the kings of Shakespeare's great Histories, who seem to embody the spirit of their time, he is a hero only in name. His faults and shortcomings are carefully brought out, his ruthlessness, sensuality, and cruelty, but they are presented in such a way that we regard them leniently; and the result is that he is a somewhat indeterminate character, the more especially as it is only towards the end of the play that we have a glimpse of his better qualities. Herein he is in striking contrast to Katharine. The magnificent portrayal of her uprightness and charity, her quiet dignity and calm resignation, has been universally admired. "The meek sorrows and virtuous distress of Katharine", says Dr. Johnson, "have furnished some scenes which may be justly numbered among the greatest efforts of tragedy." But when the critic goes on to state that "the genius of Shakespeare comes in and goes out with Katharine", and that "every other part may be

easily conceived and easily written", it is impossible to continue our assent in view of the description of the fall of Wolsey. Apart from its intrinsic power and beauty, it has a special interest in being the only passage in the play which enforces a moral lesson. The fall of Wolsey is the punishment of unscrupulous self-interest. Here alone have we the poet's utterance on the greater questions of humanity. But this is only an episode. As a whole, the play is lacking in a fundamental idea. Its power rests entirely on the greatness of individual passages.

DRAMATIS PERSONÆ

KING HENRY THE EIGHTH.
CARDINAL WOLSEY.
CARDINAL CAMPEIUS.
CAPUCIUS, Ambassador from the Emperor Charles V.
CRANMER, Archbishop of Canterbury.
DUKE OF NORFOLK.
DUKE OF BUCKINGHAM.
DUKE OF SUFFOLK.
EARL OF SURREY.
Lord Chamberlain.
Lord Chancellor.
GARDINER, Bishop of Winchester.
Bishop of Lincoln.
LORD ABERGAVENNY.
LORD SANDS.
SIR HENRY GUILDFORD.
SIR THOMAS LOVELL.
SIR ANTHONY DENNY.
SIR NICHOLAS VAUX.
Secretaries to Wolsey.
CROMWELL, Servant to Wolsey.
GRIFFITH, Gentleman-usher to Queen Katharine.
Three Gentlemen.
DOCTOR BUTTS, Physician to the King.
Garter King-at-Arms.
Surveyor to the Duke of Buckingham.
BRANDON, and a Sergeant-at-Arms.
Door-keeper of the Council-chamber.   Porter, and his Man.
Page to Gardiner.   A Crier.

QUEEN KATHARINE, wife to King Henry, afterwards divorced.
ANNE BULLEN, her Maid of Honour, afterwards Queen.
An old Lady, friend to Anne Bullen.
PATIENCE, woman to Queen Katharine.

Several Lords and Ladies in the Dumb Shows; Women attending upon the
Queen; Scribes, Officers, Guards, and other Attendants.
Spirits.

SCENE: *London; Westminster; Kimbolton.*

THE FAMOUS HISTORY

OF THE LIFE OF

KING HENRY THE EIGHTH.

THE PROLOGUE.

I come no more to make you laugh: things now,
That bear a weighty and a serious brow,
Sad, high, and working, full of state and woe,
Such noble scenes as draw the eye to flow,
We now present.   Those that can pity, here
May, if they think it well, let fall a tear;
The subject will deserve it.   Such as give
Their money out of hope they may believe,
May here find truth too.   Those that come to see
Only a show or two, and so agree   10
The play may pass, if they be still and willing,
I 'll undertake may see away their shilling
Richly in two short hours.   Only they
That come to hear a merry bawdy play,
A noise of targets, or to see a fellow
In a long motley coat guarded with yellow,
Will be deceived; for, gentle hearers, know,
To rank our chosen truth with such a show
As fool and fight is, beside forfeiting
Our own brains and the opinion that we bring   20

To make that only true we now intend,
Will leave us never an understanding friend.
Therefore, for goodness' sake, and as you are known
The first and happiest hearers of the town,
Be sad, as we would make ye: think ye see
The very persons of our noble story
As they were living; think you see them great,
And follow'd with the general throng and sweat
Of thousand friends; then, in a moment, see
How soon this mightiness meets misery: 30
And if you can be merry then, I 'll say
A man may weep upon his wedding-day.

ACT I.

Scene I.   *London.   An ante-chamber in the palace.*

Enter the Duke of Norfolk *at one door; at the other, the* Duke of Buckingham *and the* Lord Abergavenny.

Buck. Good morrow, and well met.   How have ye done
Since last we saw in France?
    Nor.   I thank your grace,
Healthful, and ever since a fresh admirer
Of what I saw there.
    Buck.   An untimely ague
Stay'd me a prisoner in my chamber when
Those suns of glory, those two lights of men,
Met in the vale of Andren.
    Nor.   'Twixt Guynes and Arde:
I was then present, saw them salute on horseback;
Beheld them, when they lighted, how they clung
In their embracement, as they grew together;   10

Which had they, what four throned ones could have
    weigh'd
Such a compounded one?

Buck.   All the whole time
I was my chamber's prisoner.

Nor.   Then you lost
The view of earthly glory: men might say,
Till this time pomp was single, but now married
To one above itself.   Each following day
Became the next day's master, till the last
Made former wonders its.   To-day the French,
All clinquant, all in gold, like heathen gods,
Shone down the English; and to-morrow they   20
Made Britain India: every man that stood
Show'd like a mine.   There dwarfish pages were
As cherubins, all gilt: the madams too,
Not used to toil, did almost sweat to bear
The pride upon them, that their very labour
Was to them as a painting: now this masque
Was cried incomparable; and the ensuing night
Made it a fool and beggar.   The two kings,
Equal in lustre, were now best, now worst,
As presence did present them; him in eye,   30
Still him in praise; and being present both,
'T was said they saw but one; and no discerner
Durst wag his tongue in censure.   When these suns—
For so they phrase 'em—by their heralds challenged
The noble spirits to arms, they did perform
Beyond thought's compass; that former fabulous story,
Being now seen possible enough, got credit,
That Bevis was believed.

Buck.   O, you go far.

Nor. As I belong to worship, and affect
In honour honesty, the tract of every thing   40
Would by a good discourser lose some life,

Which action's self was tongue to. All was royal;
To the disposing of it nought rebell'd;
Order gave each thing view; the office did
Distinctly his full function.

 Buck.   Who did guide,
I mean, who set the body and the limbs
Of this great sport together, as you guess?

 Nor. One, certes, that promises no element
In such a business.

 Buck.   I pray you, who, my lord?

 Nor. All this was order'd by the good discretion   50
Of the right reverend Cardinal of York.

 Buck. The devil speed him! no man's pie is freed
From his ambitious finger. What had he
To do in these fierce vanities? I wonder
That such a keech can with his very bulk
Take up the rays o' the beneficial sun,
And keep it from the earth.

 Nor.   Surely, sir,
There's in him stuff that puts him to these ends;
For, being not propp'd by ancestry, whose grace
Chalks successors their way, nor call'd upon   60
For high feats done to the crown; neither allied
To eminent assistants; but, spider-like,
Out of his self-drawing web, he gives us note,
The force of his own merit makes his way;
A gift that heaven gives for him, which buys
A place next to the king.

 Aber.   I cannot tell
What heaven hath given him; let some graver eye
Pierce into that; but I can see his pride
Peep through each part of him: whence has he that?
If not from hell, the devil is a niggard,   70
Or has given all before, and he begins
A new hell in himself.

Buck.   Why the devil,
Upon this French going out, took he upon him,
Without the privity o' the king, to appoint
Who should attend on him?   He makes up the file
Of all the gentry; for the most part such
To whom as great a charge as little honour
He meant to lay upon: and his own letter,
The honourable board of council out,
Must fetch him in he papers.

Aber.   I do know   80
Kinsmen of mine, three at the least, that have
By this so sicken'd their estates that never
They shall abound as formerly.

Buck.   O, many
Have broke their backs with laying manors on 'em
For this great journey.   What did this vanity
But minister communication of
A most poor issue?

Nor.   Grievingly I think,
The peace between the French and us not values
The cost that did conclude it.

Buck.   Every man,
After the hideous storm that follow'd, was   90
A thing inspired, and not consulting broke
Into a general prophecy; That this tempest,
Dashing the garment of this peace, aboded
The sudden breach on 't.

Nor.   Which is budded out;
For France hath flaw'd the league, and hath attach'd
Our merchants' goods at Bordeaux.

Aber.   Is it therefore
The ambassador is silenced?

Nor.   Marry, is 't.

Aber. A proper title of a peace, and purchased
At a superfluous rate!

Buck.   Why, all this business
Our reverend cardinal carried.

   Nor.   Like it your grace,   100
The state takes notice of the private difference
Betwixt you and the cardinal. I advise you—
And take it from a heart that wishes towards you
Honour and plenteous safety—that you read
The cardinal's malice and his potency
Together; to consider further that
What his high hatred would effect wants not
A minister in his power. You know his nature,
That he's revengeful, and I know his sword
Hath a sharp edge; it's long and 't may be said   110
It reaches far, and where 't will not extend,
Thither he darts it. Bosom up my counsel;
You 'll find it wholesome. Lo, where comes that rock
That I advise your shunning.

Enter CARDINAL WOLSEY, *the purse borne before him, certain
of the* Guard, *and two* Secretaries *with papers. The*
CARDINAL *in his passage fixeth his eye on* BUCKINGHAM,
and BUCKINGHAM *on him, both full of disdain.*

   Wol. The Duke of Buckingham's surveyor, ha?
Where's his examination?

   First Secr.   Here, so please you.

   Wol. Is he in person ready?

   First Secr.   Ay, please your grace.

   Wol. Well, we shall then know more; and Buckingham
Shall lessen this big look. [*Exeunt Wolsey and his Train.*

   Buck. This butcher's cur is venom-mouth'd, and I   120
Have not the power to muzzle him; therefore best
Not wake him in his slumber. A beggar's book
Outworths a noble's blood.

   Nor.   What, are you chafed?

Ask God for temperance; that's the appliance only
Which your disease requires.

    Buck.   I read in 's looks
Matter against me, and his eye reviled
Me as his abject object: at this instant
He bores me with some trick: he's gone to the king;
I'll follow and outstare him.

    Nor.   Stay, my lord,
And let your reason with your choler question   130
What 't is you go about: to climb steep hills
Requires slow pace at first: anger is like
A full-hot horse, who being allow'd his way,
Self-mettle tires him.   Not a man in England
Can advise me like you: be to yourself
As you would to your friend.

    Buck.   I'll to the king;
And from a mouth of honour quite cry down
This Ipswich fellow's insolence, or proclaim
There's difference in no persons.

    Nor.   Be advised;
Heat not a furnace for your foe so hot   140
That it do singe yourself: we may outrun,
By violent swiftness, that which we run at,
And lose by over-running.   Know you not,
The fire that mounts the liquor till 't run o'er,
In seeming to augment it wastes it?   Be advised:
I say again, there is no English soul
More stronger to direct you than yourself,
If with the sap of reason you would quench,
Or but allay, the fire of passion.

    Buck.   Sir,
I am thankful to you; and I'll go along   150
By your prescription: but this top-proud fellow—
Whom from the flow of gall I name not, but
From sincere motions—by intelligence

And proofs as clear as founts in July when
We see each grain of gravel, I do know
To be corrupt and treasonous.

   Nor.   Say not 'treasonous'.

   Buck. To the king I 'll say 't; and make my vouch as
      strong
As shore of rock.   Attend.   This holy fox,
Or wolf, or both—for he is equal ravenous
As he is subtle, and as prone to mischief   160
As able to perform 't; his mind and place
Infecting one another, yea, reciprocally—
Only to show his pomp as well in France
As here at home, suggests the king our master
To this last costly treaty, the interview,
That swallow'd so much treasure, and like a glass
Did break i' the rinsing.

   Nor.   Faith, and so it did.

   Buck. Pray, give me favour, sir.   This cunning cardinal
The articles o' the combination drew
As himself pleased; and they were ratified   170
As he cried 'Thus let be', to as much end
As give a crutch to the dead: but our count-cardinal
Has done this, and 't is well; for worthy Wolsey,
Who cannot err, he did it.   Now this follows,—
Which, as I take it, is a kind of puppy
To the old dam, treason,—Charles the emperor,
Under pretence to see the queen his aunt,—
For 't was indeed his colour, but he came
To whisper Wolsey,—here makes visitation:
His fears were that the interview betwixt   180
England and France might through their amity
Breed him some prejudice; for from this league
Peep'd harms that menaced him: he privily
Deals with our cardinal; and, as I trow—
Which I do well, for I am sure the emperor

Paid ere he promised; whereby his suit was granted
Ere it was ask'd; but when the way was made
And paved with gold, the emperor thus desired,
That he would please to alter the king's course,
And break the foresaid peace. Let the king know, 190
As soon he shall by me, that thus the cardinal
Does buy and sell his honour as he pleases,
And for his own advantage.

Nor.   I am sorry
To hear this of him, and could wish he were
Something mistaken in 't.

Buck.   No, not a syllable:
I do pronounce him in that very shape
He shall appear in proof.

Enter BRANDON, *a* Sergeant-at-arms *before him, and
two or three of the* Guard.

Bran. Your office, sergeant; execute it.
Serg.   Sir,
My lord the Duke of Buckingham, and Earl
Of Hereford, Stafford, and Northampton, I 200
Arrest thee of high treason, in the name
Of our most sovereign king.

Buck.   Lo you, my lord,
The net has fall'n upon me! I shall perish
Under device and practice.

Bran.   I am sorry
To see you ta'en from liberty, to look on
The business present: 't is his highness' pleasure
You shall to the Tower.

Buck.   It will help me nothing
To plead mine innocence; for that dye is on me
Which makes my whitest part black. The will of heaven
Be done in this and all things! I obey. 210
O my Lord Abergavenny, fare you well!

Bran. Nay, he must bear you company. [*To Aberga-
venny*] The king
Is pleased you shall to the Tower, till you know
How he determines further.

    Aber.   As the duke said,
The will of heaven be done, and the king's pleasure
By me obey'd!

    Bran.   Here is a warrant from
The king to attach Lord Montacute; and the bodies
Of the duke's confessor, John de la Car,
One Gilbert Peck, his chancellor,—

    Buck.   So, so;
These are the limbs o' the plot: no more, I hope.   220

    Bran. A monk o' the Chartreux.

    Buck.   O, Nicholas Hopkins?

    Bran.   He.

    Buck. My surveyor is false; the o'er-great cardinal
Hath show'd him gold; my life is spann'd already:
I am the shadow of poor Buckingham,
Whose figure even this instant cloud puts on,
By darkening my clear sun. My lord, farewell. [*Exeunt.*

SCENE II. *The same. The council-chamber.*

Cornets. Enter KING HENRY, *leaning on the* CARDINAL'S
shoulder; the Nobles, *and* SIR THOMAS LOVELL: *the*
CARDINAL *places himself under the* KING'S *feet on his
right side.*

    King. My life itself, and the best heart of it,
Thanks you for this great care: I stood i' the level
Of a full-charged confederacy, and give thanks
To you that choked it. Let be call'd before us
That gentleman of Buckingham's; in person
I'll hear him his confessions justify;

And point by point the treasons of his master
He shall again relate.

A noise within, crying 'Room for the Queen!' *Enter* QUEEN
    KATHARINE, *ushered by the* DUKE OF NORFOLK, *and
    the* DUKE OF SUFFOLK: *she kneels. The* KING *riseth
    from his state, takes her up, kisses and placeth her by him.*

Q. Kath. Nay, we must longer kneel: I am a suitor.

King. Arise, and take place by us: half your suit   10
Never name to us; you have half our power:
The other moiety ere you ask is given;
Repeat your will and take it.

Q. Kath.   Thank your majesty.
That you would love yourself, and in that love
Not unconsider'd leave your honour nor
The dignity of your office, is the point
Of my petition.

King.   Lady mine, proceed.

Q. Kath. I am solicited, not by a few,
And those of true condition, that your subjects
Are in great grievance: there have been commissions   20
Sent down among 'em, which have flaw'd the heart
Of all their loyalties: wherein although,
My good lord cardinal, they vent reproaches
Most bitterly on you as putter on
Of these exactions, yet the king our master—
Whose honour heaven shield from soil!—even he escapes not
Language unmannerly, yea, such which breaks
The sides of loyalty, and almost appears
In loud rebellion.

Nor.   Not almost appears;
It doth appear; for, upon these taxations,   30
The clothiers all, not able to maintain
The many to them longing, have put off
The spinsters, carders, fullers, weavers, who,

Unfit for other life, compell'd by hunger
And lack of other means, in desperate manner
Daring the event to the teeth, are all in uproar,
And danger serves among them.

    King.   Taxation!
Wherein? and what taxation? My lord cardinal,
You that are blamed for it alike with us,
Know you of this taxation?

    Wol.   Please you, sir,   40
I know but of a single part in aught
Pertains to the state, and front but in that file
Where others tell steps with me.

    Q. Kath.   No, my lord,
You know no more than others: but you frame
Things that are known alike, which are not wholesome
To those which would not know them, and yet must
Perforce be their acquaintance. These exactions,
Whereof my sovereign would have note, they are
Most pestilent to the hearing; and, to bear 'em,
The back is sacrifice to the load. They say   50
They are devised by you; or else you suffer
Too hard an exclamation.

    King.   Still exaction!
The nature of it? in what kind, let's know,
Is this exaction?

    Q. Kath.   I am much too venturous
In tempting of your patience, but am bolden'd
Under your promised pardon. The subjects' grief
Comes through commissions, which compel from each
The sixth part of his substance to be levied
Without delay; and the pretence for this
Is named your wars in France: this makes bold mouths: 60
Tongues spit their duties out, and cold hearts freeze
Allegiance in them; their curses now
Live where their prayers did: and it's come to pass,

This tractable obedience is a slave
To each incensed will.   I would your highness
Would give it quick consideration, for
There is no primer business.
  King.   By my life,
This is against our pleasure.
    Wol.   And for me,
I have no further gone in this than by
A single voice, and that not pass'd me but   70
By learned approbation of the judges.   If I am
Traduced by ignorant tongues, which neither know
My faculties nor person, yet will be
The chronicles of my doing, let me say
'T is but the fate of place, and the rough brake
That virtue must go through.   We must not stint
Our necessary actions, in the fear
To cope malicious censurers; which ever,
As ravenous fishes, do a vessel follow
That is new-trimm'd, but benefit no further   80
Than vainly longing.   What we oft do best,
By sick interpreters, once weak ones, is
Not ours, or not allow'd; what worst, as oft,
Hitting a grosser quality, is cried up
For our best act.   If we shall stand still,
In fear our motion will be mock'd or carp'd at,
We should take root here where we sit, or sit
State-statues only.
    King.   Things done well,
And with a care, exempt themselves from fear;
Things done without example, in their issue   90
Are to be fear'd.   Have you a precedent
Of this commission?   I believe, not any.
We must not rend our subjects from our laws,
And stick them in our will.   Sixth part of each?
A trembling contribution!   Why, we take

From every tree lop, bark, and part o' the timber,
And though we leave it with a root, thus hack'd,
The air will drink the sap.   To every county
Where this is question'd send our letters, with
Free pardon to each man that has denied   100
The force of this commission: pray, look to 't;
I put it to your care.

 Wol. [*To the Secretary*] A word with you.
Let there be letters writ to every shire,
Of the king's grace and pardon.   The grieved commons
Hardly conceive of me: let it be noised
That through our intercession this revokement
And pardon comes: I shall anon advise you
Further in the proceeding.   [*Exit Secretary.*

Enter Surveyor.

 Q. Kath.   I am sorry that the Duke of Buckingham
Is run in your displeasure.

 King.   It grieves many: 110
The gentleman is learn'd and a most rare speaker;
To nature none more bound; his training such
That he may furnish and instruct great teachers,
And never seek for aid out of himself.   Yet see,
When these so noble benefits shall prove
Not well disposed, the mind growing once corrupt,
They turn to vicious forms, ten times more ugly
Than ever they were fair.   This man so complete,
Who was enroll'd 'mongst wonders, and when we,
Almost with ravish'd listening, could not find   120
His hour of speech a minute; he, my lady,
Hath into monstrous habits put the graces
That once were his, and is become as black
As if besmear'd in hell.   Sit by us; you shall hear—
This was his gentleman in trust—of him
Things to strike honour sad.   Bid him recount

The fore-recited practices; whereof
We cannot feel too little, hear too much.

    Wol. Stand forth, and with bold spirit relate what
      you,
Most like a careful subject, have collected   130
Out of the Duke of Buckingham.

    King.   Speak freely.

    Surv. First, it was usual with him, every day
It would infect his speech, that if the king
Should without issue die, he'll carry it so
To make the sceptre his: these very words
I've heard him utter to his son-in-law,
Lord Abergavenny, to whom by oath he menaced
Revenge upon the cardinal.

    Wol.   Please your highness, note
This dangerous conception in this point.
Not friended by his wish, to your high person   140
His will is most malignant, and it stretches
Beyond you, to your friends.

    Q. Kath.   My learn'd lord cardinal,
Deliver all with charity.

    King.   Speak on:
How grounded he his title to the crown
Upon our fail? to this point hast thou heard him
At any time speak aught?

    Surv.   He was brought to this
By a vain prophecy of Nicholas Henton.

    King. What was that Henton?

    Surv.   Sir, a Chartreux friar,
His confessor, who fed him every minute
With words of sovereignty.

    King.   How know'st thou this?   150

    Surv. Not long before your highness sped to France,
The duke being at the Rose, within the parish
Saint Lawrence Poultney, did of me demand

What was the speech among the Londoners
Concerning the French journey: I replied,
Men fear'd the French would prove perfidious,
To the king's danger.   Presently the duke
Said, 't was the fear indeed, and that he doubted
'T would prove the verity of certain words
Spoke by a holy monk; 'that oft', says he,   160
'Hath sent to me, wishing me to permit
John de la Car, my chaplain, a choice hour
To hear from him a matter of some moment:
Whom after under the confession's seal
He solemnly had sworn, that what he spoke
My chaplain to no creature living but
To me should utter, with demure confidence
This pausingly ensued: Neither the king nor 's heirs,
Tell you the duke, shall prosper: bid him strive
To gain the love o' the commonalty: the duke   170
Shall govern England.'

    Q. Kath.   If I know you well,
You were the duke's surveyor and lost your office
On the complaint o' the tenants: take good heed
You charge not in your spleen a noble person
And spoil your nobler soul: I say, take heed;
Yes, heartily beseech you.

    King.   Let him on.
Go forward.

    Surv.   On my soul, I 'll speak but truth.
I told my lord the duke, by the devil's illusions
The monk might be deceived; and that 't was dangerous for
    him
To ruminate on this so far, until   180
It forged him some design, which, being believed,
It was much like to do: he answer'd 'Tush,
It can do me no damage'; adding further,
That, had the king in his last sickness fail'd,

The cardinal's and Sir Thomas Lovell's heads
Should have gone off.

 King.   Ha! what, so rank?   Ah, ha!
There's mischief in this man: canst thou say further?

 Surv. I can, my liege.

 King.   Proceed.

 Surv.   Being at Greenwich,
After your highness had reproved the duke
About Sir William Bulmer,—

 King.   I remember   190
Of such a time: being my sworn servant,
The duke retain'd him his.   But on; what hence?

 Surv. 'If', quoth he, 'I for this had been committed,
As, to the Tower, I thought, I would have play'd
The part my father meant to act upon
The usurper Richard; who, being at Salisbury,
Made suit to come in 's presence; which if granted,
As he made semblance of his duty, would
Have put his knife into him.'

 King.   A giant traitor!

 Wol. Now, madam, may his highness live in freedom, 200
And this man out of prison?

 Q. Kath.   God mend all!

 King. There's something more would out of thee; what
  say'st?

 Surv. After 'the duke his father', with the 'knife',
He stretch'd him, and, with one hand on his dagger,
Another spread on 's breast, mounting his eyes,
He did discharge a horrible oath, whose tenour
Was, were he evil used, he would outgo
His father by as much as a performance
Does an irresolute purpose.

 King.   There's his period,
To sheathe his knife in us.   He is attach'd; 210
Call him to present trial: if he may

 (M 548)

            4

Find mercy in the law, 't is his; if none,
Let him not seek 't of us: by day and night,
He 's traitor to the height.   [*Exeunt.*

SCENE III.   *An ante-chamber in the palace.*

Enter the LORD CHAMBERLAIN *and* LORD SANDS.

Cham. Is 't possible the spells of France should juggle
Men into such strange mysteries?
    Sands.   New customs,
Though they be never so ridiculous,
Nay, let 'em be unmanly, yet are follow'd.
    Cham. As far as I see, all the good our English
Have got by the late voyage is but merely
A fit or two o' the face; but they are shrewd ones;
For when they hold 'em, you would swear directly
Their very noses had been counsellors
To Pepin or Clotharius, they keep state so.   10
    Sands. They have all new legs, and lame ones: one would
      take it,
That never saw 'em pace before, the spavin
Or springhalt reign'd among 'em.
    Cham.   Death! my lord,
Their clothes are after such a pagan cut too,
That, sure, they 've worn out Christendom.

Enter SIR THOMAS LOVELL.

                       How now!
What news, Sir Thomas Lovell?
    Lov.   Faith, my lord,
I hear of none but the new proclamation
That 's clapp'd upon the court-gate.
    Cham.   What is 't for?
    Lov. The reformation of our travell'd gallants,
That fill the court with quarrels, talk, and tailors.   20
    Cham. I 'm glad 't is there: now I would pray our monsieurs

To think an English courtier may be wise,
And never see the Louvre.
  Lov.   They must either,
For so run the conditions, leave those remnants
Of fool and feather that they got in France,
With all their honourable points of ignorance
Pertaining thereunto, as fights and fireworks,
Abusing better men than they can be
Out of a foreign wisdom, renouncing clean
The faith they have in tennis and tall stockings,   30
Short blister'd breeches and those types of travel,
And understand again like honest men,
Or pack to their old playfellows: there, I take it,
They may, 'cum privilegio', wear away
The lag end of their lewdness, and be laugh'd at.
  Sands. 'T is time to give 'm physic, their diseases
Are grown so catching.
  Cham.   What a loss our ladies
Will have of these trim vanities!
  Lov.   Ay, marry,
A French song and a fiddle has no fellow.
  Sands. The devil fiddle 'em! I am glad they are going, 40
For, sure, there 's no converting of 'em: now
An honest country lord, as I am, beaten
A long time out of play, may bring his plain-song
And have an hour of hearing; and, by 'r lady,
Held current music too.
  Cham.   Well said, Lord Sands;
Your colt's tooth is not cast yet.
  Sands.   No, my lord;
Nor shall not, while I have a stump.
  Cham.   Sir Thomas,
Whither were you a-going?
  Lov.   To the cardinal's:
Your lordship is a guest too.

Cham.   O, 't is true:
This night he makes a supper, and a great one,   50
To many lords and ladies; there will be
The beauty of this kingdom, I 'll assure you.

Lov. That churchman bears a bounteous mind indeed,
A hand as fruitful as the land that feeds us;
His dews fall every where.

Cham.   No doubt he 's noble;
He had a black mouth that said other of him.

Sands. He may, my lord; has wherewithal: in him
Sparing would show a worse sin than ill doctrine:
Men of his way should be most liberal;
They are set here for examples.

Cham.   True, they are so;   60
But few now give so great ones.   My barge stays;
Your lordship shall along.   Come, good Sir Thomas,
We shall be late else; which I would not be,
For I was spoke to, with Sir Henry Guildford
This night to be comptrollers.

Sands.   I am your lordship's.   [*Exeunt.*

SCENE IV.   *A hall in York Place.*

Hautboys.   A small table under a state for the CARDINAL, *a
longer table for the guests.   Then enter* ANNE BULLEN
and divers other Ladies *and* Gentlemen *as guests, at one
door; at another door, enter* SIR HENRY GUILDFORD.

Guild. Ladies, a general welcome from his grace
Salutes ye all; this night he dedicates
To fair content and you: none here, he hopes,
In all this noble bevy, has brought with her
One care abroad; he would have all as merry
As, first, good company, good wine, good welcome,
Can make good people.

Enter LORD CHAMBERLAIN, LORD SANDS, *and*
SIR THOMAS LOVELL.

       O, my lord, you 're tardy:
The very thought of this fair company
Clapp'd wings to me.

  Cham.   You are young, Sir Harry Guildford.

  Sands. Sir Thomas Lovell, had the cardinal 10
But half my lay thoughts in him, some of these
Should find a running banquet ere they rested,
I think would better please 'em: by my life,
They are a sweet society of fair ones.

  Lov. O, that your lordship were but now confessor
To one or two of these!

  Sands.   I would I were;
They should find easy penance.

  Lov.   Faith, how easy?

  Sands. As easy as a down-bed would afford it.

  Cham. Sweet ladies, will it please you sit? Sir
  Harry,
Place you that side; I 'll take the charge of this: 20
His grace is entering. Nay, you must not freeze;
Two women placed together makes cold weather:
My Lord Sands, you are one will keep 'em waking;
Pray, sit between these ladies.

  Sands.   By my faith,
And thank your lordship. By your leave, sweet ladies:
If I chance to talk a little wild, forgive me;
I had it from my father.

  Anne.   Was he mad, sir?

  Sands. O, very mad, exceeding mad, in love too:
But he would bite none; just as I do now,
He would kiss you twenty with a breath. [*Kisses her.*

  Cham.   Well said, my lord.
So, now you 're fairly seated. Gentlemen, 31

The penance lies on you, if these fair ladies
Pass away frowning.

    Sands.   For my little cure,
Let me alone.

Hautboys. Enter CARDINAL WOLSEY, *and takes his state.*

    Wol. You 're welcome, my fair guests: that noble lady
Or gentleman that is not freely merry,
Is not my friend: this, to confirm my welcome;
And to you all, good health.   *[Drinks.*

    Sands.   Your grace is noble:
Let me have such a bowl may hold my thanks,
And save me so much talking.

    Wol.   My Lord Sands,   40
I am beholding to you: cheer your neighbours.
Ladies, you are not merry: gentlemen,
Whose fault is this?

    Sands.   The red wine first must rise
In their fair cheeks, my lord; then we shall have 'em
Talk us to silence.

    Anne.   You are a merry gamester,
My Lord Sands.

    Sands.   Yes, if I make my play.
Here 's to your ladyship: and pledge it, madam,
For 't is to such a thing—

    Anne.   You cannot show me.

    Sands. I told your grace they would talk anon.
               [Drum and trumpet: chambers discharged.

    Wol.   What 's that?

    Cham. Look out there, some of ye.   *[Exit Servant.*

    Wol.   What warlike voice,   50
And to what end, is this? Nay, ladies, fear not;
By all the laws of war you 're privileged.

Re-enter Servant.

Cham. How now! what is 't?
Serv.   A noble troop of strangers;
For so they seem: they 've left their barge and landed;
And hither make, as great ambassadors
From foreign princes.
Wol.   Good lord chamberlain,
Go, give 'em welcome; you can speak the French tongue;
And, pray, receive 'em nobly and conduct 'em
Into our presence, where this heaven of beauty
Shall shine at full upon them. Some attend him.   60
                    [*Exit Chamberlain, attended. All rise,
                        and tables removed.*
You have now a broken banquet; but we 'll mend it.
A good digestion to you all: and once more
I shower a welcome on ye; welcome all.

Hautboys.   Enter the KING *and others, as masquers, habited
    like shepherds, ushered by the* LORD CHAMBERLAIN.
    They pass directly before the CARDINAL, *and gracefully
    salute him.*

A noble company! what are their pleasures?
    Cham. Because they speak no English, thus they pray'd
To tell your grace, that, having heard by fame
Of this so noble and so fair assembly
This night to meet here, they could do no less,
Out of the great respect they bear to beauty,
But leave their flocks, and under your fair conduct   70
Crave leave to view these ladies and entreat
An hour of revels with 'em.
    Wol.   Say, lord chamberlain,
They have done my poor house grace; for which I pay 'em
A thousand thanks, and pray 'em take their pleasure.
                    [*They choose Ladies for the dance. The
                        King chooses Anne Bullen.*

King. The fairest hand I ever touch'd!   O beauty,
Till now I never knew thee!   [*Music.   Dance.*
   Wol. My lord!
   Cham.   Your grace?
   Wol.   Pray, tell 'em thus much from me:
There should be one amongst 'em, by his person,
More worthy this place than myself; to whom,
If I but knew him, with my love and duty   80
I would surrender it.
   Cham.   I will, my lord. [*Whispers the Masquers.*
   Wol. What say they?
   Cham.   Such a one, they all confess,
There is indeed; which they would have your grace
Find out, and he will take it.
   Wol.   Let me see then.
By all your good leaves, gentlemen; here I'll make
My royal choice.
   King. [*Unmasking*] Ye have found him, cardinal:
You hold a fair assembly; you do well, lord:
You are a churchman, or, I'll tell you, cardinal,
I should judge now unhappily.
   Wol.   I am glad
Your grace is grown so pleasant.
   King.   My lord chamberlain,   90
Prithee, come hither: what fair lady's that?
   Cham. An't please your grace, Sir Thomas Bullen's
        daughter,
The Viscount Rochford, one of her highness' women.
   King. By heaven, she is a dainty one.   Sweetheart,
I were unmannerly to take you out
And not to kiss you.   A health, gentlemen!
Let it go round.
   Wol. Sir Thomas Lovell, is the banquet ready
I' the privy chamber?
   Lov.   Yes, my lord.

Wol.   Your grace,
I fear, with dancing is a little heated.   100
    King. I fear, too much.
    Wol.   There's fresher air, my lord,
In the next chamber.
    King. Lead in your ladies, every one.   Sweet partner,
I must not yet forsake you.   Let's be merry,
Good my lord cardinal: I have half a dozen healths
To drink to these fair ladies, and a measure
To lead 'em once again; and then let's dream
Who's best in favour.   Let the music knock it.
                                    [*Exeunt with trumpets.*

ACT II.

SCENE I.   *Westminster.   A street.*

Enter two Gentlemen, *meeting.*

    First Gent. Whither away so fast?
    Sec. Gent.   O, God save ye!
Even to the hall, to hear what shall become
Of the great Duke of Buckingham.
    First Gent.   I'll save you
That labour, sir.   All's now done, but the ceremony
Of bringing back the prisoner.
    Sec. Gent.   Were you there?
    First Gent. Yes, indeed was I.
    Sec. Gent.   Pray, speak what has happen'd.
    First Gent. You may guess quickly what.
    Sec. Gent.   Is he found guilty?
    First Gent. Yes, truly is he, and condemn'd upon 't.
    Sec. Gent. I am sorry for 't.
    First Gent.   So are a number more.
    Sec. Gent. But, pray, how pass'd it?   10

First Gent. I 'll tell you in a little.   The great duke
Came to the bar; where to his accusations
He pleaded still not guilty and alleged
Many sharp reasons to defeat the law.
The king's attorney on the contrary
Urged on the examinations, proofs, confessions
Of divers witnesses; which the duke desired
To have brought viva voce to his face:
At which appear'd against him his surveyor;
Sir Gilbert Peck his chancellor; and John Car,   20
Confessor to him; with that devil monk,
Hopkins, that made this mischief.
   Sec. Gent.   That was he
That fed him with his prophecies?
   First Gent.   The same.
All these accused him strongly; which he fain
Would have flung from him, but indeed he could not:
And so his peers upon this evidence
Have found him guilty of high treason.   Much
He spoke, and learnedly, for life; but all
Was either pitied in him or forgotten.
   Sec. Gent. After all this, how did he bear himself?   30
   First Gent. When he was brought again to the bar, to hear
His knell rung out, his judgment, he was stirr'd
With such an agony, he sweat extremely,
And something spoke in choler, ill and hasty:
But he fell to himself again, and sweetly
In all the rest show'd a most noble patience.
   Sec. Gent. I do not think he fears death.
   First Gent.   Sure, he does not:
He never was so womanish; the cause
He may a little grieve at.
   Sec. Gent.   Certainly
The cardinal is the end of this.
   First Gent.   'T is likely,   40

By all conjectures: first, Kildare's attainder,
Then deputy of Ireland; who removed,
Earl Surrey was sent thither, and in haste too,
Lest he should help his father.

 Sec. Gent.   That trick of state
Was a deep envious one.

 First Gent.   At his return
No doubt he will requite it.   This is noted,
And generally, whoever the king favours,
The cardinal instantly will find employment,
And far enough from court too.

 Sec. Gent.   All the commons
Hate him perniciously, and, o' my conscience, 50
Wish him ten fathom deep: this duke as much
They love and dote on; call him bounteous Buckingham,
The mirror of all courtesy—

 First Gent.   Stay there, sir,
And see the noble ruin'd man you speak of.

Enter BUCKINGHAM *from his arraignment, tipstaves before
 him, the axe with the edge towards him, halberds on
 each side, accompanied with* SIR THOMAS LOVELL, SIR
 NICHOLAS VAUX, SIR WILLIAM SANDS, *and common
 people,* &c.

 Sec. Gent. Let's stand close, and behold him.
 Buck.   All good people,
You that thus far have come to pity me,
Hear what I say, and then go home and lose me.
I have this day received a traitor's judgment,
And by that name must die: yet, heaven bear witness,
And if I have a conscience, let it sink me, 60
Even as the axe falls, if I be not faithful!
The law I bear no malice for my death;
'T has done upon the premises but justice:
But those that sought it I could wish more Christians:

Be what they will, I heartily forgive 'em:
Yet let 'em look they glory not in mischief,
Nor build their evils on the graves of great men;
For then my guiltless blood must cry against 'em.
For further life in this world I ne'er hope,
Nor will I sue, although the king have mercies   70
More than I dare make faults.   You few that loved me
And dare be bold to weep for Buckingham,
His noble friends and fellows, whom to leave
Is only bitter to him, only dying,
Go with me, like good angels, to my end,
And, as the long divorce of steel falls on me,
Make of your prayers one sweet sacrifice,
And lift my soul to heaven.   Lead on, o' God's name.
    Lov. I do beseech your grace, for charity,
If ever any malice in your heart   80
Were hid against me, now to forgive me frankly.
    Buck. Sir Thomas Lovell, I as free forgive you
As I would be forgiven: I forgive all;
There cannot be those numberless offences
'Gainst me, that I cannot take peace with: no black envy
Shall mark my grave.   Commend me to his grace;
And if he speak of Buckingham, pray tell him
You met him half in heaven: my vows and prayers
Yet are the king's, and, till my soul forsake,
Shall cry for blessings on him: may he live   90
Longer than I have time to tell his years!
Ever beloved and loving may his rule be!
And when old time shall lead him to his end,
Goodness and he fill up one monument!
    Lov. To the water side I must conduct your grace;
Then give my charge up to Sir Nicholas Vaux,
Who undertakes you to your end.
    Vaux.   Prepare there;
The duke is coming: see the barge be ready,

And fit it with such furniture as suits
The greatness of his person.
  Buck.   Nay, Sir Nicholas, 100
Let it alone; my state now will but mock me.
When I came hither, I was lord high constable
And Duke of Buckingham; now, poor Edward Bohun:
Yet I am richer than my base accusers,
That never knew what truth meant: I now seal it;
And with that blood will make 'em one day groan
  for 't.
My noble father, Henry of Buckingham,
Who first raised head against usurping Richard,
Flying for succour to his servant Banister,
Being distress'd, was by that wretch betray'd, 110
And without trial fell; God's peace be with him!
Henry the Seventh succeeding, truly pitying
My father's loss, like a most royal prince,
Restored me to my honours, and out of ruins
Made my name once more noble.   Now his son,
Henry the Eighth, life, honour, name and all
That made me happy, at one stroke has taken
For ever from the world.   I had my trial,
And, must needs say, a noble one; which makes me
A little happier than my wretched father: 120
Yet thus far we are one in fortunes: both
Fell by our servants, by those men we loved most;
A most unnatural and faithless service!
Heaven has an end in all: yet, you that hear me,
This from a dying man receive as certain:
Where you are liberal of your loves and counsels
Be sure you be not loose; for those you make friends
And give your hearts to, when they once perceive
The least rub in your fortunes, fall away
Like water from ye, never found again 130
But where they mean to sink ye.   All good people,

Pray for me!   I must now forsake ye: the last hour
Of my long weary life is come upon me.
Farewell:
And when you would say something that is sad,
Speak how I fell.   I have done; and God forgive me!

                            [*Exeunt Duke and Train.*

   First Gent.   O, this is full of pity!   Sir, it calls,
I fear, too many curses on their heads
That were the authors.
   Sec. Gent.   If the duke be guiltless,
'T is full of woe: yet I can give you inkling   140
Of an ensuing evil, if it fall,
Greater than this.
   First Gent.   Good angels keep it from us!
What may it be?   You do not doubt my faith, sir?
   Sec. Gent. This secret is so weighty, 't will require
A strong faith to conceal it.
   First Gent.   Let me have it;
I do not talk much.
   Sec. Gent.   I am confident;
You shall, sir: did you not of late days hear
A buzzing of a separation
Between the king and Katharine?
   First Gent.   Yes, but it held not:
For when the king once heard it, out of anger   150
He sent command to the lord mayor straight
To stop the rumour and allay those tongues
That durst disperse it.
   Sec. Gent.   But that slander, sir,
Is found a truth now: for it grows again
Fresher than e'er it was, and held for certain
The king will venture at it.   Either the cardinal,
Or some about him near, have, out of malice
To the good queen, possess'd him with a scruple
That will undo her: to confirm this too,

Cardinal Campeius is arrived, and lately: 160
As all think, for this business.
 First Gent.   'T is the cardinal;
And merely to revenge him on the emperor
For not bestowing on him at his asking
The archbishopric of Toledo, this is purposed.
 Sec. Gent. I think you have hit the mark: but is't not cruel
That she should feel the smart of this? The cardinal
Will have his will, and she must fall.
 First Gent.   'T is woeful.
We are too open here to argue this;
Let's think in private more.   [*Exeunt.*

   Scene II. *An ante-chamber in the palace.*

  Enter the Lord Chamberlain, *reading a letter.*

 Cham. 'My lord, the horses your lordship sent for, with
all the care I had, I saw well chosen, ridden, and furnished.
They were young and handsome, and of the best breed in the
north. When they were ready to set out for London, a man
of my lord cardinal's, by commission and main power, took
'em from me; with this reason: His master would be served
before a subject, if not before the king; which stopped our
mouths, sir.'
I fear he will indeed: well, let him have them:
He will have all, I think.   10

  Enter, to the Lord Chamberlain, *the* Dukes of
    Norfolk *and* Suffolk.

 Nor. Well met, my lord chamberlain.
 Cham. Good day to both your graces.
 Suf. How is the king employ'd?
 Cham.   I left him private,
Full of sad thoughts and troubles.
 Nor.   What's the cause?

Cham. It seems the marriage with his brother's wife
Has crept too near his conscience.

Suf.   No, his conscience
Has crept too near another lady.

Nor.   'T is so:
This is the cardinal's doing, the king-cardinal:
That blind priest, like the eldest son of fortune,
Turns what he list.   The king will know him one day.   20

Suf. Pray God he do! he'll never know himself else.

Nor. How holily he works in all his business!
And with what zeal! for, now he has crack'd the league
Between us and the emperor, the queen's great nephew,
He dives into the king's soul, and there scatters
Dangers, doubts, wringing of the conscience,
Fears, and despairs; and all these for his marriage:
And out of all these to restore the king,
He counsels a divorce; a loss of her
That, like a jewel, has hung twenty years   30
About his neck, yet never lost her lustre;
Of her that loves him with that excellence
That angels love good men with; even of her
That, when the greatest stroke of fortune falls,
Will bless the king: and is not this course pious?

Cham. Heaven keep me from such counsel!   'T is most
     true
These news are every where; every tongue speaks 'em,
And every true heart weeps for 't: all that dare
Look into these affairs see this main end,
The French king's sister.   Heaven will one day open   40
The king's eyes, that so long have slept upon
This bold bad man.

Suf.   And free us from his slavery.

Nor. We had need pray,
And heartily, for our deliverance;
Or this imperious man will work us all

From princes into pages: all men's honours
Lie like one lump before him, to be fashion'd
Into what pitch he please.

Suf.   For me, my lords,
I love him not, nor fear him; there's my creed:
As I am made without him, so I'll stand,   50
If the king please; his curses and his blessings
Touch me alike; they're breath I not believe in.
I knew him, and I know him; so I leave him
To him that made him proud, the pope.

Nor.   Let's in;
And with some other business put the king
From these sad thoughts that work too much upon him:
My lord, you'll bear us company?

Cham.   Excuse me;
The king has sent me otherwhere: besides,
You'll find a most unfit time to disturb him:
Health to your lordships.   (

Nor.   Thanks, my good lord chamberlain.

[*Exit Lord Chamberlain; and the King draws
the curtain and sits reading pensively.*

Suf. How sad he looks! sure, he is much afflicted.   6 (

King. Who's there, ha?

Nor.   Pray God he be not angry.

King. Who's there, I say? How dare you thrust your-
selves
Into my private meditations?
Who am I? ha?

Nor. A gracious king that pardons all offences
Malice ne'er meant: our breach of duty this way
Is business of estate, in which we come
To know your royal pleasure.

King.   Ye are too bold;
Go to; I'll make ye know your times of business: 70
Is this an hour for temporal affairs, ha?

Enter WOLSEY *and* CAMPEIUS, *with a commission.*

Who 's there? my good lord cardinal?   O my Wolsey,
The quiet of my wounded conscience,
Thou art a cure fit for a king.   [*To Camp.*] You 're wel-
          come,
Most learned reverend sir, into our kingdom:
Use us and it. [*To Wol.*] My good lord, have great care
I be not found a talker.
     Wol.   Sir, you cannot.
I would your grace would give us but an hour
Of private conference.
     King. [*To Nor. and Suf.*] We are busy; go.
     Nor. [*Aside to Suf.*] This priest has no pride in him?
     Suf.   [*Aside to Nor.*] Not to speak of:
I would not be so sick though for his place: 81
But this cannot continue.
     Nor.   [*Aside to Suf.*] If it do,
I 'll venture one have-at-him.
     Suf.   [*Aside to Nor.*] I another.
                    [*Exeunt Norfolk and Suffolk.*

     Wol. Your grace has given a precedent of wisdom
Above all princes, in committing freely
Your scruple to the voice of Christendom:
Who can be angry now? what envy reach you?
The Spaniard, tied by blood and favour to her,
Must now confess, if they have any goodness,
The trial just and noble.   All the clerks,   90
I mean the learned ones, in Christian kingdoms
Have their free voices: Rome, the nurse of judgment,
Invited by your noble self, hath sent
One general tongue unto us, this good man,
This just and learned priest, Cardinal Campeius;
Whom once more I present unto your highness.
     King. And once more in mine arms I bid him welcome,

And thank the holy conclave for their loves:
They have sent me such a man I would have wish'd for.

   Cam. Your grace must needs deserve all strangers' loves,
You are so noble.   To your highness' hand   101
I tender my commission: by whose virtue,
The court of Rome commanding, you, my lord
Cardinal of York, are join'd with me their servant
In the unpartial judging of this business.

   King. Two equal men.   The queen shall be acquainted
Forthwith for what you come.   Where 's Gardiner?

   Wol. I know your majesty has always loved her
So dear in heart, not to deny her that
A woman of less place might ask by law,   110
Scholars allow'd freely to argue for her.

   King. Ay, and the best she shall have; and my favour
To him that does best: God forbid else.   Cardinal,
Prithee, call Gardiner to me, my new secretary:
I find him a fit fellow.   *[Exit Wolsey.*

     Re-enter WOLSEY, *with* GARDINER.

   Wol. [*Aside to Gar.*] Give me your hand: much joy and
    favour to you:
You are the king's now.

   Gar. [*Aside to Wol.*] But to be commanded
For ever by your grace, whose hand has raised me.

   King. Come hither, Gardiner.   [*Walks and whispers.*

   Cam. My lord of York, was not one Doctor Pace   120
In this man's place before him?

   Wol.   Yes, he was.

   Cam. Was he not held a learned man?

   Wol.   Yes, surely.

   Cam. Believe me, there 's an ill opinion spread then,
Even of yourself, lord cardinal.

   Wol.   How! of me?

   Cam. They will not stick to say you envied him,

And fearing he would rise, he was so virtuous,
Kept him a foreign man still; which so grieved him
That he ran mad and died.

Wol.   Heaven's peace be with him!
That 's Christian care enough; for living murmurers
There 's places of rebuke.   He was a fool;   130
For he would needs be virtuous; that good fellow,
If I command him, follows my appointment:
I will have none so near else.   Learn this, brother,
We live not to be grip'd by meaner persons.

King. Deliver this with modesty to the queen.
                                        [*Exit Gardiner*
The most convenient place that I can think of
For such receipt of learning is Black-Friars;
There ye shall meet about this weighty business.
My Wolsey, see it furnish'd.   O, my lord,
Would it not grieve an able man to leave   140
So sweet a bedfellow?   But conscience, conscience!
O, 't is a tender place; and I must leave her.   [*Exeunt.*

SCENE III.   *An ante-chamber of the Queen's apartments.*

Enter ANNE BULLEN *and an* Old Lady.

Anne. Not for that neither: here 's the pang that
    pinches:
His highness having lived so long with her, and she
So good a lady that no tongue could ever
Pronounce dishonour of her—by my life,
She never knew harm-doing—O, now, after
So many courses of the sun enthroned,
Still growing in a majesty and pomp, the which
To leave a thousand-fold more bitter than
'T is sweet at first to acquire,—after this process,
To give her the avaunt! it is a pity   10
Would move a monster.

Old L.   Hearts of most hard temper
Melt and lament for her.
    Anne.   O, God's will! much better
She ne'er had known pomp: though 't be temporal,
Yet, if that quarrel, fortune, do divorce
It from the bearer, 't is a sufferance panging
As soul and body's severing.
    Old L.   Alas, poor lady!
She 's a stranger now again.
    Anne.   So much the more
Must pity drop upon her.   Verily,
I swear, 't is better to be lowly born,
And range with humble livers in content,   20
Than to be perk'd up in a glistering grief
And wear a golden sorrow.
    Old L.   Our content
Is our best having.
    Anne.   By my troth and maidenhead,
I would not be a queen.
    Old L.   Beshrew me, I would,
And venture maidenhead for 't; and so would you,
For all this spice of your hypocrisy:
You, that have so fair parts of woman on you,
Have too a woman's heart; which ever yet
Affected eminence, wealth, sovereignty;
Which, to say sooth, are blessings; and which gifts,   30
Saving your mincing, the capacity
Of your soft cheveril conscience would receive,
If you might please to stretch it.
    Anne.   Nay, good troth.
    Old L. Yes, troth, and troth; you would not be a queen?
    Anne. No, not for all the riches under heaven.
    Old L. 'T is strange: a three-pence bow'd would hire
      me,
Old as I am, to queen it; but, I pray you,

What think you of a duchess? have you limbs
To bear that load of title?

    Anne.   No, in truth.

    Old L. Then you are weakly made: pluck off a little; 40
I would not be a young count in your way,
For more than blushing comes to: if your back
Cannot vouchsafe this burthen, 't is too weak
Ever to get a boy.

    Anne.   How you do talk!
I swear again, I would not be a queen
For all the world.

    Old L.   In faith, for little England
You 'ld venture an emballing: I myself
Would for Carnarvonshire, although there long'd
No more to the crown but that.   Lo, who comes here?

              Enter the LORD CHAMBERLAIN.

    Cham. Good morrow, ladies. What were 't worth to
       know
The secret of your conference?

    Anne.   My good lord,   51
Not your demand: it values not your asking:
Our mistress' sorrows we were pitying.

    Cham. It was a gentle business, and becoming
The action of good women: there is hope
All will be well.

    Anne.   Now, I pray God, amen!

    Cham. You bear a gentle mind, and heavenly bless-
       ings
Follow such creatures.   That you may, fair lady,
Perceive I speak sincerely, and high note 's
Ta'en of your many virtues, the king's majesty   60
Commends his good opinion of you, and
Does purpose honour to you no less flowing
Than Marchioness of Pembroke; to which title

A thousand pound a year, annual support,
Out of his grace he adds.

   Anne.   I do not know
What kind of my obedience I should tender;
More than my all is nothing: nor my prayers
Are not words duly hallowed, nor my wishes
More worth than empty vanities; yet prayers and wishes
Are all I can return.   Beseech your lordship,   70
Vouchsafe to speak my thanks and my obedience,
As from a blushing handmaid, to his highness,
Whose health and royalty I pray for.

   Cham.   Lady,
I shall not fail to approve the fair conceit
The king hath of you.   [*Aside*] I have perused her well;
Beauty and honour in her are so mingled
That they have caught the king: and who knows yet
But from this lady may proceed a gem
To lighten all this isle?   I 'll to the king,
And say I spoke with you.   [*Exit Lord Chamberlain.*

   Anne.   My honour'd lord.   80

   Old L. Why, this it is; see, see!
I have been begging sixteen years in court.
Am yet a courtier beggarly, nor could
Come pat betwixt too early and too late
For any suit of pounds; and you, O fate!
A very fresh fish here—fie, fie, fie upon
This compell'd fortune!—have your mouth fill'd up
Before you open it.

   Anne.   This is strange to me.

   Old L. How tastes it? is it bitter? forty pence, no.
There was a lady once, 't is an old story,   90
That would not be a queen, that would she not,
For all the mud in Egypt: have you heard it?

   Anne. Come, you are pleasant.

   Old L.   With your theme, I could

O'ermount the lark.   The Marchioness of Pembroke!
A thousand pounds a year for pure respect!
No other obligation!   By my life,
That promises mo thousands: honour's train
Is longer than his foreskirt.   By this time
I know your back will bear a duchess: say,
Are you not stronger than you were?

   Anne.   Good lady,   100
Make yourself mirth with your particular fancy,
And leave me out on 't.   Would I had no being,
If this salute my blood a jot: it faints me,
To think what follows.
The queen is comfortless, and we forgetful
In our long absence: pray, do not deliver
What here you 've heard to her.

   Old L.   What do you think me?

                                   [*Exeunt.*

SCENE IV.   *A hall in Black-Friars.*

Trumpets, sennet, and cornets.   Enter two Vergers, *with
short silver wands; next them, two* Scribes, *in the habit
of doctors; after them, the* ARCHBISHOP OF CANTER-
BURY *alone; after him, the* BISHOPS OF LINCOLN, ELY,
ROCHESTER, *and* SAINT ASAPH; *next them, with some
small distance, follows a* Gentleman *bearing the purse,
with the great seal, and a cardinal's hat; then two*
Priests, *bearing each a silver cross; then a* Gentleman-
usher *bare-headed, accompanied with a* Sergeant-at-arms
bearing a silver mace; then two Gentlemen *bearing two
great silver pillars; after them, side by side, the two*
CARDINALS; *two* Noblemen *with the sword and mace.
The* KING *takes place under the cloth of state; the two*
CARDINALS *sit under him as judges.   The* QUEEN *takes
place some distance from the* KING.   *The* Bishops *place
themselves on each side the court, in manner of a consis-*

tory; below them, the Scribes.   *The* Lords *sit next the*
Bishops.   *The rest of the* Attendants *stand in convenient
order about the stage.*

Wol. Whilst our commission from Rome is read,
Let silence be commanded.
   King.   What's the need?
It hath already publicly been read,
And on all sides the authority allow'd;
You may then spare that time.
   Wol.   Be't so.   Proceed.
   Scribe. Say, Henry King of England, come into the
   court.
   Crier. Henry King of England, &c.
   King. Here.
   Scribe. Say, Katharine Queen of England, come into the
   court.   15
   Crier. Katharine Queen of England, &c.

        [*The Queen makes no answer, rises out of her
          chair, goes about the court, comes to the
          King, and kneels at his feet; then speaks.*

   Q. Kath. Sir, I desire you do me right and justice,
And to bestow your pity on me; for
I am a most poor woman, and a stranger,
Born out of your dominions; having here
No judge indifferent, nor no more assurance,
Of equal friendship and proceeding.   Alas, sir,
In what have I offended you? what cause
Hath my behaviour given to your displeasure,   20
That thus you should proceed to put me off,
And take your good grace from me?   Heaven witness,
I have been to you a true and humble wife,
At all times to your will conformable,
Ever in fear to kindle your dislike,
Yea, subject to your countenance, glad or sorry

As I saw it inclined: when was the hour
I ever contradicted your desire,
Or made it not mine too?   Or which of your friends
Have I not strove to love, although I knew   30
He were mine enemy? what friend of mine
That had to him derived your anger, did I
Continue in my liking? nay, gave notice
He was from thence discharged?   Sir, call to mind
That I have been your wife, in this obedience,
Upward of twenty years, and have been blest
With many children by you: if in the course
And process of this time you can report,
And prove it too, against mine honour aught,
My bond to wedlock, or my love and duty,   40
Against your sacred person, in God's name,
Turn me away, and let the foul'st contempt
Shut door upon me, and so give me up
To the sharp'st kind of justice.   Please you, sir,
The king, your father, was reputed for
A prince most prudent, of an excellent
And unmatch'd wit and judgment: Ferdinand,
My father, king of Spain, was reckon'd one
The wisest prince that there had reign'd by many
A year before: it is not to be question'd   50
That they had gather'd a wise council to them
Of every realm, that did debate this business,
Who deem'd our marriage lawful: wherefore I humbly
Beseech you, sir, to spare me, till I may
Be by my friends in Spain advised, whose counsel
I will implore: if not, i' the name of God,
Your pleasure be fulfill'd!

Wol.   You have here, lady,
And of your choice, these reverend fathers; men
Of singular integrity and learning,
Yea, the elect o' the land, who are assembled   60

To plead your cause: it shall be therefore bootless
That longer you desire the court, as well
For your own quiet, as to rectify
What is unsettled in the king.

 Cam.   His grace
Hath spoken well and justly: therefore, madam,
It's fit this royal session do proceed,
And that without delay their arguments
Be now produced and heard.

 Q. Kath.   Lord cardinal,
To you I speak.

 Wol.   Your pleasure, madam?

 Q. Kath.   Sir,
I am about to weep; but, thinking that   70
We are a queen, or long have dream'd so, certain
The daughter of a king, my drops of tears
I'll turn to sparks of fire.

 Wol.   Be patient yet.

 Q. Kath. I will, when you are humble; nay, before,
Or God will punish me. I do believe,
Induced by potent circumstances, that
You are mine enemy, and make my challenge
You shall not be my judge: for it is you
Have blown this coal betwixt my lord and me;
Which God's dew quench! Therefore I say again, 80
I utterly abhor, yea, from my soul
Refuse you for my judge; whom, yet once more,
I hold my most malicious foe, and think not
At all a friend to truth.

 Wol.   I do profess
You speak not like yourself; who ever yet
Have stood to charity, and display'd the effects
Of disposition gentle, and of wisdom
O'ertopping woman's power. Madam, you do me wrong.
I have no spleen against you, nor injustice

For you or any: how far I have proceeded,   90
Or how far further shall, is warranted
By a commission from the consistory,
Yea, the whole consistory of Rome.   You charge me
That I have blown this coal: I do deny it:
The king is present: if it be known to him
That I gainsay my deed, how may he wound,
And worthily, my falsehood! yea, as much
As you have done my truth.   If he know
That I am free of your report, he knows
I am not of your wrong.   Therefore in him   100
It lies to cure me: and the cure is to
Remove these thoughts from you: the which before
His highness shall speak in, I do beseech
You, gracious madam, to unthink your speaking,
And to say so no more.
   Q. Kath.   My lord, my lord,
I am a simple woman, much too weak
To oppose your cunning.   You 're meek and humble-mouth'd:
You sign your place and calling, in full seeming,
With meekness and humility; but your heart
Is cramm'd with arrogancy, spleen, and pride.   110
You have, by fortune and his highness' favours,
Gone slightly o'er low steps and now are mounted
Where powers are your retainers, and your words,
Domestics to you, serve your will as 't please
Yourself pronounce their office.   I must tell you
You tender more your person's honour than
Your high profession spiritual: that again
I do refuse you for my judge, and here,
Before you all, appeal unto the pope,
To bring my whole cause 'fore his holiness,   120
And to be judged by him.
               [*She curtsies to the King, and offers to depart.*
   Cam.   The queen is obstinate,

Stubborn to justice, apt to accuse it, and
Disdainful to be tried by 't: 't is not well.
She 's going away.

    King. Call her again.

    Crier. Katharine Queen of England, come into the court.

    Gent. Ush. Madam, you are call'd back.

    Q. Kath. What need you note it? pray you, keep your
      way:
When you are call'd, return.   Now the Lord help!
They vex me past my patience.   Pray you, pass on: 130
I will not tarry, no, nor ever more
Upon this business my appearance make
In any of their courts. [*Exeunt Queen, and her Attendants.*

    King.   Go thy ways, Kate:
That man i' the world who shall report he has
A better wife, let him in nought be trusted,
For speaking false in that: thou art, alone,
If thy rare qualities, sweet gentleness,
Thy meekness saint-like, wife-like government,
Obeying in commanding, and thy parts
Sovereign and pious else, could speak thee out,   140
The queen of earthly queens.   She 's noble born,
And like her true nobility she has
Carried herself towards me.

    Wol.   Most gracious sir,
In humblest manner I require your highness,
That it shall please you to declare in hearing
Of all these ears—for where I am robb'd and bound,
There must I be unloosed, although not there
At once and fully satisfied—whether ever I
Did broach this business to your highness, or
Laid any scruple in your way which might   150
Induce you to the question on 't? or ever
Have to you, but with thanks to God for such
A royal lady, spake one the least word that might

Be to the prejudice of her present state,
Or touch of her good person?
  King.   My lord cardinal,
I do excuse you; yea, upon mine honour,
I free you from 't. You are not to be taught
That you have many enemies that know not
Why they are so, but, like to village-curs,
Bark when their fellows do: by some of these   160
The queen is put in anger. You 're excused:
But will you be more justified? you ever
Have wish'd the sleeping of this business, never desired
It to be stirr'd, but oft have hinder'd, oft,
The passages made toward it: on my honour,
I speak my good lord cardinal to this point,
And thus far clear him. Now, what moved me to 't,
I will be bold with time and your attention:
Then mark the inducement. Thus it came; give heed to 't:
My conscience first received a tenderness,   170
Scruple, and prick, on certain speeches utter'd
By the Bishop of Bayonne, then French ambassador;
Who had been hither sent on the debating
A marriage 'twixt the Duke of Orleans and
Our daughter Mary: i' the progress of this business,
Ere a determinate resolution, he,
I mean the bishop, did require a respite,
Wherein he might the king his lord advertise
Whether our daughter were legitimate,
Respecting this our marriage with the dowager,   180
Sometimes our brother's wife. This respite shook
The bosom of my conscience, enter'd me,
Yea, with a splitting power, and made to tremble
The region of my breast; which forced such way
That many mazed considerings did throng
And press'd in with this caution. First, methought
I stood not in the smile of heaven, who had

Commanded nature that my lady's womb,
If it conceived a male child by me, should
Do no more offices of life to 't than   190
The grave does to the dead; for her male issue
Or died where they were made, or shortly after
This world had air'd them: hence I took a thought,
This was a judgment on me, that my kingdom,
Well worthy the best heir o' the world, should not
Be gladded in 't by me: then follows that
I weigh'd the danger which my realms stood in
By this my issue's fail; and that gave to me
Many a groaning throe.   Thus hulling in
The wild sea of my conscience, I did steer   200
Toward this remedy whereupon we are
Now present here together; that 's to say,
I meant to rectify my conscience, which
I then did feel full sick and yet not well,
By all the reverend fathers of the land
And doctors learn'd.   First I began in private
With you, my Lord of Lincoln; you remember
How under my oppression I did reek,
When I first moved you.

   Lin.   Very well, my liege.

   King. I have spoken long: be pleased yourself to say 210
How far you satisfied me.

   Lin.   So please your highness,
The question did at first so stagger me,
Bearing a state of mighty moment in 't
And consequence of dread, that I committed
The daring'st counsel which I had to doubt,
And did entreat your highness to this course
Which you are running here.

   King.   I then moved you,
My Lord of Canterbury, and got your leave
To make this present summons: unsolicited

I left no reverend person in this court;　　　　　　　220
But by particular consent proceeded
Under your hands and seals: therefore, go on;
For no dislike i' the world against the person
Of the good queen, but the sharp thorny points
Of my alleged reasons, drive this forward:
Prove but our marriage lawful, by my life
And kingly dignity, we are contented
To wear our mortal state to come with her,
Katharine our queen, before the primest creature
That 's paragon'd o' the world.

Cam.　　　　　　　　　So please your highness, 230
The queen being absent, 't is a needful fitness
That we adjourn this court till further day:
Meanwhile must be an earnest motion
Made to the queen, to call back her appeal
She intends unto his holiness.

King.　　　　　　　　　[*Aside*] I may perceive
These cardinals trifle with me: I abhor
This dilatory sloth and tricks of Rome.
My learn'd and well-beloved servant, Cranmer,
Prithee, return: with thy approach, I know,
My comfort comes along.—Break up the court:　　240
I say, set on.　　　　　　[*Exeunt in manner as they entered.*

ACT III.

SCENE I.　*London.　The* QUEEN'S *apartments.*

The QUEEN *and her Women, as at work.*

Q. Kath. Take thy lute, wench: my soul grows sad with
　　troubles;
Sing, and disperse 'em, if thou canst: leave working.

SONG.

Orpheus with his lute made trees,
And the mountain tops that freeze
   Bow themselves when he did sing:
To his music plants and flowers
Ever sprung, as sun and showers
   There had made a lasting spring.

Every thing that heard him play,
Even the billows of the sea,   10
   Hung their heads, and then lay by
In sweet music is such art,
Killing care and grief of heart
   Fall asleep, or hearing die.

Enter a Gentleman.

Q. Kath. How now!

Gent. An 't please your grace, the two great cardinals
Wait in the presence.

Q. Kath.   Would they speak with me?

Gent. They will'd me say so, madam.

Q. Kath.   Pray their graces
To come near. [*Exit Gent.*] What can be their business
With me, a poor weak woman, fall'n from favour?   20
I do not like their coming.   Now I think on 't,
They should be good men, their affairs as righteous:
But all hoods make not monks.

Enter the two Cardinals, WOLSEY *and* CAMPEIUS.

Wol.   Peace to your highness!

Q. Kath. Your graces find me here part of a housewife;
I would be all, against the worst may happen.
What are your pleasures with me, reverend lords?

Wol. May it please you, noble madam, to withdraw

Into your private chamber, we shall give you
The full cause of our coming.

    Q. Kath.   Speak it here:
There's nothing I have done yet, o' my conscience,   30
Deserves a corner: would all other women
Could speak this with as free a soul as I do!
My lords, I care not, so much I am happy
Above a number, if my actions
Were tried by every tongue, every eye saw 'em,
Envy and base opinion set against 'em,
I know my life so even.   If your business
Seek me out, and that way I am wife in,
Out with it boldly: truth loves open dealing.

    Wol. Tanta est erga te mentis integritas, regina serenis-
sima,—   41

    Q. Kath. O, good my lord, no Latin;
I am not such a truant since my coming,
As not to know the language I have lived in:
A strange tongue makes my cause more strange, suspi-
    cious;
Pray speak in English: here are some will thank you,
If you speak truth, for their poor mistress' sake;
Believe me, she has had much wrong: lord cardinal,
The willing'st sin I ever yet committed
May be absolved in English.

    Wol.   Noble lady,   50
I am sorry my integrity should breed,
And service to his majesty and you,
So deep suspicion, where all faith was meant.
We come not by the way of accusation,
To taint that honour every good tongue blesses,
Nor to betray you any way to sorrow—
You have too much, good lady—but to know
How you stand minded in the weighty difference
Between the king and you, and to deliver,

Like free and honest men, our just opinions   60
And comforts to your cause.

Cam.   Most honour'd madam,
My Lord of York, out of his noble nature,
Zeal and obedience he still bore your grace,
Forgetting, like a good man, your late censure
Both of his truth and him, which was too far,
Offers, as I do, in a sign of peace,
His service and his counsel.

Q. Kath.   [*Aside*] To betray me.—
My lords, I thank you both for your good wills;
Ye speak like honest men; pray God, ye prove so!
But how to make ye suddenly an answer,   70
In such a point of weight, so near mine honour,
More near my life, I fear, with my weak wit,
And to such men of gravity and learning,
In truth, I know not.   I was set at work
Among my maids, full little, God knows, looking
Either for such men or such business.
For her sake that I have been—for I feel
The last fit of my greatness—good your graces,
Let me have time and counsel for my cause:
Alas, I am a woman, friendless, hopeless!   80

Wol. Madam, you wrong the king's love with these fears:
Your hopes and friends are infinite.

Q. Kath.   In England
But little for my profit: can you think, lords,
That any Englishman dare give me counsel?
Or be a known friend, 'gainst his highness' pleasure—
Though he be grown so desperate to be honest—
And live a subject?   Nay, forsooth, my friends,
They that must weigh out my afflictions,
They that my trust must grow to, live not here:
They are, as all my other comforts, far hence   90
In mine own country, lords.

    Cam.   I would your grace
Would leave your griefs, and take my counsel.
    Q. Kath.   How, sir?
    Cam. Put your main cause into the king's protection;
He's loving and most gracious: 't will be much
Both for your honour better and your cause;
For if the trial of the law o'ertake ye,
You'll part away disgraced.
    Wol.   He tells you rightly.
    Q. Kath. Ye tell me what ye wish for both, my ruin:
Is this your Christian counsel? out upon ye!
Heaven is above all yet; there sits a judge   100
That no king can corrupt.
    Cam.   Your rage mistakes us.
    Q. Kath. The more shame for ye: holy men I thought ye,
Upon my soul, two reverend cardinal virtues;
But cardinal sins and hollow hearts I fear ye:
Mend 'em, for shame, my lords.   Is this your comfort?
The cordial that ye bring a wretched lady,
A woman lost among you, laugh'd at, scorn'd?
I will not wish ye half my miseries;
I have more charity: but say, I warn'd ye;
Take heed, for heaven's sake, take heed, lest at once   110
The burthen of my sorrows fall upon ye.
    Wol. Madam, this is a mere distraction;
You turn the good we offer into envy.
    Q. Kath. Ye turn me into nothing: woe upon ye
And all such false professors! would you have me—
If you have any justice, any pity,
If ye be any thing but churchmen's habits—
Put my sick cause into his hands that hates me?
Alas, has banish'd me his bed already,
His love, too long ago! I am old, my lords,   120
And all the fellowship I hold now with him
Is only my obedience. What can happen

To me above this wretchedness? all your studies
Make me a curse like this.

    Cam.   Your fears are worse.

    Q. Kath. Have I lived thus long—let me speak myself,
Since virtue finds no friends—a wife, a true one?
A woman, I dare say without vain-glory,
Never yet branded with suspicion?
Have I with all my full affections
Still met the king? loved him next heaven? obey'd him? 130
Been, out of fondness, superstitious to him?
Almost forgot my prayers to content him?
And am I thus rewarded? 't is not well, lords.
Bring me a constant woman to her husband,
One that ne'er dream'd a joy beyond his pleasure,
And to that woman, when she has done most,
Yet will I add an honour, a great patience.

    Wol. Madam, you wander from the good we aim at.

    Q. Kath. My lord, I dare not make myself so guilty,
To give up willingly that noble title   140
Your master wed me to: nothing but death
Shall e'er divorce my dignities.

    Wol.   Pray, hear me.

    Q. Kath. Would I had never trod this English earth,
Or felt the flatteries that grow upon it!
Ye have angels' faces, but heaven knows your hearts.
What will become of me now, wretched lady!
I am the most unhappy woman living.
Alas, poor wenches, where are now your fortunes?
Shipwreck'd upon a kingdom, where no pity,
No friends, no hope; no kindred weep for me;   150
Almost no grave allow'd me: like the lily,
That once was mistress of the field and flourish'd,
I 'll hang my head and perish.

    Wol.   If your grace
Could but be brought to know our ends are honest,

You 'ld feel more comfort: why should we, good lady,
Upon what cause, wrong you? alas, our places,
The way of our profession is against it:
We are to cure such sorrows, not to sow 'em.
For goodness' sake, consider what you do;
How you may hurt yourself, ay, utterly   160
Grow from the king's acquaintance, by this carriage.
The hearts of princes kiss obedience,
So much they love it; but to stubborn spirits
They swell, and grow as terrible as storms.
I know you have a gentle, noble temper,
A soul as even as a calm: pray think us
Those we profess, peace-makers, friends, and servants.

    Cam. Madam, you 'll find it so.   You wrong your virtues
With these weak women's fears: a noble spirit,
As yours was put into you, ever casts   170
Such doubts, as false coin, from it.   The king loves you;
Beware you lose it not: for us, if you please
To trust us in your business, we are ready
To use our utmost studies in your service.

    Q. Kath. Do what ye will, my lords: and pray forgive me,
If I have used myself unmannerly;
You know I am a woman, lacking wit
To make a seemly answer to such persons.
Pray do my service to his majesty:
He has my heart yet, and shall have my prayers   180
While I shall have my life.   Come, reverend fathers,
Bestow your counsels on me: she now begs,
That little thought, when she set footing here,
She should have bought her dignities so dear.   [*Exeunt.*

SCENE II. *Ante-chamber to the King's apartment.*

Enter the DUKE OF NORFOLK, *the* DUKE OF SUFFOLK,
the EARL OF SURREY, *and the* LORD CHAMBERLAIN.

Nor. If you will now unite in your complaints,
And force them with a constancy, the cardinal
Cannot stand under them: if you omit
The offer of this time, I cannot promise
But that you shall sustain mo new disgraces,
With these you bear already.
Sur.   I am joyful
To meet the least occasion that may give me
Remembrance of my father-in-law, the duke,
To be revenged on him.
Suf.   Which of the peers
Have uncontemn'd gone by him, or at least   10
Strangely neglected? when did he regard
The stamp of nobleness in any person
Out of himself?
Cham.   My lords, you speak your pleasures:
What he deserves of you and me I know;
What we can do to him, though now the time
Gives way to us, I much fear.   If you cannot
Bar his access to the king, never attempt
Any thing on him; for he hath a witchcraft
Over the king in 's tongue.
Nor.   O, fear him not;
His spell in that is out: the king hath found   20
Matter against him that for ever mars
The honey of his language.   No, he 's settled,
Not to come off, in his displeasure.
Sur.   Sir,
I should be glad to hear such news as this
Once every hour.

Nor.   Believe it, this is true:
In the divorce his contrary proceedings
Are all unfolded; wherein he appears
As I would wish mine enemy.
     Sur.   How came
His practices to light?
     Suf.   Most strangely.
     Sur.   O, how, how?
     Suf. The cardinal's letters to the pope miscarried,   30
And came to the eye o' the king: wherein was read
How that the cardinal did entreat his holiness
To stay the judgment o' the divorce; for if
It did take place, 'I do', quoth he, 'perceive
My king is tangled in affection to
A creature of the queen's, Lady Anne Bullen'.
     Sur. Has the king this?
     Suf.   Believe it.
     Sur.   Will this work?
     Cham. The king in this perceives him, how he coasts
And hedges his own way.   But in this point
All his tricks founder, and he brings his physic   40
After his patient's death: the king already
Hath married the fair lady.
     Sur.   Would he had!
     Suf. May you be happy in your wish, my lord!
For, I profess, you have it.
     Sur.   Now, all my joy
Trace the conjunction!
     Suf.   My amen to 't!
     Nor.   All men's!
     Suf. There's order given for her coronation:
Marry, this is yet but young, and may be left
To some ears unrecounted.   But, my lords,
She is a gallant creature and complete
In mind and feature: I persuade me, from her   50

Will fall some blessing to this land, which shall
In it be memorized.

 Sur.   But will the king
Digest this letter of the cardinal's?
The Lord forbid!

 Nor.   Marry, amen!

 Suf.   No, no;
There be mo wasps that buzz about his nose
Will make this sting the sooner.   Cardinal Campeius
Is stol'n away to Rome; hath ta'en no leave;
Has left the cause o' the king unhandled; and
Is posted as the agent of our cardinal,
To second all his plot.   I do assure you   60
The king cried Ha! at this.

 Cham.   Now, God incense him,
And let him cry Ha! louder!

 Nor.   But, my lord,
When returns Cranmer?

 Suf. He is return'd in his opinions, which
Have satisfied the king for his divorce,
Together with all famous colleges
Almost in Christendom: shortly, I believe,
His second marriage shall be publish'd, and
Her coronation.   Katharine no more
Shall be call'd queen, but princess dowager 70
And widow to Prince Arthur.

 Nor.   This same Cranmer's
A worthy fellow, and hath ta'en much pain
In the king's business.

 Suf.   He has; and we shall see him
For it an archbishop.

 Nor.   So I hear.

 Suf.   'T is so.
The cardinal!

Enter WOLSEY *and* CROMWELL.

Nor.   Observe, observe, he's moody.

Wol. The packet, Cromwell,
Gave't you the king?

Crom.   To his own hand, in's bedchamber.

Wol. Look'd he o' the inside of the paper?

Crom.   Presently
He did unseal them: and the first he view'd,
He did it with a serious mind; a heed   8c
Was in his countenance. You he bade
Attend him here this morning.

Wol.   Is he ready
To come abroad?

Crom.   I think, by this he is.

Wol. Leave me awhile.   [*Exit Cromwell.*
[*Aside*] It shall be to the Duchess of Alençon,
The French king's sister: he shall marry her.
Anne Bullen! No; I'll no Anne Bullens for him:
There's more in't than fair visage. Bullen!
No, we'll no Bullens. Speedily I wish
To hear from Rome. The Marchioness of Pembroke! 90

Nor. He's discontented.

Suf.   May be, he hears the king
Does whet his anger to him.

Sur.   Sharp enough,
Lord, for thy justice.

Wol. [*Aside*] The late queen's gentlewoman, a knight's
          daughter,
To be her mistress' mistress! the queen's queen!
This candle burns not clear: 't is I must snuff it;
Then out it goes. What though I know her virtuous
And well deserving? yet I know her for
A spleeny Lutheran, and not wholesome to
Our cause, that she should lie i' the bosom of   100

Our hard-ruled king.   Again, there is sprung up
An heretic, an arch one, Cranmer, one
Hath crawl'd into the favour of the king,
And is his oracle.

    Nor.   He is vex'd at something.

    Sur. I would 't were something that would fret the string,
The master-cord on 's heart!

Enter the KING, *reading of a schedule, and* LOVELL.

    Suf.   The king, the king!

    King. What piles of wealth hath he accumulated
To his own portion! and what expense by the hour
Seems to flow from him!   How, i' the name of thrift,
Does he rake this together?   Now, my lords,   110
Saw you the cardinal?

    Nor.   My lord, we have
Stood here observing him: some strange commotion
Is in his brain: he bites his lip, and starts;
Stops on a sudden, looks upon the ground,
Then lays his finger on his temple; straight
Springs out into fast gait; then stops again,
Strikes his breast hard, and anon he casts
His eye against the moon: in most strange postures
We have seen him set himself.

    King.   It may well be;
There is a mutiny in 's mind.   This morning   120
Papers of state he sent me to peruse,
As I required: and wot you what I found
There, on my conscience, put unwittingly?
Forsooth, an inventory, thus importing,
The several parcels of his plate, his treasure,
Rich stuffs, and ornaments of household, which
I find at such proud rate that it out-speaks
Possession of a subject.

    Nor.   It 's heaven's will:

Some spirit put this paper in the packet,
To bless your eye withal.

    King.   If we did think   130
His contemplations were above the earth,
And fix'd on spiritual object, he should still
Dwell in his musings: but I am afraid
His thinkings are below the moon, not worth
His serious considering.

                [*King takes his seat; whispers Lovell,*
                     who goes to the Cardinal.

    Wol.   Heaven forgive me!
Ever God bless your highness!

    King.   Good my lord,
You are full of heavenly stuff, and bear the inventory
Of your best graces in your mind; the which
You were now running o'er: you have scarce time
To steal from spiritual leisure a brief span   140
To keep your earthly audit: sure, in that
I deem you an ill husband, and am glad
To have you therein my companion.

    Wol.   Sir,
For holy offices I have a time; a time
To think upon the part of business which
I bear i' the state; and nature does require
Her times of preservation, which perforce
I, her frail son, amongst my brethren mortal,
Must give my tendance to.

    King.   You have said well.

    Wol. And ever may your highness yoke together,   150
As I will lend you cause, my doing well
With my well saying!

    King.   'T is well said again;
And 't is a kind of good deed to say well:
And yet words are no deeds. My father loved you:
He said he did, and with his deed did crown

His word upon you.   Since I had my office,
I have kept you next my heart; have not alone
Employ'd you where high profits might come home,
But pared my present havings, to bestow
My bounties upon you.

Wol.   [*Aside*] What should this mean? 160

Sur. [*Aside*] The Lord increase this business!

King.   Have I not made you
The prime man of the state?   I pray you, tell me,
If what I now pronounce you have found true:
And, if you may confess it, say withal,
If you are bound to us or no.   What say you?

Wol. My sovereign, I confess your royal graces,
Shower'd on me daily, have been more than could
My studied purposes requite; which went
Beyond all man's endeavours: my endeavours
Have ever come too short of my desires,   170
Yet filed with my abilities: mine own ends
Have been mine so that evermore they pointed
To the good of your most sacred person and
The profit of the state.   For your great graces
Heap'd upon me, poor undeserver, I
Can nothing render but allegiant thanks,
My prayers to heaven for you, my loyalty,
Which ever has and ever shall be growing,
Till death, that winter, kill it.

King.   Fairly answer'd;
A loyal and obedient subject is   180
Therein illustrated: the honour of it
Does pay the act of it; as, i' the contrary,
The foulness is the punishment.   I presume
That, as my hand has open'd bounty to you,
My heart dropp'd love, my power rain'd honour, more
On you than any; so your hand and heart,
Your brain, and every function of your power,

Should, notwithstanding that your bond of duty,
As 't were in love's particular, be more
To me, your friend, than any.

Wol.   I do profess   190
That for your highness' good I ever labour'd
More than mine own; that am, have, and will be—
Though all the world should crack their duty to you,
And throw it from their soul; though perils did
Abound, as thick as thought could make 'em, and
Appear in forms more horrid—yet my duty,
As doth a rock against the chiding flood,
Should the approach of this wild river break,
And stand unshaken yours.

King.   'T is nobly spoken.
Take notice, lords, he has a loyal breast,   200
For you have seen him open 't.   Read o'er this.
                          [*Giving him papers.*
And after, this: and then to breakfast with
What appetite you have.
            [*Exit King, frowning upon the Cardinal: the Nobles
                throng after him, smiling and whispering.*

Wol.   What should this mean?
What sudden anger 's this? how have I reap'd it?
He parted frowning from me, as if ruin
Leap'd from his eyes: so looks the chafed lion
Upon the daring huntsman that has gall'd him;
Then makes him nothing.   I must read this paper;
I fear, the story of his anger.   'T is so;
This paper has undone me: 't is the account   210
Of all that world of wealth I have drawn together
For mine own ends; indeed, to gain the popedom,
And fee my friends in Rome.   O negligence!
Fit for a fool to fall by: what cross devil
Made me put this main secret in the packet
I sent the king?   Is there no way to cure this?

No new device to beat this from his brains?
I know 't will stir him strongly; yet I know
A way, if it take right, in spite of fortune
Will bring me off again. What 's this? 'To the Pope!' 220
The letter, as I live, with all the business
I writ to 's holiness.   Nay then, farewell!
I have touch'd the highest point of all my greatness;
And, from that full meridian of my glory,
I haste now to my setting: I shall fall
Like a bright exhalation in the evening,
And no man see me more.

Re-enter to WOLSEY *the* DUKES OF NORFOLK *and* SUFFOLK,
    the EARL OF SURREY, *and the* LORD CHAMBERLAIN.

  Nor. Hear the king's pleasure, cardinal: who commands
    you
To render up the great seal presently
Into our hands; and to confine yourself   230
To Asher House, my Lord of Winchester's,
Till you hear further from his highness.
  Wol.   Stay:
Where 's your commission, lords? words cannot carry
Authority so weighty.
  Suf.   Who dare cross 'em,
Bearing the king's will from his mouth expressly?
  Wol. Till I find more than will or words to do it,
I mean your malice, know, officious lords,
I dare and must deny it.   Now I feel
Of what coarse metal ye are moulded, envy:
How eagerly ye follow my disgraces,   240
As if it fed ye! and how sleek and wanton
Ye appear in every thing may bring my ruin!
Follow your envious courses, men of malice;
You have Christian warrant for 'em, and, no doubt,
In time will find their fit rewards.   That seal

You ask with such a violence, the king,
Mine and your master, with his own hand gave me;
Bade me enjoy it, with the place and honours,
During my life; and, to confirm his goodness,
Tied it by letters-patents: now, who'll take it?   250

    Sur. The king, that gave it.

    Wol.   It must be himself, then.

    Sur. Thou art a proud traitor, priest.

    Wol.   Proud lord, thou liest:
Within these forty hours Surrey durst better
Have burnt that tongue than said so.

    Sur.   Thy ambition,
Thou scarlet sin, robb'd this bewailing land
Of noble Buckingham, my father-in-law:
The heads of all thy brother cardinals,
With thee and all thy best parts bound together,
Weigh'd not a hair of his.   Plague of your policy!
You sent me deputy for Ireland;   260
Far from his succour, from the king, from all
That might have mercy on the fault thou gavest him;
Whilst your great goodness, out of holy pity,
Absolved him with an axe.

    Wol.   This, and all else
This talking lord can lay upon my credit,
I answer is most false.   The duke by law
Found his deserts.   How innocent I was
From any private malice in his end,
His noble jury and foul cause can witness.
If I loved many words, lord, I should tell you   270
You have as little honesty as honour,
That in the way of loyalty and truth
Toward the king, my ever royal master,
Dare mate a sounder man than Surrey can be,
And all that love his follies.

    Sur.   By my soul,

Your long coat, priest, protects you; thou shouldst feel
My sword i' the life-blood of thee else.   My lords,
Can ye endure to hear this arrogance?
And from this fellow?   If we live thus tamely,
To be thus jaded by a piece of scarlet,   280
Farewell nobility; let his grace go forward,
And dare us with his cap like larks.
    Wol.   All goodness
Is poison to thy stomach.
    Sur.   Yes, that goodness
Of gleaning all the land's wealth into one,
Into your own hands, cardinal, by extortion;
The goodness of your intercepted packets
You writ to the pope against the king: your goodness,
Since you provoke me, shall be most notorious.
My Lord of Norfolk, as you are truly noble,
As you respect the common good, the state   290
Of our despised nobility, our issues,
Who, if he live, will scarce be gentlemen,
Produce the grand sum of his sins, the articles
Collected from his life.   I 'll startle you
Worse than the sacring bell, when the brown wench
Lay kissing in your arms, lord cardinal.
    Wol. How much, methinks, I could despise this man,
But that I am bound in charity against it!
    Nor. Those articles, my lord, are in the king's hand:
But, thus much, they are foul ones.
    Wol.   So much fairer   300
And spotless shall mine innocence arise,
When the king knows my truth.
    Sur.   This cannot save you:
I thank my memory, I yet remember
Some of these articles, and out they shall.
Now, if you can blush and cry 'guilty', cardinal,
You 'll show a little honesty.

Wol.   Speak on, sir;
I dare your worst objections: if I blush,
It is to see a nobleman want manners.

    Sur. I had rather want those than my head.   Have at
       you!
First that, without the king's assent or knowledge,   310
You wrought to be a legate; by which power
You maim'd the jurisdiction of all bishops.

    Nor. Then that in all you writ to Rome, or else
To foreign princes, 'Ego et Rex meus'
Was still inscribed; in which you brought the king
To be your servant.

    Suf.   Then that, without the knowledge
Either of king or council, when you went
Ambassador to the emperor, you made bold
To carry into Flanders the great seal.

    Sur. Item, you sent a large commission   320
To Gregory de Cassado, to conclude,
Without the king's will or the state's allowance,
A league between his highness and Ferrara.

    Suf. That, out of mere ambition, you have caused
Your holy hat to be stamp'd on the king's coin.

    Sur. Then that you have sent innumerable substance—
By what means got, I leave to your own conscience—
To furnish Rome, and to prepare the ways
You have for dignities, to the mere undoing
Of all the kingdom.   Many more there are;   330
Which, since they are of you, and odious,
I will not taint my mouth with.

    Cham.   O my lord!
Press not a falling man too far; 't is virtue:
His faults lie open to the laws; let them,
Not you, correct him.   My heart weeps to see him
So little of his great self.

    Sur.   I forgive him.

Suf. Lord cardinal, the king's further pleasure is,
Because all those things you have done of late,
By your power legatine, within this kingdom,
Fall into the compass of a præmunire,   340
That therefore such a writ be sued against you;
To forfeit all your goods, lands, tenements,
Chattels, and whatsoever, and to be
Out of the king's protection.   This is my charge.

Nor. And so we'll leave you to your meditations
How to live better.   For your stubborn answer
About the giving back the great seal to us,
The king shall know it, and, no doubt, shall thank you.
So fare you well, my little good lord cardinal.

　　　　　　　　　　　　　[Exeunt all but Wolsey.

Wol. So farewell to the little good you bear me.   350
Farewell! a long farewell, to all my greatness!
This is the state of man: to-day he puts forth
The tender leaves of hopes; to-morrow blossoms,
And bears his blushing honours thick upon him;
The third day comes a frost, a killing frost,
And, when he thinks, good easy man, full surely
His greatness is a-ripening, nips his root,
And then he falls, as I do.   I have ventured,
Like little wanton boys that swim on bladders,
This many summers in a sea of glory,   360
But far beyond my depth: my high-blown pride
At length broke under me, and now has left me,
Weary and old with service, to the mercy
Of a rude stream that must for ever hide me.
Vain pomp and glory of this world, I hate ye:
I feel my heart new open'd.   O, how wretched
Is that poor man that hangs on princes' favours!
There is, betwixt that smile we would aspire to,
That sweet aspect of princes, and their ruin,
More pangs and fears than wars or women have: 370

And when he falls, he falls like Lucifer,
Never to hope again.

Enter CROMWELL, *and stands amazed.*

                      Why, how now, Cromwell!
  Crom. I have no power to speak, sir.
  Wol.   What, amazed
At my misfortunes? can thy spirit wonder
A great man should decline? Nay, an you weep,
I am fall'n indeed.
  Crom.   How does your grace?
  Wol.   Why, well;
Never so truly happy, my good Cromwell.
I know myself now; and I feel within me
A peace above all earthly dignities,
A still and quiet conscience. The king has cured me, 380
I humbly thank his grace; and from these shoulders,
These ruin'd pillars, out of pity, taken
A load would sink a navy, too much honour:
O, 't is a burden, Cromwell, 't is a burden
Too heavy for a man that hopes for heaven!
  Crom. I am glad your grace has made that right use of it.
  Wol. I hope I have: I am able now, methinks,
Out of a fortitude of soul I feel,
To endure more miseries and greater far
Than my weak-hearted enemies dare offer.   390
What news abroad?
  Crom.   The heaviest and the worst
Is your displeasure with the king.
  Wol.   God bless him!
  Crom. The next is, that Sir Thomas More is chosen
Lord chancellor in your place.
  Wol.   That 's somewhat sudden:
But he 's a learned man. May he continue
Long in his highness' favour, and do justice

For truth's sake and his conscience; that his bones,
When he has run his course and sleeps in blessings,
May have a tomb of orphans' tears wept on 'em!
What more?

 Crom. That Cranmer is return'd with welcome. 400
Install'd lord archbishop of Canterbury.

 Wol. That's news indeed.

 Crom.   Last, that the Lady Anne,
Whom the king hath in secrecy long married,
This day was view'd in open as his queen,
Going to chapel; and the voice is now
Only about her coronation.

 Wol. There was the weight that pull'd me down. O
  Cromwell,
The king has gone beyond me; all my glories
In that one woman I have lost for ever:
No sun shall ever usher forth mine honours, 410
Or gild again the noble troops that waited
Upon my smiles. Go, get thee from me, Cromwell;
I am a poor fall'n man, unworthy now
To be thy lord and master: seek the king:
That sun, I pray, may never set! I have told him
What and how true thou art: he will advance thee;
Some little memory of me will stir him—
I know his noble nature—not to let
Thy hopeful service perish too: good Cromwell,
Neglect him not; make use now, and provide 420
For thine own future safety.

 Crom.   O my lord,
Must I then leave you? must I needs forgo
So good, so noble and so true a master?
Bear witness, all that have not hearts of iron,
With what a sorrow Cromwell leaves his lord.
The king shall have my service; but my prayers
For ever and for ever shall be yours.

Wol. Cromwell, I did not think to shed a tear
In all my miseries; but thou hast forced me,
Out of thy honest truth, to play the woman.   430
Let's dry our eyes: and thus far hear me, Cromwell;
And, when I am forgotten, as I shall be,
And sleep in dull cold marble, where no mention
Of me more must be heard of, say, I taught thee;
Say, Wolsey, that once trod the ways of glory,
And sounded all the depths and shoals of honour,
Found thee a way, out of his wreck, to rise in;
A sure and safe one, though thy master miss'd it.
Mark but my fall and that that ruin'd me.
Cromwell, I charge thee, fling away ambition: 440
By that sin fell the angels; how can man then,
The image of his Maker, hope to win by it?
Love thyself last: cherish those hearts that hate thee;
Corruption wins not more than honesty.
Still in thy right hand carry gentle peace,
To silence envious tongues.   Be just, and fear not:
Let all the ends thou aim'st at be thy country's,
Thy God's, and truth's; then if thou fall'st, O Cromwell,
Thou fall'st a blessed martyr!   Serve the king;
And prithee, lead me in: 450
There take an inventory of all I have;
To the last penny, 't is the king's: my robe,
And my integrity to heaven, is all
I dare now call mine own.   O Cromwell, Cromwell!
Had I but served my God with half the zeal
I served my king, he would not in mine age
Have left me naked to mine enemies.
    Crom. Good sir, have patience.
    Wol.   So I have.   Farewell
The hopes of court! my hopes in heaven do dwell. [*Exeunt.*

ACT IV.

Scene I. *A street in Westminster.*

Enter two Gentlemen, *meeting one another.*

First Gent. You 're well met once again.

Sec. Gent.   So are you.

First Gent. You come to take your stand here and behold
The Lady Anne pass from her coronation?

Sec. Gent. 'T is all my business.   At our last encounter
The Duke of Buckingham came from his trial.

First Gent. 'T is very true: but that time offer'd sorrow;
This, general joy.

Sec. Gent.   'T is well: the citizens,
I am sure, have shown at full their royal minds—
As, let 'em have their rights, they are ever forward—
In celebration of this day with shows,   10
Pageants, and sights of honour.

First Gent.   Never greater,
Nor, I 'll assure you, better taken, sir.

Sec. Gent. May I be bold to ask what that contains,
That paper in your hand?

First Gent.   Yes; 't is the list
Of those that claim their offices this day
By custom of the coronation.
The Duke of Suffolk is the first, and claims
To be high-steward; next, the Duke of Norfolk,
He to be earl marshal: you may read the rest.

Sec. Gent. I thank you, sir: had I not known those cus-
toms,   20
I should have been beholding to your paper.
But, I beseech you, what 's become of Katharine,
The princess dowager? how goes her business?

First Gent. That I can tell you too. The Archbishop
Of Canterbury, accompanied with other
Learned and reverend fathers of his order,
Held a late court at Dunstable, six miles off
From Ampthill, where the princess lay; to which
She was often cited by them, but appear'd not:
And, to be short, for not appearance and   30
The king's late scruple, by the main assent
Of all these learned men she was divorced,
And the late marriage made of none effect:
Since which she was removed to Kimbolton,
Where she remains now sick.
    Sec. Gent.   Alas, good lady! [*Trumpets.*
The trumpets sound: stand close, the queen is coming.
                                 [*Hautboys.*

THE ORDER OF THE CORONATION.

1. *A lively flourish of trumpets.*
2. *Then two* Judges.
3. LORD CHANCELLOR, *with purse and mace before him.*
4. Choristers, *singing. Music.*
5. MAYOR OF LONDON, *bearing the mace. Then* Garter, *in his coat of arms, and on his head a gilt copper crown.*
6. MARQUESS DORSET, *bearing a sceptre of gold, on his head a demi-coronal of gold. With him, the* EARL OF SURREY, *bearing the rod of silver with the dove, crowned with an earl's coronet. Collars of SS.*
7. DUKE OF SUFFOLK, *in his robe of estate, his coronet on his head, bearing a long white wand, as high-steward. With him, the* DUKE OF NORFOLK, *with the rod of marshalship, a coronet on his head. Collars of SS.*
8. *A canopy borne by four of the* Cinque-ports; *under it, the* QUEEN *in her robe; in her hair richly adorned with pearl, crowned. On each side her, the* Bishops of London *and* Winchester.

9. *The old* DUCHESS OF NORFOLK, *in a coronal of gold,
   wrought with flowers, bearing the* QUEEN'S *train.*
10. *Certain* Ladies *or* Countesses, *with plain circlets of gold
    without flowers.*
   They pass over the stage in order and state.

Sec. Gent. A royal train, believe me. These I know:
Who's that that bears the sceptre?
   First Gent.   Marquess Dorset:
And that the Earl of Surrey, with the rod.
   Sec. Gent. A bold brave gentleman. That should be 40
The Duke of Suffolk?
   First Gent.   'T is the same: high-steward.
   Sec. Gent. And that my Lord of Norfolk?
   First Gent.   Yes.
   Sec. Gent. [*Looking on the Queen*]   Heaven bless thee!
Thou hast the sweetest face I ever look'd on.
Sir, as I have a soul, she is an angel;
Our king has all the Indies in his arms,
And more and richer, when he strains that lady:
I cannot blame his conscience.
   First Gent.   They that bear
The cloth of honour over her, are four barons
Of the Cinque-ports.
   Sec. Gent. Those men are happy; and so are all are near
her.   50
I take it, she that carries up the train
Is that old noble lady, Duchess of Norfolk.
   First Gent. It is; and all the rest are countesses.
   Sec. Gent. Their coronets say so. These are stars indeed,
And sometimes falling ones.
   First Gent.   No more of that.
                          [*Exit procession; and then a great
                            flourish of trumpets.*

Enter a third Gentleman.

    First Gent. God save you, sir! where have you been
    broiling?
    Third Gent. Among the crowd i' the Abbey; where a
    finger
Could not be wedged in more: I am stifled
With the mere rankness of their joy.
    Sec. Gent.   You saw
The ceremony?
    Third Gent. That I did.
    First Gent.   How was it?   60
    Third Gent. Well worth the seeing.
    Sec. Gent.   Good sir, speak it to us.
    Third Gent. As well as I am able.   The rich stream
Of lords and ladies, having brought the queen
To a prepared place in the choir, fell off
A distance from her; while her grace sat down
To rest awhile, some half an hour or so,
In a rich chair of state, opposing freely
The beauty of her person to the people.
Believe me, sir, she is the goodliest woman
That ever lay by man: which when the people   70
Had the full view of, such a noise arose
As the shrouds make at sea in a stiff tempest,
As loud, and to as many tunes: hats, cloaks,—
Doublets, I think,—flew up; and had their faces
Been loose, this day they had been lost. Such joy
I never saw before.   Great-bellied women,
That had not half a week to go, like rams
In the old time of war, would shake the press,
And make 'em reel before 'em.   No man living
Could say 'This is my wife' there, all were woven   80
So strangely in one piece.
    Sec. Gent.   But what follow'd?

Third Gent. At length her grace rose, and with modest
    paces
Came to the altar, where she kneel'd and saintlike
Cast her fair eyes to heaven and pray'd devoutly;
Then rose again and bow'd her to the people;
When by the Archbishop of Canterbury
She had all the royal makings of a queen,
As holy oil, Edward Confessor's crown,
The rod, and bird of peace, and all such emblems
Laid nobly on her: which perform'd, the choir,   90
With all the choicest music of the kingdom,
Together sung 'Te Deum'. So she parted,
And with the same full state paced back again
To York-place, where the feast is held.

First Gent.   Sir,
You must no more call it York-place; that's past;
For, since the cardinal fell, that title's lost:
'T is now the king's, and call'd Whitehall.

Third Gent.   I know it;
But 't is so lately alter'd, that the old name
Is fresh about me.

Sec. Gent.   What two reverend bishops
Were those that went on each side of the queen?   100

Third Gent. Stokesly and Gardiner; the one of Winchester
Newly preferr'd from the king's secretary,
The other, London.

Sec. Gent.   He of Winchester
Is held no great good lover of the archbishop's,
The virtuous Cranmer.

Third Gent.   All the land knows that:
However, yet there is no great breach; when it comes,
Cranmer will find a friend will not shrink from him.

Sec. Gent. Who may that be, I pray you?

Third Gent.   Thomas Cromwell;
A man in much esteem with the king, and truly

A worthy friend.   The king has made him master   110
O' the jewel house,
And one, already, of the privy council.
    Sec. Gent. He will deserve more.
    Third Gent.   Yes, without all doubt.
Come, gentlemen, ye shall go my way,
Which is to the court, and there ye shall be my guests:
Something I can command.   As I walk thither,
I 'll tell ye more.
    Both.   You may command us, sir.   [*Exeunt.*

Scene II.   *Kimbolton.*

Enter Katharine, *Dowager, sick; led between* Griffith,
    her Gentleman-usher, and Patience, *her woman.*

    Grif. How does your grace?
    Kath.   O Griffith, sick to death!
My legs, like loaden branches, bow to the earth,
Willing to leave their burthen.   Reach a chair:
So; now, methinks, I feel a little ease.
Didst thou not tell me, Griffith, as thou led'st me,
That the great child of honour, Cardinal Wolsey,
Was dead?
    Grif.   Yes, madam; but I think your grace,
Out of the pain you suffer'd, gave no ear to 't.
    Kath. Prithee, good Griffith, tell me how he died:
If well, he stepp'd before me, happily,   10
For my example.
    Grif.   Well, the voice goes, madam:
For after the stout Earl Northumberland
Arrested him at York, and brought him forward,
As a man sorely tainted, to his answer,
He fell sick suddenly, and grew so ill
He could not sit his mule.
    Kath.   Alas, poor man!

Grif. At last, with easy roads, he came to Leicester,
Lodged in the abbey; where the reverend abbot,
With all his covent, honourably received him;
To whom he gave these words, 'O father abbot,   20
An old man, broken with the storms of state,
Is come to lay his weary bones among ye;
Give him a little earth for charity!'
So went to bed; where eagerly his sickness
Pursued him still; and three nights after this,
About the hour of eight, which he himself
Foretold should be his last, full of repentance,
Continual meditations, tears, and sorrows,
He gave his honours to the world again,
His blessed part to heaven, and slept in peace.   30
    Kath. So, may he rest; his faults lie gently on him!
Yet thus far, Griffith, give me leave to speak him,
And yet with charity.   He was a man
Of an unbounded stomach, ever ranking
Himself with princes; one that by suggestion
Tied all the kingdom: simony was fair-play:
His own opinion was his law: i' the presence
He would say untruths, and be ever double
Both in his words and meaning: he was never,
But where he meant to ruin, pitiful: 40
His promises were, as he then was, mighty;
But his performance, as he is now, nothing:
Of his own body he was ill, and gave
The clergy ill example.
    Grif.   Noble madam,
Men's evil manners live in brass; their virtues
We write in water.   May it please your highness
To hear me speak his good now?
    Kath.   Yes, good Griffith;
I were malicious else.
    Grif.   This cardinal,

Though from an humble stock, undoubtedly
Was fashion'd to much honour from his cradle.   50
He was a scholar, and a ripe and good one;
Exceeding wise, fair-spoken, and persuading:
Lofty and sour to them that loved him not,
But to those men that sought him, sweet as summer.
And though he were unsatisfied in getting,
Which was a sin, yet in bestowing, madam,
He was most princely: ever witness for him
Those twins of learning that he raised in you,
Ipswich and Oxford! one of which fell with him,
Unwilling to outlive the good that did it;   60
The other, though unfinish'd, yet so famous,
So excellent in art, and still so rising,
That Christendom shall ever speak his virtue.
His overthrow heap'd happiness upon him;
For then, and not till then, he felt himself,
And found the blessedness of being little:
And, to add greater honours to his age
Than man could give him, he died fearing God.

    Kath. After my death I wish no other herald,
No other speaker of my living actions,   70
To keep mine honour from corruption,
But such an honest chronicler as Griffith.
Whom I most hated living, thou hast made me,
With thy religious truth and modesty,
Now in his ashes honour: peace be with him!
Patience, be near me still; and set me lower:
I have not long to trouble thee.   Good Griffith,
Cause the musicians play me that sad note
I named my knell, whilst I sit meditating
On that celestial harmony I go to.   80

                [Sad and solemn music.

    Grif. She is asleep: good wench, let's sit down quiet,
For fear we wake her: softly, gentle Patience.

The vision.   Enter, solemnly tripping one after another, six
   personages, clad in white robes, wearing on their heads
   garlands of bays, and golden vizards on their faces;
   branches of bays or palm in their hands.   They first
   congee unto her, then dance; and, at certain changes, the
   first two hold a spare garland over her head; at which
   the other four make reverent curtsies; then the two that
   held the garland deliver the same to the other next two,
   who observe the same order in their changes, and holding
   the garland over her head: which done, they deliver the
   same garland to the last two, who likewise observe the
   same order: at which, as it were by inspiration, she
   makes in her sleep signs of rejoicing, and holdeth up her
   hands to heaven: and so in their dancing vanish, carry-
   ing their garland with them.   The music continues.

   Kath.   Spirits of peace, where are ye? are ye all
      gone,
And leave me here in wretchedness behind ye?
   Grif.   Madam, we are here.
   Kath.   It is not you I call for:
Saw ye none enter since I slept?
   Grif.   None, madam.
   Kath.   No?   Saw you not even now a blessed troop
Invite me to a banquet, whose bright faces
Cast thousand beams upon me, like the sun?
They promised me eternal happiness,   90
And brought me garlands, Griffith, which I feel
I am not worthy yet to wear: I shall, assuredly.
   Grif.   I am most joyful, madam, such good dreams
Possess your fancy.
   Kath.   Bid the music leave;
They are harsh and heavy to me.   [*Music ceases.*
   Pat.   Do you note
How much her grace is alter'd on the sudden?

How long her face is drawn! how pale she looks,
And of an earthy cold!   Mark her eyes!
 Grif. She is going, wench: pray, pray.
 Pat.   Heaven comfort her!

    Enter a Messenger.

 Mess. An 't like your grace,—
 Kath.   You are a saucy fellow: 100
Deserve we no more reverence?
 Grif.   You are to blame,
Knowing she will not lose her wonted greatness,
To use so rude behaviour: go to, kneel.
 Mess. I humbly do entreat your highness' pardon;
My haste made me unmannerly.   There is staying
A gentleman, sent from the king, to see you.
 Kath. Admit him entrance, Griffith: but this fellow
Let me ne'er see again.   [*Exeunt Griffith and Messenger.*

  Re-enter GRIFFITH *with* CAPUCIUS.

      If my sight fail not,
You should be lord ambassador from the emperor,
My royal nephew, and your name Capucius.   110
 Cap. Madam, the same; your servant.
 Kath.   O, my lord,
The times and titles now are alter'd strangely
With me since first you knew me.   But, I pray you,
What is your pleasure with me?
 Cap.   Noble lady,
First, mine own service to your grace; the next,
The king's request that I would visit you;
Who grieves much for your weakness, and by me
Sends you his princely commendations,
And heartily entreats you take good comfort.
 Kath. O my good lord, that comfort comes too late; 120
'T is like a pardon after execution:

That gentle physic, given in time, had cured me;
But now I am past all comforts here but prayers.
How does his highness?

   Cap.   Madam, in good health.

   Kath. So may he ever do! and ever flourish,
When I shall dwell with worms, and my poor name
Banish'd the kingdom!   Patience, is that letter,
I caused you write, yet sent away?

   Pat.   No, madam.

                          [Giving it to Katharine.

   Kath. Sir, I most humbly pray you to deliver
This to my lord the king.

   Cap.   Most willing, madam.   130

   Kath. In which I have commended to his goodness
The model of our chaste loves, his young daughter,—
The dews of heaven fall thick in blessings on her!—
Beseeching him to give her virtuous breeding—
She is young and of a noble modest nature:
I hope she will deserve well—and a little
To love her for her mother's sake, that loved him,
Heaven knows how dearly.   My next poor petition
Is that his noble grace would have some pity
Upon my wretched women, that so long   140
Have follow'd both my fortunes faithfully:
Of which there is not one, I dare avow,—
And now I should not lie—but will deserve,
For virtue and true beauty of the soul,
For honesty and decent carriage,
A right good husband, let him be a noble:
And, sure, those men are happy that shall have 'em.
The last is, for my men; they are the poorest,
But poverty could never draw 'em from me;
That they may have their wages duly paid 'em,   150
And something over to remember me by:
If heaven had pleased to have given me longer life

(M 548)   8

And able means, we had not parted thus.
These are the whole contents: and, good my lord,
By that you love the dearest in this world,
As you wish Christian peace to souls departed,
Stand these poor people's friend, and urge the king
To do me this last right.

  Cap.   By heaven, I will,
Or let me lose the fashion of a man!

  Kath. I thank you, honest lord. Remember me   160
In all humility unto his highness:
Say his long trouble now is passing
Out of this world; tell him, in death I bless'd him,
For so I will. Mine eyes grow dim. Farewell,
My lord. Griffith, farewell. Nay, Patience,
You must not leave me yet: I must to bed;
Call in more women. When I am dead, good wench,
Let me be used with honour: strew me over
With maiden flowers, that all the world may know
I was a chaste wife to my grave: embalm me,   170
Then lay me forth: although unqueen'd, yet like
A queen, and daughter to a king, inter me.
I can no more.   *[Exeunt, leading Katharine.*

ACT V.

Scene I.   *London. A gallery in the palace.*

Enter Gardiner, Bishop of Winchester, *a* Page *with a
torch before him, met by* Sir Thomas Lovell.

  Gar. It's one o'clock, boy, is't not?
  Boy.   It hath struck.
  Gar. These should be hours for necessities,
Not for delights; times to repair our nature

With comforting repose, and not for us
To waste these times.   Good hour of night, Sir Thomas!
Whither so late?

   Lov.   Came you from the king, my lord?

   Gar. I did, Sir Thomas; and left him at primero
With the Duke of Suffolk.

   Lov.   I must to him too,
Before he go to bed.   I'll take my leave.

   Gar. Not yet, Sir Thomas Lovell.   What's the matter? 10
It seems you are in haste: an if there be
No great offence belongs to't, give your friend
Some touch of your late business: affairs that walk,
As they say spirits do, at midnight, have
In them a wilder nature than the business
That seeks dispatch by day.

   Lov.   My lord, I love you;
And durst commend a secret to your ear
Much weightier than this work.   The queen's in labour,
They say, in great extremity; and fear'd
She'll with the labour end.

   Gar.   The fruit she goes with   20
I pray for heartily, that it may find
Good time, and live: but for the stock, Sir Thomas,
I wish it grubb'd up now.

   Lov.   Methinks I could
Cry the amen; and yet my conscience says
She's a good creature, and, sweet lady, does
Deserve our better wishes.

   Gar.   But, sir, sir,
Hear me, Sir Thomas: you're a gentleman
Of mine own way; I know you wise, religious;
And, let me tell you, it will ne'er be well,
'T will not, Sir Thomas Lovell, take 't of me,   30
Till Cranmer, Cromwell, her two hands, and she,
Sleep in their graves.

 Lov.   Now, sir, you speak of two
The most remark'd i' the kingdom.   As for Cromwell,
Beside that of the jewel house, is made master
O' the rolls, and the king's secretary; further, sir,
Stands in the gap and trade of mo preferments,
With which the time will load him.   The archbishop
Is the king's hand and tongue; and who dare speak
One syllable against him?

 Gar.   Yes, yes, Sir Thomas,
There are that dare; and I myself have ventured   40
To speak my mind of him: and indeed this day,
Sir, I may tell it you, I think I have
Incensed the lords o' the council, that he is—
For so I know he is, they know he is—
A most arch-heretic, a pestilence
That does infect the land: with which they moved
Have broken with the king; who hath so far
Given ear to our complaint, of his great grace
And princely care foreseeing those fell mischiefs
Our reasons laid before him, hath commanded   50
To-morrow morning to the council-board
He be convented.   He 's a rank weed, Sir Thomas,
And we must root him out.   From your affairs
I hinder you too long: good night, Sir Thomas.

 Lov. Many good nights, my lord: I rest your servant.

         [Exeunt Gardiner and Page.

Enter KING *and* SUFFOLK.

 King. Charles, I will play no more to-night;
My mind 's not on 't; you are too hard for me.

 Suf. Sir, I did never win of you before.

 King. But little, Charles;
Nor shall not, when my fancy 's on my play.   60
Now, Lovell, from the queen what is the news?

 Lov. I could not personally deliver to her

What you commanded me, but by her woman
I sent your message; who return'd her thanks
In the great'st humbleness, and desired your highness
Most heartily to pray for her.

   King.   What say'st thou, ha?
To pray for her? what, is she crying out?

   Lov. So said her woman, and that her sufferance made
Almost each pang a death.

   King.   Alas, good lady!

   Suf. God safely quit her of her burthen, and   70
With gentle travail, to the gladding of
Your highness with an heir!

   King.   'T is midnight, Charles;
Prithee, to bed; and in thy prayers remember
The estate of my poor queen. Leave me alone;
For I must think of that which company
Would not be friendly to.

   Suf.   I wish your highness
A quiet night, and my good mistress will
Remember in my prayers.

   King.   Charles, good night. [*Exit Suffolk.*

      Enter SIR ANTHONY DENNY.

Well, sir, what follows?

   Den. Sir, I have brought my lord the archbishop,   80
As you commanded me.

   King.   Ha! Canterbury?

   Den. Ay, my good lord.

   King.   'T is true: where is he, Denny?

   Den. He attends your highness' pleasure.

   King.   Bring him to us.
                                [*Exit Denny.*

   Lov. [*Aside*] This is about that which the bishop spake:
I am happily come hither.

Re-enter DENNY, *with* CRANMER.

King. Avoid the gallery. [*Lovell seems to stay.*] Ha! I
    have said. Be gone.
What!   [*Exeunt Lovell and Denny.*

   Cran. [*Aside*] I am fearful: wherefore frowns he thus?
'T is his aspect of terror. All's not well.

   King. How now, my lord! you do desire to know
Wherefore I sent for you.

   Cran.   [*Kneeling*] It is my duty   90
To attend your highness' pleasure.

   King.   Pray you, arise,
My good and gracious Lord of Canterbury.
Come, you and I must walk a turn together;
I have news to tell you: come, come, give me your hand.
Ah, my good lord, I grieve at what I speak,
And am right sorry to repeat what follows:
I have, and most unwillingly, of late
Heard many grievous, I do say, my lord,
Grievous complaints of you; which, being consider'd,
Have moved us and our council, that you shall   100
This morning come before us; where, I know,
You cannot with such freedom purge yourself,
But that, till further trial in those charges
Which will require your answer, you must take
Your patience to you and be well contented
To make your house our Tower: you a brother of us,
It fits we thus proceed, or else no witness
Would come against you.

   Cran.   [*Kneeling*] I humbly thank your highness;
And am right glad to catch this good occasion
Most throughly to be winnow'd, where my chaff   110
And corn shall fly asunder: for, I know,
There's none stands under more calumnious tongues
Than I myself, poor man.

King.   Stand up, good Canterbury:
Thy truth and thy integrity is rooted
In us, thy friend: give me thy hand, stand up:
Prithee, let's walk.   Now, by my holidame,
What manner of man are you?   My lord, I look'd
You would have given me your petition, that
I should have ta'en some pains to bring together
Yourself and your accusers, and to have heard you,   120
Without indurance further.

Cran.   Most dread liege,
The good I stand on is my truth and honesty:
If they shall fail, I, with mine enemies,
Will triumph o'er my person; which I weigh not,
Being of those virtues vacant.   I fear nothing
What can be said against me.

King.   Know you not
How your state stands i' the world, with the whole world?
Your enemies are many, and not small; their practices
Must bear the same proportion; and not ever
The justice and the truth o' the question carries   130
The due o' the verdict with it: at what ease
Might corrupt minds procure knaves as corrupt
To swear against you?   Such things have been done.
You are potently opposed, and with a malice
Of as great size.   Ween you of better luck,
I mean, in perjured witness, than your master,
Whose minister you are, whiles here he lived
Upon this naughty earth?   Go to, go to;
You take a precipice for no leap of danger,
And woo your own destruction.

Cran.   God and your majesty   140
Protect mine innocence, or I fall into
The trap is laid for me!

King.   Be of good cheer;
They shall no more prevail than we give way to.

Keep comfort to you; and this morning see
You do appear before them.   If they shall chance,
In charging you with matters, to commit you,
The best persuasions to the contrary
Fail not to use, and with what vehemency
The occasion shall instruct you: if entreaties
Will render you no remedy, this ring   150
Deliver them, and your appeal to us
There make before them.   Look, the good man weeps!
He's honest, on mine honour.   God's blest mother!
I swear he is true-hearted, and a soul
None better in my kingdom.   Get you gone,
And do as I have bid you. [*Exit Cranmer.*] He has strangled
His language in his tears.

Enter Old Lady, LOVELL *following.*

 Gent. [*Within*] Come back: what mean you?
 Old L. I'll not come back; the tidings that I bring
Will make my boldness manners.   Now, good angels
Fly o'er thy royal head, and shade thy person   160
Under their blessed wings!
 King.   Now, by thy looks
I guess thy message.   Is the queen deliver'd?
Say, ay, and of a boy.
 Old L.   Aÿ, ay, my liege;
And of a lovely boy: the God of heaven
Both now and ever bless her! 't is a girl,
Promises boys hereafter.   Sir, your queen
Desires your visitation, and to be
Acquainted with this stranger: 't is as like you
As cherry is to cherry.
 King.   Lovell!
 Lov.   Sir?
 King. Give her an hundred marks. I'll to the queen. [*Exit.*
 Old L. An hundred marks! By this light, I'll ha' more.   171

An ordinary groom is for such payment.
I will have more, or scold it out of him.
Said I for this, the girl was like to him?
I will have more, or else unsay 't; and now,
While it is hot, I 'll put it to the issue.   [*Exeunt.*

SCENE II.   *Before the council-chamber.*
Pursuivants, Pages, &c., attending.

Enter CRANMER, *Archbishop of Canterbury.*

Cran. I hope I am not too late; and yet the gentleman
That was sent to me from the council, pray'd me
To make great haste.   All fast? what means this?   Ho!
Who waits there?   Sure, you know me?

Enter Keeper.

Keep.   Yes, my lord;
But yet I cannot help you.
   Cran. Why?

Enter DOCTOR BUTTS.

Keep. Your grace must wait till you be call'd for.
   Cran.   So.
   Butts. [*Aside*] This is a piece of malice.   I am glad
I came this way so happily: the king
Shall understand it presently.   [*Exit.*
   Cran.   [*Aside*] 'T is Butts,   10
The king's physician: as he pass'd along,
How earnestly he cast his eyes upon me!
Pray heaven, he sound not my disgrace!   For certain,
This is of purpose laid by some that hate me—
God turn their hearts!   I never sought their malice—
To quench mine honour: they would shame to make me
Wait else at door, a fellow-councillor,
'Mong boys, grooms, and lackeys.   But their pleasures
Must be fulfill'd, and I attend with patience.

Enter the KING *and* BUTTS *at a window above.*

Butts. I 'll show your grace the strangest sight—
King.   What 's that, Butts?
Butts. I think your highness saw this many a day.   21
King. Body o' me, where is it?
Butts.   There, my lord:
The high promotion of his grace of Canterbury;
Who holds his state at door, 'mongst pursuivants,
Pages, and footboys.
King.   Ha! 't is he, indeed:
Is this the honour they do one another?
'T is well there 's one above 'em yet.   I had thought
They had parted so much honesty among 'em,
At least good manners, as not thus to suffer
A man of his place, and so near our favour,   30
To dance attendance on their lordships' pleasures,
And at the door too, like a post with packets.
By holy Mary, Butts, there 's knavery:
Let 'em alone, and draw the curtain close:
We shall hear more anon.   [*Exeunt.*

SCENE III.   *The council-chamber.*

Enter LORD CHANCELLOR, *places himself at the upper end
    of the table on the left hand; a seat being left void above
    him, as for* CANTERBURY'S *seat.*   DUKE OF SUFFOLK,
    DUKE OF NORFOLK, SURREY, LORD CHAMBERLAIN,
    GARDINER, *seat themselves in order on each side.*
    CROMWELL *at lower end, as secretary.*   Keeper *at the
    door.*

Chan. Speak to the business, master secretary:
Why are we met in council?
Crom.   Please your honours,
The chief cause concerns his grace of Canterbury.

Gar. Has he had knowledge of it?
Crom.   Yes.
Nor.   Who waits there?
Keep. Without, my noble lords?
Gar.   Yes.
Keep.   My lord archbishop;
And has done half an hour, to know your pleasures.
Chan. Let him come in.
Keep.   Your grace may enter now.
            [*Cranmer enters and approaches the council-table.*
Chan. My good lord archbishop, I'm very sorry
To sit here at this present and behold
That chair stand empty: but we all are men,   10
In our own natures frail and capable
Of our flesh; few are angels: out of which frailty
And want of wisdom, you, that best should teach us,
Have misdemean'd yourself, and not a little,
Toward the king first, then his laws, in filling
The whole realm, by your teaching and your chaplains,
For so we are inform'd, with new opinions,
Divers and dangerous; which are heresies,
And, not reform'd, may prove pernicious.
    Gar. Which reformation must be sudden too,   20
My noble lords; for those that tame wild horses
Pace 'em not in their hands to make 'em gentle,
But stop their mouths with stubborn bits and spur 'em,
Till they obey the manage.   If we suffer,
Out of our easiness and childish pity
To one man's honour, this contagious sickness,
Farewell all physic: and what follows then?
Commotions, uproars, with a general taint
Of the whole state: as of late days our neighbours,
The upper Germany, can dearly witness,   30
Yet freshly pitied in our memories.
    Cran. My good lords, hitherto, in all the progress

Both of my life and office, I have labour'd,
And with no little study, that my teaching
And the strong course of my authority
Might go one way, and safely; and the end
Was ever to do well: nor is there living,
I speak it with a single heart, my lords,
A man that more detests, more stirs against,
Both in his private conscience and his place,   40
Defacers of a public peace, than I do.
Pray heaven, the king may never find a heart
With less allegiance in it! Men that make
Envy and crooked malice nourishment
Dare bite the best. I do beseech your lordships,
That, in this case of justice, my accusers,
Be what they will, may stand forth face to face,
And freely urge against me.

   Suf.   Nay, my lord,
That cannot be: you are a councillor,
And, by that virtue, no man dare accuse you.   50

   Gar. My lord, because we have business of more moment,
We will be short with you. 'T is his highness' pleasure,
And our consent, for better trial of you,
From hence you be committed to the Tower;
Where, being but a private man again,
You shall know many dare accuse you boldly,
More than, I fear, you are provided for.

   Cran. Ah, my good Lord of Winchester, I thank
     you;
You are always my good friend; if your will pass,
I shall both find your lordship judge and juror,   60
You are so merciful. I see your end;
'T is my undoing. Love and meekness, lord,
Become a churchman better than ambition:
Win straying souls with modesty again,
Cast none away. That I shall clear myself,

Lay all the weight ye can upon my patience,
I make as little doubt as you do conscience
In doing daily wrongs.   I could say more,
But reverence to your calling makes me modest.

Gar. My lord, my lord, you are a sectary;   70
That's the plain truth: your painted gloss discovers,
To men that understand you, words and weakness.

Crom. My Lord of Winchester, you are a little,
By your good favour, too sharp; men so noble,
However faulty, yet should find respect
For what they have been: 't is a cruelty
To load a falling man.

Gar.   Good master secretary,
I cry your honour mercy; you may, worst
Of all this table, say so.

Crom.   Why, my lord?

Gar. Do not I know you for a favourer   80
Of this new sect? ye are not sound.

Crom.   Not sound?

Gar. Not sound, I say.

Crom.   Would you were half so honest!
Men's prayers then would seek you, not their fears.

Gar. I shall remember this bold language.

Crom.   Do.
Remember your bold life too.

Chan.   This is too much;
Forbear, for shame, my lords.

Gar.   I have done.

Crom.   And I.

Chan. Then thus for you, my lord: it stands agreed,
I take it, by all voices, that forthwith
You be convey'd to the Tower a prisoner;
There to remain till the king's further pleasure   90
Be known unto us: are you all agreed, lords?

All. We are.

Cran.   Is there no other way of mercy,
But I must needs to the Tower, my lords?
  Gar.   What other
Would you expect? you are strangely troublesome.
Let some o' the guard be ready there.

Enter Guard.

  Cran.   For me?
Must I go like a traitor thither?
  Gar.   Receive him,
And see him safe i' the Tower.
  Cran.   Stay, good my lords,
I have a little yet to say.   Look there, my lords;
By virtue of that ring, I take my cause
Out of the gripes of cruel men, and give it   101
To a most noble judge, the king my master.
  Cham. This is the king's ring.
  Sur.   'T is no counterfeit.
  Suf. 'T is the right ring, by heaven: I told ye all,
When we first put this dangerous stone a-rolling,
'T would fall upon ourselves.
  Nor.   Do you think, my lords,
The king will suffer but the little finger
Of this man to be vex'd?
  Cham.   'T is now too certain:
How much more is his life in value with him?
Would I were fairly out on 't!
  Crom.   My mind gave me,
In seeking tales and informations   110
Against this man, whose honesty the devil
And his disciples only envy at,
Ye blew the fire that burns ye: now have at ye!

Enter KING, *frowning on them; takes his seat.*

Gar. Dread sovereign, how much are we bound to heaven
In daily thanks, that gave us such a prince,
Not only good and wise, but most religious:
One that, in all obedience, makes the church
The chief aim of his honour; and, to strengthen
That holy duty, out of dear respect,
His royal self in judgment comes to hear   120
The cause betwixt her and this great offender.
   King. You were ever good at sudden commendations,
Bishop of Winchester.   But know, I come not
To hear such flattery now, and in my presence
They are too thin and bare to hide offences.
To me you cannot reach you play the spaniel,
And think with wagging of your tongue to win me;
But, whatsoe'er thou takest me for, I 'm sure
Thou hast a cruel nature and a bloody.
[*To Cranmer*] Good man, sit down.   Now let me see the
          proudest   130
He, that dares most, but wag his finger at thee:
By all that 's holy he had better starve
Than but once think this place becomes thee not.
   Sur. May it please your grace,—
   King.   No, sir, it does not please me.
I had thought I had had men of some understanding
And wisdom of my council; but I find none.
Was it discretion, lords, to let this man,
This good man,—few of you deserve that title,—
This honest man, wait like a lousy footboy
At chamber-door? and one as great as you are?   140
Why, what a shame was this!   Did my commission
Bid ye so far forget yourselves?   I gave ye
Power as he was a councillor to try him,
Not as a groom: there 's some of ye, I see,

More out of malice than integrity,
Would try him to the utmost, had ye mean;
Which ye shall never have while I live.

Chan.   Thus far,
My most dread sovereign, may it like your grace
To let my tongue excuse all.   What was purposed
Concerning his imprisonment, was rather,   150
If there be faith in men, meant for his trial
And fair purgation to the world, than malice,
I 'm sure, in me.

King.   Well, well, my lords, respect him;
Take him and use him well; he 's worthy of it.
I will say thus much for him, if a prince
May be beholding to a subject, I
Am, for his love and service, so to him.
Make me no more ado, but all embrace him:
Be friends, for shame, my lords!   My Lord of Canterbury,
I have a suit which you must not deny me;   160
That is, a fair young maid that yet wants baptism;
You must be godfather, and answer for her.

Cran. The greatest monarch now alive may glory
In such an honour: how may I deserve it,
That am a poor and humble subject to you?

King. Come, come, my lord, you 'ld spare your spoons:
you shall have two noble partners with you; the old Duchess
of Norfolk, and Lady Marquess Dorset: will these please you?
Once more, my Lord of Winchester, I charge you,
Embrace and love this man.

Gar.   With a true heart   170
And brother-love I do it.

Cran.   And let heaven
Witness how dear I hold this confirmation.

King. Good man, those joyful tears show thy true heart:
The common voice, I see, is verified
Of thee, which says thus: 'Do my Lord of Canterbury

A shrewd turn, and he is your friend for ever'.
Come, lords, we trifle time away; I long
To have this young one made a Christian.
As I have made ye one, lords, one remain;   179
So I grow stronger, you more honour gain.   [*Exeunt.*

SCENE IV.   *The palace yard.*

Noise and tumult within. Enter Porter *and his* Man.

Port. You'll leave your noise anon, ye rascals: do you take
the court for Parish-garden? ye rude slaves, leave your gaping.
    [*Within*] Good master porter, I belong to the larder.
    Port. Belong to the gallows, and be hanged, ye rogue! Is
this a place to roar in?   Fetch me a dozen crab-tree staves,
and strong ones: these are but switches to 'em.   I'll scratch
your heads: you must be seeing christenings? do you look
for ale and cakes here, you rude rascals?
    Man. Pray, sir, be patient; 't is as much impossible—
Unless we sweep 'em from the door with cannons—   10
To scatter 'em, as 't is to make 'em sleep
On May-day morning; which will never be:
We may as well push against Powle's as stir 'em.
    Port. How got they in, and be hang'd?
    Man. Alas, I know not; how gets the tide in?
As much as one sound cudgel of four foot—
You see the poor remainder—could distribute,
I made no spare, sir.
    Port.   You did nothing, sir.
    Man. I am not Samson, nor Sir Guy, nor Colbrand,
To mow 'em down before me: but if I spared any   20
That had a head to hit, either young or old,
He or she, cuckold or cuckold-maker,
Let me ne'er hope to see a chine again;
And that I would not for a cow, God save her!
    [*Within*] Do you hear, master porter?

Port. I shall be with you presently, good master puppy. Keep the door close, sirrah.

Man. What would you have me do?   28

Port. What should you do, but knock 'em down by the dozens? Is this Moorfields to muster in? On my Christian conscience, this one christening will beget a thousand; here will be father, godfather, and all together.

Man. The spoons will be the bigger, sir. There is a fellow somewhat near the door, he should be a brazier by his face, for, o' my conscience, twenty of the dog-days now reign in 's nose; all that stand about him are under the line, they need no other penance: that fire-drake did I hit three times on the head, and three times was his nose discharged against me; he stands there, like a mortar-piece, to blow us. There was a haberdasher's wife of small wit near him, that railed upon me till her pinked porringer fell off her head, for kindling such a combustion in the state. I missed the meteor once, and hit that woman, who cried out 'Clubs!' when I might see from far some forty truncheoners draw to her succour, which were the hope o' the Strand, where she was quartered. They fell on; I made good my place: at length they came to the broomstaff to me; I defied 'em still: when suddenly a file of boys behind 'em, loose shot, delivered such a shower of pebbles, that I was fain to draw mine honour in and let 'em win the work: the devil was amongst 'em, I think, surely.   51

Port. These are the youths that thunder at a playhouse, and fight for bitten apples; that no audience, but the tribulation of Tower-hill, or the limbs of Limehouse, their dear brothers, are able to endure. I have some of 'em in Limbo Patrum, and there they are like to dance these three days; besides the running banquet of two beadles that is to come.

Enter LORD CHAMBERLAIN.

Cham. Mercy o' me, what a multitude are here!
They grow still too; from all parts they are coming,
As if we kept a fair here!   Where are these porters,   60
These lazy knaves?   Ye have made a fine hand, fellows!
There 's a trim rabble let in: are all these
Your faithful friends o' the suburbs?   We shall have
Great store of room, no doubt, left for the ladies,
When they pass back from the christening.
Port.   An 't please your honour
We are but men; and what so many may do,
Not being torn a-pieces, we have done:
An army cannot rule 'em.
Cham.   As I live,
If the king blame me for 't, I 'll lay ye all
By the heels, and suddenly; and on your heads   70
Clap round fines for neglect: ye are lazy knaves;
And here ye lie baiting of bombards when
Ye should do service.   Hark! the trumpets sound;
They 're come already from the christening:
Go, break among the press, and find a way out
To let the troop pass fairly, or I 'll find
A Marshalsea shall hold ye play these two months.
Port. Make way there for the princess.
Man.   You great fellow,
Stand close up, or I 'll make your head ache.
Port. You i' the camlet, get up o' the rail;   80
I 'll peck you o'er the pales else.   [*Exeunt.*

SCENE V. *The palace.*

Enter trumpets, sounding; then two Aldermen, LORD
    MAYOR, GARTER, CRANMER, DUKE OF NORFOLK *with
    his marshal's staff,* DUKE OF SUFFOLK, *two* Noble-
    men *bearing great standing-bowls for the christening-*

gifts ; then four Noblemen *bearing a canopy, under
which the* DUCHESS OF NORFOLK, *godmother, bearing
the child richly habited in a mantle, &c., train borne
by a* Lady; *then follows the* MARCHIONESS DORSET,
the other godmother, and Ladies. *The troop pass once
about the stage, and* GARTER *speaks.*

Gart. Heaven, from thy endless goodness, send prosperous
life, long, and ever happy, to the high and mighty princess
of England, Elizabeth!

Flourish.   Enter KING *and* Guard.

Cran. [*Kneeling.*] And to your royal grace, and the good
    queen,
My noble partners and myself thus pray
All comfort, joy, in this most gracious lady,
Heaven ever laid up to make parents happy,
May hourly fall upon ye!
    King.   Thank you, good lord archbishop:
What is her name?
    Cran.   Elizabeth.
    King.   Stand up, lord.
                [*The King kisses the child.*
With this kiss take my blessing: God protect thee!   10
Into whose hand I give thy life.
    Cran.   Amen.
    King. My noble gossips, ye have been too prodigal:
I thank ye heartily; so shall this lady,
When she has so much English.
    Cran.   Let me speak, sir,
For heaven now bids me; and the words I utter
Let none think flattery, for they 'll find 'em truth.
This royal infant—heaven still move about her!—
Though in her cradle, yet now promises
Upon this land a thousand thousand blessings,

Which time shall bring to ripeness: she shall be—   20
But few now living can behold that goodness—
A pattern to all princes living with her,
And all that shall succeed: Saba was never
More covetous of wisdom and fair virtue
Than this pure soul shall be: all princely graces,
That mould up such a mighty piece as this is,
With all the virtues that attend the good,
Shall still be doubled on her: truth shall nurse her,
Holy and heavenly thoughts still counsel her:
She shall be loved and fear'd: her own shall bless her;   30
Her foes shake like a field of beaten corn,
And hang their heads with sorrow.   Good grows with
     her:
In her days every man shall eat in safety,
Under his own vine, what he plants, and sing
The merry songs of peace to all his neighbours:
God shall be truly known; and those about her
From her shall read the perfect ways of honour,
And by those claim their greatness, not by blood.
Nor shall this peace sleep with her: but, as when
The bird of wonder dies, the maiden phœnix,   40
Her ashes new create another heir
As great in admiration as herself,
So shall she leave her blessedness to one—
When heaven shall call her from this cloud of darkness—
Who from the sacred ashes of her honour
Shall star-like rise, as great in fame as she was,
And so stand fix'd.   Peace, plenty, love, truth, terror,
That were the servants to this chosen infant,
Shall then be his, and like a vine grow to him:
Wherever the bright sun of heaven shall shine,   50
His honour and the greatness of his name
Shall be, and make new nations: he shall flourish,
And, like a mountain cedar, reach his branches

To all the plains about him.   Our children's children
Shall see this, and bless heaven.

 King.   Thou speakest wonders.

 Cran. She shall be, to the happiness of England,
An aged princess; many days shall see her,
And yet no day without a deed to crown it.
Would I had known no more! but she must die,
She must, the saints must have her; yet a virgin,   60
A most unspotted lily shall she pass
To the ground, and all the world shall mourn her.

 King. O lord archbishop,
Thou hast made me now a man! never, before
This happy child, did I get any thing:
This oracle of comfort has so pleased me,
That when I am in heaven I shall desire
To see what this child does, and praise my Maker.
I thank ye all.   To you, my good lord mayor,
And your good brethren, I am much beholding;   70
I have received much honour by your presence,
And ye shall find me thankful.   Lead the way, lords:
Ye must all see the queen, and she must thank ye;
She will be sick else.   This day, no man think
Has business at his house; for all shall stay:
This little one shall make it holiday.   *[Exeunt.*

EPILOGUE.

 'T is ten to one this play can never please
All that are here: some come to take their ease,
And sleep an act or two; but those, we fear,
We have frighted with our trumpets; so, 't is clear,
They 'll say 't is naught: others, to hear the city
Abused extremely, and to cry 'That 's witty!'
Which we have not done neither; that, I fear,
All the expected good we 're like to hear

For this play at this time, is only in
The merciful construction of good women;   10
For such a one we show'd 'em: if they smile,
And say 't will do, I know, within a while
All the best men are ours; for 't is ill hap,
If they hold when their ladies bid 'em clap.

NOTES.

Abbott ...Dr. E. Abbott's *Shakespearian Grammar*.
Kellner...L. Kellner's *Historical Outlines of English Syntax*.
O.E......Old English (Anglo-Saxon).
M.E......Middle English.
E.E......Elizabethan English.
Mod. E. ...Modern English.

The quotations from Hall and Holinshed are taken from the 1809 reprint of Hall's *Chronicle*, and the second edition (1587) of Holinshed's *Chronicle*. The longer passages in Holinshed of direct bearing on the play are given in Appendix A.

DRAMATIS PERSONÆ.

This list is not in the Folios. It was first given, imperfectly, by Rowe (1709).

HENRY VIII., born in 1491, became heir to the crown in 1502 by the death of his brother Arthur, and succeeded his father Henry VII. in April, 1509. In June he married Katharine of Aragon, his brother's widow, and five years his senior. The only child of the marriage who survived was Mary; and as Henry was anxious for an heir, so as to avoid the recurrence of a disputed succession, no queen having yet ruled in England, he hoped to get a divorce from Katharine. His plea was that his marriage with his brother's wife was illegal; but his scruples were largely prompted by the fact that he was growing tired of Katharine and had cast his eyes on Anne Bullen. An alliance with the Emperor Charles, Katharine's nephew, for a while balked him of his plans, but in 1527, when he was veering towards an alliance with France, he took the matter up seriously. As the Pope Clement would not give his consent, Henry sent Stephen Gardiner to Rome in 1528 to urge the appointment of legates who should decide in Henry's favour. The Pope so far acceded as to appoint Wolsey and Campeggio, but he refused to consider any decision they might come to as valid before it had his approval. The legates opened proceedings at Blackfriars on 31st May, 1529, and the trial proper began on 21st June. The only result, however, was that Katharine appealed directly to the Pope. It was at this juncture that Henry contrived to make himself acknowledged the supreme head of the English church, and to forbid any appeals, as well in spiritual as in temporal matters, to be made to any authority outside the kingdom. He was accordingly now free to act as he pleased in the divorce, and had no longer to await the Pope's consent. On 23rd May, 1533, Cranmer gave judgment in his favour. Previous to this, on 25th January, he had secretly married Anne Bullen, who, on 7th September, gave birth to Elizabeth. It was not till 1537 that Henry had—by his third wife, Jane Seymour—a son who lived.

CARDINAL WOLSEY was born at Ipswich in 1471. (For his parentage, see i. 1. 120.) In 1506 he became chaplain to Henry VII., who subsequently sent him on several embassies, and conferred on him the deanery of Lincoln. Shortly after the accession of Henry VIII. he was made king's almoner and called to the council. His great genius for administration speedily made him the trusted servant of the king, who in 1514 appointed him Archbishop of York, and in 1515 Lord Chancellor; and in the same year the Pope made him a Cardinal. Henceforward he practically directed the home and foreign administration of England. His position was apparently never more secure than in 1527; but the case of the divorce was to bring about a change in his fortunes. Though he worked honestly in Henry's cause, circumstances were such that he could not but fail, and he became the victim of Henry's wrath. On 9th October, 1529, proceedings were taken against him under the Statute of Præmunire (see notes, iii. 2. 337–341), and though the charge was iniquitous, for Wolsey had exercised his legatine authority only at the king's wish and in his interests, he had no other course to follow than to submit. (See quotation, note iii. 2. 342–344.) On 17th October he was deprived of the great seal, and ordered to retire to Esher (iii. 2. 229, 231). The king's anger had somewhat relaxed, however, by the following February, when he received a full pardon, and was restored to the Archbishopric of York, whither he retired. But his old enemies were implacable, and searched for something to ruin him utterly. This they found in his indiscreet but harmless communications with the French and imperial envoys. Henry now ordered him to be charged with high treason. He was arrested at Cawood (not at York, as in iv. 2. 13) on 4th November; but on the way to his trial in London he died at Leicester Abbey on 29th November, 1530. It should be remarked that the dramatist's characterization of Wolsey was suggested directly by Holinshed, and is accordingly largely unjust. "The figure of Wolsey was long left to the portraiture of prejudice, and he was regarded only as the type of the arrogant ecclesiastic whom it was the great work of the Reformation to have rendered impossible in the future. . . . Not till the mass of documents relating to the reign of Henry VIII. was published did it become possible for Dr. Brewer to show the significance of the schemes of the great cardinal, and to estimate his merits and his faults" (Mandell Creighton).

CARDINAL CAMPEIUS (Lorenzo Campeggio) was sent as a legate to England in October, 1528, to try, along with Wolsey, the case of the king's divorce. He refused to deliver judgment without reference to the Pope. He prorogued the court in July, 1529, and in September departed for Rome. This was his second mission to England. In 1524 he had been made Bishop of Salisbury, but he was deprived of the see by Act of Parliament in 1534. He died in 1539.

CAPUCIUS (Eustace Chapuys) came to England as imperial ambassador in 1529. In December, 1535, he obtained permission from the king to visit Katharine at Kimbolton in what proved to be her last illness. He arrived on 2nd January, and left on the 5th. Katharine died two days later. The historical inaccuracy of making Capucius present at the time of her death is due to a misleading statement in Holinshed (p. 939): "This in effect was all that she requested [*of Capucius*], and so immediatlie herevpon she departed this life".

CRANMER, THOMAS (1489–1556), first came into notice in connection with the divorce. It was he who recommended Henry to find out the opinions of the universities, and he was abroad on this errand in 1529 (ii. 4. 238; iii. 2. 64). In 1533 he was appointed Archbishop of Canterbury, in succession to William Warham (iii. 2. 400). In May of the same year he pronounced Katharine's marriage invalid (iv. 1. 24, &c.), and in October was godfather to the princess Elizabeth (v. 5). He was in great favour with the king, who found him a pliable servant. The unsuccessful attempt of his enemies to convict him of heresy in 1544–45 (v. 3) strengthened his position, for nobody thereafter dared to oppose him as long as Henry lived. But in 1556, in the reign of Mary, he was burned at the stake as a heretic, despite several recantations.

DUKE OF NORFOLK, Thomas Howard (1443–1524), first Earl of Surrey and second Duke of Norfolk. Henry conferred the dukedom of Norfolk on him on 1st February, 1514. In the previous year he (while still Earl of Surrey) had defeated the Scots at Flodden. In 1520 he was left guardian of the kingdom while Henry was at the Field of the Cloth of Gold (see note i. 1, *init.*). "In May, 1521, he was appointed lord high steward for the trial of Edward, Duke of Buckingham, on the charge of treason. Buckingham was his friend, and father of the wife of his eldest son; and few incidents are more characteristic of the temper of the time than that Norfolk should have consented to preside at such a trial, of which the issue was a foregone conclusion. With tears streaming down his face, Norfolk passed sentence of death on a man with whose sentiments he entirely agreed, but had his reward in a grant of manors from Buckingham's forfeitures" (*Dict. Nat. Biog.*). It is to be noted that all mention of Norfolk's part in this trial is studiously omitted in the play. As Norfolk died in 1524, his appearance in Acts iii., iv., and v. is anachronous. See note iii. 2, *init.*

DUKE OF BUCKINGHAM, Edward Stafford (1478–1521), third Duke. He was restored by Henry VII. in 1485 to the family honours forfeited by his father's attainder. For a while he was in high favour with Henry VIII., whom he accompanied to the Field of the Cloth of Gold (see note i. 1. *init.*); but his career was checked by the rise of Wolsey, and he "became the mouthpiece of the great nobles who resented their exclusion from office and hated Wolsey as a low-born ecclesiastic" (*Dict. Nat. Biog.*). He was executed 17th May, 1521. (See *Norfolk*, supra, and ii. 1. *init.*) The dramatist follows Holinshed in describing Buckingham's fall as due to Wolsey; but "the popular account of Wolsey's inveterate malice and his supposed designs against the life of the Duke rest on no certain foundation" (Brewer, *Henry VIII.*, i. 381). It seems to be the case, too, that he was betrayed, not by Charles Knyvet, the surveyor whom he had dismissed, but by Robert Gilbert (see note i. 1. 219), his chancellor. In i. 1. 199, 200 his full title is given as "Duke of Buckingham and Earl of Hereford, Stafford, and Northampton". He was the great-great-grandson of Edmund, fifth Earl of Stafford, whose wife Anne was the representative of Humphrey de Bohun, last Earl of Hereford, Northampton, and Essex. Their son Humphrey, the first Duke of Buckingham, used the title Earl of Hereford; but "it does not appear that he was ever created Earl of Hereford; and in *Richard III.*, iv. 2. 93, it will be remembered that the Buckingham of that play incurred the anger of the king by pressing his claim to the earldom" (Wright).

DUKE OF SUFFOLK. Charles Brandon, created Duke of Suffolk in 1514, was a special favourite of the king (see v. 1. 56, &c.) and his brother-in-law, being the second husband of Henry's younger sister Mary, the widow of Louis XII. of France. He was present at the Field of the Cloth of Gold, and was one of the judges at the trial of Buckingham. He had been befriended by Wolsey, but he became one of his bitterest enemies. He died in 1545.

EARL OF SURREY, Thomas Howard (1473–1554), second Earl of Surrey, third Duke of Norfolk. He was the son-in-law of Buckingham (see note ii. 1. 44). In 1524 he succeeded his father as Duke of Norfolk, and his appearance in iii. 2, &c., as the Earl of Surrey is therefore an anachronism (see note iii. 2, *init.*). As Duke of Norfolk he did much of what in the play is attributed to his father: *e.g.* it was he and the Duke of Suffolk who demanded the great seal from Wolsey (iii. 2. 229).

LORD CHAMBERLAIN. During the time covered by *Henry VIII.* (1520–1544) this office was held by: (1) Charles Somerset, Earl of Worcester, chamberlain from 1509; (2) William Sands or Sandys, Baron Sandys of the Vine, chamberlain from 1526; and (3) William Paulet, Baron St. John, afterwards Marquis of Winchester, chamberlain from 1543.

LORD CHANCELLOR. "If the date of Cranmer's appearance

before the council was 1544 or 1545, the Chancellor was Sir Thomas Wriothesley, afterwards Earl of Southampton, the grandfather of Shakespeare's friend. It is probable that the dramatist supposed it was Sir Thomas More; but, as Theobald pointed out, he had surrendered the seals on May 16, 1532, a year and more before the birth of Elizabeth, and was succeeded by Sir Thomas Audley, who resigned April 21, 1544, and died on April 30 following" (Wright).

GARDINER, STEPHEN (1483–1555), became secretary to the king on 28th July, 1529. He had previously been secretary to Wolsey. He was consecrated Bishop of Winchester in December, 1531.

BISHOP OF LINCOLN. John Longland (1476–1547), Bishop of Lincoln from 1528.

LORD ABERGAVENNY, George Neville (1471–1535), third Baron. He was present at the Field of the Cloth of Gold. He was imprisoned in May, 1521, for complicity in Buckingham's treason, but he was pardoned in March, 1522. He was Buckingham's son-in-law (see note i. 2. 136).

LORD SANDS. See *Lord Chamberlain*, supra, and note I. 4, *init.* He was raised to the peerage on 27th April, 1523, and died in 1540.

SIR HENRY GUILDFORD (1489–1532), Master of the Horse and Privy Councillor.

SIR THOMAS LOVELL (died 1524), Chancellor of the Exchequer under Henry VII., gradually withdrew from public affairs on the rise of Wolsey. At the time of the trial of Buckingham he was Constable of the Tower.

SIR ANTHONY DENNY (1501–1549) was Remembrancer and Groom of the Stole to Henry VIII., a member of his Privy Council, and one of the executors of his will. He was knighted at Boulogne, 30th September, 1544.

SIR NICHOLAS VAUX, "son of Sir William Vaux who appears in *2 Henry VI.*, iii. 2. 366, was knighted after the battle of Stoke in 1487, and created Lord Vaux of Harrowden 27th April, 15 Henry VIII. (1523), in which year he died" (Wright).

CROMWELL, THOMAS (1485–1540), succeeded Gardiner as Wolsey's secretary in 1529. In November of this year he successfully pleaded Wolsey's cause in the House of Commons, when the bill of articles (see notes iii. 2. 310–322) came down from the House of Lords. About the same time he entered the king's service (see note iii. 2. 455–7), and won the royal favour by suggesting that Henry should make himself head of the Church of England, so that he might have his own way in the matter of the divorce. Thereafter honours were rapidly heaped upon him. He was made a Privy Councillor at the beginning of 1531; Master of the Jewel House,

14th April, 1532; Chancellor of the Exchequer, 12th April, 1533; Secretary before April, 1534; and Master of the Rolls, 8th October, 1534. In 1535 he was appointed Vicar-general to carry the Act of Supremacy into effect. From 1536 "his personal history continues to be till his death the history of Henry VIII.'s government and policy" (*Dict. Nat. Biog.*). But in 1540, after he had been made Earl of Essex, he was found guilty of treason and executed.

GRIFFITH, described in the play as Katharine's gentleman-usher, was her receiver-general. "His proper name was Griffin Richardes" (Brewer, *Reign of Henry VIII.*, vol. ii., p. 343, note 3).

DOCTOR BUTTS. Sir William Butts, physician to Henry VIII., Anne Bullen, Jane Seymour, the Princess Mary, and Wolsey. He was born in Norfolk, and educated at Gonville Hall, Cambridge. "Some writers have spoken of him as being one of the founders of the College of Physicians, but this is an error. The college was founded in 1528, and he did not join till 1529" (*Dict. Nat. Biog.*). He died in 1545.

GARTER KING-AT-ARMS. Sir Thomas Writhe or Wriothesley, appointed Garter in 1529. He was the uncle of the Lord Chancellor of the same name.

SURVEYOR TO THE DUKE OF BUCKINGHAM. Charles Knyvet or Knevet, Buckingham's cousin, grandson of Humphrey Stafford, first Duke of Buckingham.

BRANDON. See note i. 1. 197.

KATHARINE, born in 1485, was married on 14th November, 1501, to Prince Arthur, Henry's elder brother, who died in the following April. On 11th June, 1509, she was married to Henry VIII., seven weeks after his accession. (For her children by him, see note ii. 4. 36, 37; for the divorce proceedings, see *Henry*, supra.) Her marriage was declared void on 23rd May, 1533 (see iv. 1. 24–33), and in the same year Parliament enacted that she should no longer be styled queen but princess dowager (see iii. 2. 70). In April or May, 1534, she was removed to Kimbolton, and there she died, 7th January, 1536.

ANNE BULLEN, born in 1507, was the daughter of Sir Thomas Bullen, created Viscount Rochford in 1525, and afterwards Earl of Wiltshire and Ormond. She was created Marchioness of Pembroke 1st September, 1532. On 25th January, 1533 (probably; see note on iii. 2. 41, 42), she was married secretly to Henry. She was crowned on 1st June, nine days after Cranmer had pronounced Katharine's divorce. On 7th September she gave birth to Elizabeth; but after this she gradually fell into disfavour, partly because Henry's purpose in marrying her was not realized, and on 19th May, 1536, she was executed on a charge of infidelity.

Prologue.

There is little doubt that the Prologue to *Henry VIII.* is not by Shakespeare. It is generally believed, from internal evidence, to be by Fletcher. Dr. Johnson attributed it to Ben Jonson.

There are prologues also to *2 Henry IV.* (induction), *Henry V.*, *Troilus and Cressida*, and *Romeo and Juliet*. These four prologues (which are all unmistakeably by Shakespeare), even when not an integral part of the play as in *Henry V.*, are yet closely connected with it, and could not serve to introduce another play. Thus the Prologue to *Romeo and Juliet* states that the scene is laid in Verona, and describes briefly the story of the "star-cross'd lovers". Similarly, the Prologue to *Troilus and Cressida* says that the scene lies in Troy, and recounts the chief events in the Trojan war previous to the circumstances which the play represents. But the Prologue to *Henry VIII.*, though suggested by the play, deals with it in the most vague manner, and is more or less independent.

1. Perhaps the play acted before *Henry VIII.* was a comedy.

3. **Sad**, serious: a common sense in E.E. Cf. ii. 2. 14.

working, full of pathos, moving: referring not so much to the *action* of the play, as to its effect on the audience.

9. **May here find truth too.** It seems to be the case that *Henry VIII.* had originally the alternative title *All is True* (see the quotation from Sir Henry Wotton in the Introduction). Some commentators conjecture that there are three references to this title in the Prologue, viz.—

"May here find truth too" (9),
"To rank our chosen truth with such a show" (18), and
"To make that only true we now intend" (21).

10. **Only a show or two**, &c. The play is indeed rich in pageants, with its banquet (i. 4), masque (ib.), two trial scenes (ii. 4 and v. 3), coronation procession (iv. 1), vision (iv. 2), and christening procession (v. 5).

12. **their shilling.** A shilling seems to have been the usual price of admission to the best seats in the Globe Theatre. Twopence was the price of admission to the gallery. The prices probably varied with the theatres. (See Malone's *Historical Account of the English Stage* in vol. iii. of Boswell's Shakespeare, 1821.)

14-16. These three lines are in all probability aimed at Samuel Rowley's *When you see me you know me*, a "chronicle-history of King Henry VIII." (first published 1605, revived 1613). In this play, Will Summers, the king's fool, indulges largely in gross witticisms, and the king in disguise fights a duel with Black Will, each armed with a 'sword and buckler'. Possibly the title *All is True* was intended to point the contrast to Rowley's play.

16. a long motley coat was the conventional dress of the fool; it survives in the dress of the modern clown.   It is to be noted that in Shakespeare's time the fool's coat was always "long".

guarded, trimmed, ornamented.   Cf. *Merchant of Venice*, ii. 2. 164—

> "Give him a livery
> More guarded than his fellows'".

Guard is sometimes used in the sense of trimmings; *e. g.* "velvet-guards", *1 Henry IV.*, iii. 1. 261.

20, 21. opinion, reputation.   Cf. *1 Henry IV.*, v. 4. 48, "Thou hast redeem'd thy lost opinion".   The phrase is awkward, but, as it stands, can mean only "The reputation which we bring of making what we now intend to represent strictly in accordance with truth". Malone proposed to take l. 21 as a parenthesis, and to refer *that* to *opinion*, the meaning of the line in this case being "To justify that reputation is now our intention".

24. happiest, most favourable, best disposed: a not uncommon sense of the word in Shakespeare.   Cf. the Latin *felix*.

27-29. think you see them great, &c.   Cf. the Prologue to *Henry V.*—

> "Piece out our imperfections with your thoughts;
> Into a thousand parts divide one man,
> And make imaginary puissance;
> Think, when we talk of horses, that you see them
> Printing their proud hoofs i' the receiving earth;
> For 't is your thoughts that now must deck our kings".

A comparison of the two passages may favour the view that the Prologue to *Henry VIII.* is not by Shakespeare.

Act I.—Scene I.

The division into Acts and Scenes is given in the Folios.   The places of the scenes was first supplied by Theobald (1733).   The stage-directions, which are unusually full and explicit, are also from the Folios.

In most of Shakespeare's history plays the action begins in the first scene without any preface, and in four of them—*King John*, *Richard II.*, *1 Henry IV.*, and *Richard III.*—the title-character is the first speaker.   In *Henry VIII.* the action does not begin till after the opening conversation of Norfolk and Buckingham; but this conversation serves the double purpose (1) of giving certain informa-tion which helps to explain what is to follow, and (2) of suggesting, by the remarks on Wolsey's intrigues and ambition, the greater part of the action of the drama.

The palace. This may be taken as the palace of Bridewell. "The palace at Westminster had been burnt down in 1512 and was not afterwards rebuilt, and the king did not acquire Whitehall till after the fall of Wolsey. It was not till 1531–2 that the site of St. James's Palace came into the possession of Henry" (Wright). Moreover, if Theobald be correct, the places of this and the third scene are the same, and the third scene, as the reference to the river (l. 61) shows, is undoubtedly laid at Bridewell.

The interview of Henry VIII. and Francis I. on the Field of the Cloth of Gold lasted from 7th to 24th June, 1520. The parts of Norfolk and Buckingham in this scene should have been reversed, for Norfolk was in England during the time of the pageantry he describes, while Buckingham, according to Hall and Holinshed, was one of Francis's escort. It is to be noted, however, that line 2, "Since last we saw in France", distinctly implies that both were in France at the time of the interview.

2. saw, *i.e.* saw each other, met. Cf. *Cymbeline*, i. 1. 124, "When shall we see again".

6. suns of glory, *i.e.* Henry and Francis. See line 33.

7. Guynes and **Ardres** (Shakespeare's *Arde*) were both in Picardy, the former belonging at this time to the English, the latter to the French. In the account in Hall's *Chronicle* of the meeting of the two kings, Henry refers to Guynes as "the fardest frontier of my realme". In the Second Folio the *vale of Andren* is altered to the *vale of Arde*; but the identical phrase *met in the vale of Andren* occurs in Holinshed (p. 858).

10. embracement, embrace: a common Shakespearian form.

as, as if. See Abbott, § 107, and cf. iii. 1. 7.

11. Which had they, *i.e.* had they grown together.

12. All the whole: a pleonasm not uncommon in E.E.

18. Made former wonders its, summed up the wonders of the preceding days. *Former* is sometimes taken to refer to 'former times generally'.

its, its own: spelt *it's* in the Folios. This form of the neuter possessive pronoun began about this time to replace the older "his". It is not found in Spenser, nor in the authorized version of the Bible (1611), and occurs only ten times in Shakespeare. See Abbott, § 228.

19. clinquant, glittering. See Glossary.

23. cherubins. See Glossary.

25. that, so that. Cf. lines 36 and 38.

26. Was to them as a painting, made them appear, by heighten-ing their colour, as if they were painted.

masque. Hall, who was probably an eye-witness, gives a minute account in his *Chronicle* (pp. 619, 620) of a great masque held on the last day of the interview.

33. censure, 'judgment', not 'adverse judgment'. This is the commoner acceptation of the word in Shakespeare. Contrast, how-ever, iii. 1. 64.

34–36. Jousting went on from Monday, 11th June, to Friday the 22nd, the intervening Saturday and Sunday excepted (Hall, 611–618). The two kings with their assistants held the lists against all comers. "Course after course", says Hall, "the king lost none, but euer-more he brake his spere, and so nobly ended his Iustes royal,...and of the king our souereigne lordes doynges, all men there that him beheld reported his doynges (so valiant were his factes) euermore in honor to be renoumed. The French king on his part ran valiantly breaking speres egrely, and so well ended his chalenge of Iustes, that he ought euer to be spoken of."

36. that former fabulous story, *i.e.* 'so that the stories hitherto considered fabulous'. *That* (cf. line 25) is not to be taken as a demonstrative pronoun, *story* being here used in a general sense.

38. Bevis of Hampton was the hero of a popular mediæval romance. One of his most famous exploits was the defeat of the giant Ascapard, referred to in the play on which the *2 Henry VI.* is founded: see Malone's or Knight's text of *2 Henry VI.*, ii. 3. 92. His last great exploit was the slaughter of 60,000 citizens in the streets of London.

39. As I belong to worship, as I belong to the nobility. Cf. *Winter's Tale*, i. 2. 314—

> "whom I from meaner form
> Have bench'd and rear'd to worship".

40–42. "The course of these triumphs and pleasures, however well related, must lose in the description part of that spirit and energy which were expressed in the real action" (Johnson).

44. office, a metonymy for 'officers', those intrusted with the arrangements.

45. Distinctly, 'without confusion', rather than "visibly, in a striking manner", as Schmidt defines it.

47. as you guess. In the first three Folios, Buckingham's speech begins with "All was royal" in line 42 and ends with "Of this great sport together", Norfolk's speech beginning with "As you guess". In the Fourth Folio, "As you guess" is made a part of Buckingham's speech, but otherwise the arrangement of the first three Folios is maintained. Theobald first suggested the arrange-ment which is now invariably adopted.

48. certes is here a monosyllable; but it had not a fixed pronunciation in Shakespeare's time, as it is unmistakably a dissyllable in *The Tempest*, iii. 3. 30—

> "For, certes, these are people of the island",

and in *The Comedy of Errors*, iv. 4. 78—

> "Certes, she did; the kitchen-vestal scorn'd you";

but probably a monosyllable in *Othello*, i. 1. 16—

> "Nonsuits my mediators: for, 'Certes', says he".

These are the only four examples in Shakespeare in which the word occurs in a verse.

48, 49. that promises…business, who would not be expected to take a part in such a business.

51. Wolsey was made Archbishop of York in 1514, and Cardinal in 1515.

54. fierce, wild, extravagant.

55. keech, the fat of an ox or cow rolled by a butcher into a round lump. It is here applied to Wolsey, because he was believed to be the son of a butcher (see line 120). It is the name of a butcher's wife in *2 Henry IV.*, ii. 1. 101: "Did not goodwife Keech, the butcher's wife, come in then?"

56. *I.e.* 'engross the favour of Henry VIII.'.

62–64. 'It is by his own merits, he proclaims to us, that he makes his way, just like the spider which draws the material of its web from itself.' The text is doubtful. In the First Folio line 63 reads: "Out of his self-drawing web. O gives us note." The emendation was suggested by Capell. Rowe and Capell read "self-drawn".

70. In the Folios the point of interrogation comes after "If not from hell". The emendation is Theobald's.

73. going out, expedition.

74. privity, joint knowledge: the only instance of the word in Shakespeare.

76–78. The construction is faulty, in the redundancy of *to* and *upon*. For *such to whom*, cf. i. 2. 28, and see Abbott, § 278.

79, 80. 'His own letter, without the consent of the honourable board of council, must fetch him in whomsoever he registers on the paper (containing the list of those who are to take part in the expedition).' This use of 'papers,' if not corrupt, is unique in Shakespeare; various emendations have been proposed, *e.g.* 'the papers', and 'he paupers'. Holinshed has the phrase, "without consent of the whole boord of the councell" (p. 855).

84. broke their backs, ruined themselves: note the conceit.

84. with laying manors on 'em, with selling or pawning their lands to provide their dresses. Cf. *King John*, ii. 1. 69, 70—

"Have sold their fortunes at their native homes,
Bearing their birthrights proudly on their backs".

86, 87. minister communication...issue, bring about an unproductive conference. This awkward phrase is borrowed from, and explained by, a statement in Holinshed: "He knew not for what cause so much monie should be spent about the sight of a vaine talke to be had, and communication to be ministred of things of no importance" (p. 855).

88. not values, does not value, is not worth. The auxiliary was not required in E.E. when the negative preceded the main verb. Cf. "I not believe", ii. 2. 52. See Abbott, § 305.

90. The hideous storm. "On mondaie, the eighteenth of Iune, was such an hideous storme of wind and weather, that manie coniectured it did prognosticate trouble and hatred shortlie after to follow betweene princes" (Holinshed, p. 860).

91. not consulting, spontaneously.

93. aboded, boded, foreboded. Note the play in **budded** (l. 94).

94. on't, of it; a very common Shakespearian usage. Cf. ii. 3. 102, iii. 2. 106, v. 3. 109. See Abbott, § 182.

95. flaw'd, broken, cracked. Cf. ii. 2. 23, "he has crack'd the league".

attach'd, seized. See Glossary.

96. Bordeaux. "The French king commanded all Englishmens goods, being in Burdeaux, to be attached and put vnder arrest" (Holinshed, p. 872). This took place in 1522; but the historic Duke of Buckingham had been beheaded 17th May, 1521.

97. The ambassador is silenced. "The ambassador was commanded to kepe his house in silence, and not to come in presence till he was sent for" (Hall, p. 634).

98. A proper title of a peace, a pretty thing to call a peace! Cf., for this ironical use of *proper*, Lady Macbeth's taunt at her husband, iii. 4. 60, "O proper stuff!"

100. carried, managed, carried out. Cf. i. 2. 134.

Like it, may it please. Cf. iv. 2. 100, and v. 3. 148.
Prompted by the violence of Buckingham's language, Norfolk suddenly breaks the thread of the conversation and passes to the private difference between Buckingham and Wolsey. There is a fine contrast between the characters of the two dukes. Buckingham is courageous and outspoken, but impetuous: Norfolk, who has a like hatred of Wolsey, is cautious and politic.

108. minister, agent, instrument.

Stage-direction. The *purse* borne before Wolsey was the bag containing the great seal (see stage-direction ii. 4). He was Lord Chancellor as well as Cardinal and Archbishop.

115. surveyor, overseer. See notes on Dramatis Personæ.

120. butcher's cur. Cf. l. 55. Such epithets were frequently in the mouths of Wolsey's enemies, as Hall and Holinshed show. Wolsey's father, however, was not a butcher, but a grazier and wool merchant. Cavendish refers to him simply as "an honest poor man".

venom-mouth'd. This is Pope's reading. The Folios have 'venom'd-mouth'd'.

121, 122. *I.e.* 'let sleeping dogs lie'.

122, 123. A beggar's book...blood, the learning of a low-born man is more thought of than the high-birth of a noble. For this sense of *book*, cf. *2 Henry VI.*, iv. 7. 77—

> "Large gifts have I bestow'd on learned clerks,
>   Because my book preferr'd me to the king".

124. temperance, forbearance; **appliance**, application, remedy.

128. bores, cheats, deceives. Cf. Fletcher's *Spanish Curate*, iv. 5—

> "I am abused, betrayed! I am laughed at, scorned,
>   Baffled, and bored, it seems!"

It is sometimes said to have gained this sense from the idea of undermining,—and it has been given also the sense of 'injure' from the idea of stabbing; but Dr. Murray suggests that it is connected with *bourd*, to mock, make fun of. See Glossary.

134. Self-mettle, his own ardour, spirit. Malone compares the phrase with *Lucrece*, 707—

> "Till like a jade Self-will himself doth tire".

138. Ipswich was Wolsey's birthplace.

139. *I.e.* 'rank is considered of no account'. Cf. lines, 122, 123.

140, 141. Probably, as Steevens suggests, a reference to *Daniel*, iii. 22.

152, 153. 'Whom I mention, not from the bitterness of my feelings, but from sincere motives.' According to the Elizabethan theory of the humours, it was believed that a man's temperament was directly governed by physical conditions. The theory, which is closely connected with the mediæval idea of four fluid temperaments, is thus alluded to by Ben Jonson in the induction to *Every Man out of his Humour*—

> "In every human body
>   The choler, melancholy, phlegm, and blood,
>   By reason that they flow continually
>   In some one part and are not continent,
>   Receive the name of humours".

Hence the phrase *the flow of gall*, *gall* corresponding to *choler*.

157. Buckingham forgets his good resolution to "be advised" immediately Norfolk ventures to question a remark of his about Wolsey. Note that the parenthetical statement (lines 159–162) repeats the idea already expressed by Norfolk in lines 104–112. Wright suggests on this account that "possibly this speech may be the work of another hand". But it is to be noted that if the speeches are the same in idea, they are not the same in spirit. A comparison of them brings out very well the difference in the characters of the two dukes.

159. equal ravenous, equally ravenous. See Abbott, § 1.

161, 162. If his *mind* is 'prone to mischief', his *place* makes him 'able to perform it'; and if his place gives him the opportunity of doing mischief, his mind will devise the means.

164. suggests. See Glossary.

167. i' the rinsing, Pope's emendation of the Folio reading *i' the wrenching*; but *wrenching* is probably a misprint for *renching*, a provincial cognate of *rinsing*. See Glossary.

169. combination, interview. Holinshed states that "both the kings committed the order and manner of their meeting…vnto the cardinall of Yorke", and that the "articles" he drew up were "accepted and approoued by the same princes respectiuelie" (p. 853).

175, 176. Buckingham returns exultingly to the statement at which Norfolk had demurred. See line 156.

176. Charles the Emperor, Charles V., Emperor of Germany; his mother Joanna was sister of Katharine of Aragon. He landed at Dover on 26th May, 1520. The account of the pretended and real reasons of his visit and of his bribing of Wolsey is taken from Holinshed, p. 856.

178. colour, pretext. Cf. *Antony and Cleopatra*, i. 3. 32, "seek no colour for your going".

184. as I trow, &c. The syntax is incomplete. It has been proposed to amend it by treating "Which I do well, for I am sure" as a parenthesis.

195. mistaken, misunderstood. Cf. iii. 1. 101.

197. *I.e.* in which he shall appear in proof. "The Elizabethan authors objected to scarcely any ellipsis, provided the deficiency could be easily supplied from the context." See Abbott, §§ 382, 394.

Enter Brandon, &c. This is an historical error, as Buckingham was arrested (16th April, 1521) by Sir Henry Marney, captain of the King's Guard. "Sir Thomas Brandon, master of the kings horsse", is mentioned by Holinshed (p. 801) in another connection. Note the dramatic situation. Just as Buckingham has determined to accuse Wolsey to the king, and is confident of being able to prove his charges, he is himself arrested at the instigation of Wolsey.

200. Hereford, spelt *Hertford* in the Folios; the confusion may have arisen from the name being always pronounced *Herford.* For the title, see notes on Dramatis Personæ.

202. Lo you. See Glossary.

204. practice, artifice, plot. Cf. i. 2. 127, and v. 1. 128.

204–206. Staunton explains this as "I am sorry, since it is to see you deprived of liberty, that I am a witness of this business"; but, as the sentence stands, the two clauses can be taken only as *co-ordinate.*

211. Abergavenny, spelt *Aburgany* in the Folios, and so pronounced.

217. Henry Pole, Lord Montacute, or Montague (1492–1539), was the son-in-law of Lord Abergavenny. On this occasion he was pardoned; but in 1539 he was tried for another act of treason and beheaded.

219. Gilbert Peck. Holinshed (see Appendix) and Hall give the name as Perke. This name seems to have arisen from a misreading of the word 'clerk'. In the authentic documents relating to the trial of the Duke of Buckingham (Calendar, *Henry VIII.,* vol. iii., pt. i., pp. 490–495) there is mention of "Robert Gilbert, clerk, then his chancellor".

221. A monk o' the Chartreux, *i.e.* a Carthusian monk. This, order, founded by St. Bruno in 1084, was introduced into England about 1180. The original monastery was the *Grande Chartreuse,* near Grenoble.

Nicholas Hopkins. The Folio reading is *Michaell,* probably due to confusion on the printer's part of *Nich* with *Mich.* See the quotation from Holinshed in the Appendix.

224–226. Buckingham says that he is the shadow of his former self, and that he is now standing in his own light. The expression of the idea seems faulty; certainly it has troubled commentators since the time of Johnson, and no literal interpretation yet given is satisfactory. *Instant* = present, impending.

Scene 2.

The business of the preceding scene is continued in the examination of Buckingham's surveyor. The chief dramatic value, however, lies in the unexpected petition of Katharine against the exactions imposed on the people by Wolsey. The examination merely supplies the details of Buckingham's plot, and makes his doom more certain; but the petition episode brings out strongly the characteristics of the three leading persons of the drama, and directly suggests the main motive by opposing the gentle nobility of Katharine to the selfish scheming of Wolsey. The importance of this episode in the construction of the play is emphasized by the fact that, while the examination of Buckingham is more or less a direct transcript from Holinshed, it was entirely the dramatist's own invention to make Katharine intercede on behalf of the people.

The same, *i.e.* London. "The preliminary investigation of the charge against Buckingham was really held at Greenwich. ... But it is clear that the dramatist did not suppose the scene to be at Greenwich, or he would not have made the Surveyor refer to that place as he does in line 188" (Wright).

2. i' the level, in the direct aim: a common meaning of the substantive in Shakespeare. The metaphor is continued in *full-charged*, but is broken in *choked*.

3. confederacy, conspiracy.

5. That gentleman of Buckingham's, *i.e.* the surveyor.

13. Repeat, state: commonly without any idea of repetition in Shakespeare.

18. solicited, informed by petitioners (Wright).

20. The account of these commissions for levying "the sixth part of every man's substance" (cf. l. 58), and of the hardships and dangers they caused, is taken from Holinshed.

28. The sides of loyalty. The metaphor is taken from physical convulsions.

32. put off, discharged.

41–43. 'My knowledge is only that of an individual in matters which concern the state, and I am in the front rank only in a file where others keep step with me.'

45. alike, equally to you and others.

46. those which. *Who* occurs frequently in Shakespeare, but *which* is the usual masc. and fem. relative in E.E.

52. exclamation, reproach, outcry.

56. grief, grievance.

67. no primer business, no more pressing business. The Folios read "baseness"; the emendation is Warburton's.

70. A single voice, *i.e.* his vote. Wolsey says he did not give his vote till he was assured by the judges of the legality of the commissions.

78. cope, encounter; commonly transitive in E.E. Cf. *As You Like It*, ii. 1. 67, "I love to cope him in these sullen fits".

82. once, once for all, positively. See Abbott, § 57. Cf. German *einmal*.

83. allow'd. See Glossary.

85-87. If we shall...We should. See Abbott, § 371. Cf. l. 134.

94. stick them in our will, place them under our mere whim.

95. A trembling contribution; often explained as 'a contribution which makes the giver tremble'. But *trembling* seems to refer rather to the king who exacts than to the subjects who give.

96. lop, the smaller branches *lopped* off trees.

105. Hardly, harshly, unfavourably.

106. revokement, revocation. The foregoing account of Henry's annoyance at the commissions and of Wolsey's duplicity is modelled on Holinshed.

Enter Surveyor. The events of the first part of this scene took place in 1525, four years after the trial of Buckingham. The simultaneous representation of these two matters in which Wolsey was so intimately concerned serves to bring out with greater strength the various elements in his character. It is to be noted that Wolsey plays a more important part in the first three acts than either Katharine or Henry.

110. Is run in, has run into, incurred.

111. learn'd. "Buckingham was a patron of literature. Steevens has pointed out that the French prose romance of Helyas the Knight of the Swanne was translated at his suggestion. The title is, 'Here beginneth the History of the noble Helyas Knight of the Swanne, newly translated out of Frenshe in to Englysshe at thinstigacion of the puyssant and illustryous Prynce lorde Edwarde Duke of Buckingham'" (Wright).

112-114. Cf. the remarks of Norfolk in the preceding scene, lines 134-136 and 146, 147.

116. Not well disposed, not used to a good purpose. Cf. the Latin proverb, "corruptio optimi pessima".

118. complete. In Shakespeare "the form *cómplete* always precedes a noun accented on the first syllable, *compléte* is always in the predicate....One verse only (viz. *this one*) seems to make an exception. But in consideration of the many metrical irregularities caused by a full stop in the middle of a verse, no serious difficulty can be found in this seeming anomaly" (Schmidt, ii. 1413).

119. and when we, &c. The syntax is faulty, but the sense is clear.

128. Unlike so much of the present scene, this fine speech was not suggested by Holinshed. Indeed, Holinshed describes the examination of the surveyor as being conducted by Wolsey alone. Curiously enough, however, the dramatic instinct which led the poet to make the king preside at it brought him nearer the historical facts. "With the exception of making Wolsey present at the examination

of the duke's servants and surveyor, Shakespeare has strictly adhered
to facts in this preliminary examination of the duke's servants. We
have indisputable evidence that it was conducted by the king in
person..." (Brewer, *Reign of Henry VIII.*, i. 383).

130. Note Wolsey's bland hypocrisy in calling the man whom he
has bribed "a careful subject".

132, &c. The play now returns to Holinshed's narrative; see the
Appendix. Many of the words and phrases are identical.

136. son-in-law. Abergavenny's third wife was Mary, third
daughter of Buckingham.

140. his wish, that "the king should without issue die".

141, 142. This is Wolsey's only hint at personal considerations
in his prosecution of Buckingham.

143. Deliver, relate, utter. Cf. ii. 2. 135, and ii. 3. 106.

145. Upon our fail, in case of failure of issue. Cf. ii. 4. 198.

147. Nicholas Henton. So in the Folios. It is unnecessary
to read, with Theobald, *Hopkins* instead of *Henton.* Cf. i. 1. 221.
The mistake—which is the dramatist's, and not the printer's—would
seem to have been caused by a misreading of a phrase in Holinshed,
"one Nicholas Hopkins, a monke of an house of the Chartreux
order beside Bristow, called Henton" (p. 863).

148. friar, a mistake for *monk.* Cf. i. 1. 221, and i. 2. 160.

152. the Rose, the manor of the Red Rose, belonging to the
duke. In 1561 it was converted into the Merchant Taylors' School.

164. confession's seal. The monk binds his chaplain by the
oath of secrecy which is taken by priests in regard to confessions.
The Folios read *commissions seal*; the emendation, which is due to
Theobald, is supported by Holinshed: "The duke in talke told the
monke that he had doone verie well to bind his chapleine Iohn de
la Court, vnder the seale of confession, to keepe secret such matter"
(p. 863).

170. To gain the love is the reading of the Fourth Folio, the
first three having simply 'To the love'. The addition of some such
word is necessary for the metre.

172, 173. Holinshed incidentally mentions the dismissal of Buckingham's surveyor because of complaints made by the tenants about
his bribery. In giving this information by the mouth of Katharine,
the dramatist throws into relief her honesty and sense of justice.

174. spleen, malice, spite. The spleen was anciently supposed
to be the seat of strong passions. Cf. note on i. 1. 152, 153.

179, 180. for him, &c. The obviously faulty reading of the
Folios is—

"and that was dangerous
For this to ruminate on this so far, until".

The emendation is Capell's; but it is hardly convincing, for it takes two extra syllables from one line to add them to another. It may be well to note in this connection that there is no other example in Shakespeare of *ruminate* followed by a preposition.

184. fail'd, died: a euphemism prompted by the presence of the king; or perhaps simply a synonym of *miscarried* in Holinshed's account.

190. Bulmer. The Folios read *Blumer*, which seems to be a misprint: Pope made the mistake greater in reading *Blomer*. Henry forgave Sir William Bulmer this offence, and in the following year appointed him to be present at the Field of the Cloth of Gold.

190, 191. I remember Of. The only instance in Shakespeare, according to Schmidt, of this construction.

195. my father, *i.e.* Henry Stafford, Duke of Buckingham from 1460, beheaded at Salisbury 1483. He appears in the play of *Richard III.* Cf. ii. 1. 107.

198. made semblance of his duty, *i.e.* made semblance to kneel down before him, as in the quotation from Holinshed in the Appendix.

200. may, can. Cf. ii. 4. 235. See Abbott, § 307.

201. Katharine recognizes the hopelessness of interfering any further in the cause of justice.

204. him, himself. See Abbott, § 223.

209. period, the end he aims at. Thus, *Merry Wives*, iii. 3. 46, "this is the period of my ambition".

213. by day and night: an oath. Cf. *Hamlet*, i. 5. 164, "O day and night, but this is wondrous strange!"

Scene 3.

This scene can be regarded only as a prelude to the following one. It does not in any way further the action of the drama. The quizzical criticism of the "travell'd gallants", however, supplies contrast to the sombre colouring of the preceding scene.

Mr. Boyle assumes (*New Shakspere Society's Transactions*, 1880–1886, p. 461) that this scene was intended to ridicule the "travell'd gallants" of the reign of James I. It probably has this contemporary reference; but at the same time it was directly suggested by a passage in Holinshed. "During this time (1519) remained in the French court diuerse yoong gentlemen", says Holinshed, following Hall. "And when these yoong gentlemen came againe into England, they were all French, in eating, drinking, and apparell, yea, and in French vices and brags, so that all the estates of England were by them laughed at, the ladies and gentlewomen were dispraised;

so that nothing by them was praised, but if it were after the French turne." After a time complaints about their conduct were made to Henry by his council; "to whome the king answered", continues Holinshed, "that he had chosen them of his councell, both for the maintenance of his honour, and for the defense of all things that might blemish the same: wherefore, if they saw anie about him misuse themselves, he committed it vnto their reformation. Then the kings councell caused the lord chamberleine to call before them diuerse of the priuie chamber, which had beene in the French court, and banished them the court for diuerse considerations" (pp. 850, 852).

2. **mysteries**, incomprehensible fashions.

7. **A fit...o' the face**, a grimace. Wright compares *King Lear*, ii. 2. 87, " A plague upon your epileptic visage !"

10. **Pepin**, the son of Charles Martel and the father of Charlemagne, founded the Carlovingian dynasty in 752. **Clotharius**, *i.e.* Clotaire, the son of Clovis, belonged to the earlier Merovingian dynasty. This is a case of the particular put for the general, the meaning being merely 'the great French kings of early times'.

12, 13. **spavin Or springhalt.** Verplanck's emendation of the Folio reading *spavin A springhalt*: Pope read *And springhalt*. The correction is necessary as the two diseases are not identical. The *spavin* is a disease in horses affecting the hock-joint, and ultimately causing lameness; the *springhalt* (or *stringhalt*, as Theobald read it) shows itself in a sudden twitching of the hind-legs, likewise causing lameness.

18. **clapp'd**, stuck up. *Clap* is "a vivid or picturesque equivalent of 'put', 'place', with the implication of energetic action easily performed" (*New English Dictionary*). Cf. i. 4. 9.

23. **Louvre**, the seat of the French court in Shakespeare's time. The modern buildings were begun by Francis I., the king whom Henry " met in the vale of Andren "; but the original Louvre dated from the thirteenth century.

25. **fool and feather.** The plumes worn in hats and caps, in imitation of French fashions, were of great size. Steevens thought the allusion was to a fashion of carrying fans of feathers which was once in vogue during Shakespeare's lifetime; while others hold it is to the feathers worn in the caps of professional fools. But, as is usually the case, the simplest interpretation is the best.

27. **fights and fireworks.** This is usually said to refer to the joustings at the Field of the Cloth of Gold, and to the fireworks with which the interview concluded; but it is difficult to believe that the reference is so particular.

29. **clean**, entirely. Cf. *Othello*, i. 3. 366, "it is clean out of the way".

30. tennis, the great French game. It had been introduced into this country by the thirteenth century. Henry was an enthusiastic tennis player, and the oldest existing tennis-court in this country, that at Hampton Court, was built by him.

tall-stockings, stockings reaching high above the knee.

31. blister'd, ornamented with puffs, puffed. The *New English Dictionary* quotes from Nashe, *Pierce Penilesse* (1592), "His back… blistered with light sarcenet bastings". The Fourth Folio misses the point in reading *bolstred*, for *blister'd* "describes with picturesque humour the appearance of the slashed breeches, covered as they were with little puffs of satin lining which thrust themselves out through the slashes" (Grant White). *Tall stockings and short blister'd breeches,* which was a fashion at the court of Francis I., seems to have been a fashion also in Shakespeare's time.

types, signs, marks.

32. understand, a pun, as in *The Two Gentlemen of Verona,* ii. 5. 28, "My staff understands me"; and in *Twelfth Night,* iii. 1. 89, "My legs do better understand me, sir, than I understand what you mean by bidding me taste my legs".

35. The lag end, the latter end. Cf. *1 Henry IV.,* v. 1. 24, "the lag end of my life". Note the abundant alliteration of this speech.

Though Henry's proclamation condemns the imitation of French fashions, he himself followed the example of his "good brother of France" in one or two matters.

43. plain-song, simple melody, without variations.

45. Held current music, *i.e.* have it held current music.

46. colt's tooth, youthful tastes, frolicsomeness. The phrase is common in our literature, from Chaucer, *Reeve's Prol.,* 34, "And yet I have alwey a coltes toth", to Steele, *Tatler,* No. 151, "my Aunt Margery had again a colt's tooth in her head".

57. has wherewithal. The Folios read *ha's,* perhaps an error for *'has, i.e.* he has; in any case the ellipsis is not uncommon. See Abbott, § 400.

61. My barge stays. This shows that the present scene is laid in the palace of Bridewell, which was on the banks of the Thames. The Lord Chamberlain is proceeding by the river to York Place (scene 4).

62. shall along. Cf. *Hamlet,* iii. 3. 4—

"And he to England shall along with you".

For the ellipsis of the verb of motion, cf. v. 1. 8, "I must to him", v. 3. 93, "I must needs to the Tower", &c.; and see Abbott, § 405.

65. comptrollers, stewards, masters of ceremonies.

Scene 4.

This scene is to be regarded primarily as a pageant. Its dramatic importance lies only in the meeting of the king and Anne Bullen, and in the representation of Wolsey at the height of his glory.

George Cavendish, Wolsey's gentleman-usher, who was present at the entertainment here described, gives an account of it in his *Life of Wolsey*. It is possible that the dramatist may have borrowed his material directly from this life, for, though it was not published till 1641, it had been widely circulated in MS.; but probably he was indebted to Holinshed's transcript from Stow's *Chronicle* of Cavendish's account. See Introduction (11.), and Appendix.

The entertainment took place on 3rd January, 1527. There is an historical error in making the Lord Chamberlain and Lord Sands distinct persons, for in 1526 Lord Sands had succeeded the Earl of Worcester as Lord Chamberlain.

York Place, Wolsey's residence as Archbishop of York, now Whitehall. See iv. 1. 94–97.

4. bevy, company of ladies. See Glossary.

6. first, good company. This is the reading of the first three Folios, the fourth omitting the comma after *first*. Theobald read *first-good*, explaining it as "the best company in the land, of the best rank"; Staunton considered *first* a corruption of *feast*; and Halliwell-Phillips plausibly suggested *far as*. But emendation is not necessary.

12. running banquet, a slight repast, a hasty refreshment, here used figuratively, as also in v. 4. 57. This (or "dessert") was probably the original sense of *banquet*.

20. Place you that side, place yourself on that side. Cf. i. 2. 204.

30. kiss you twenty, *i.e.* kiss you twenty times. In M.E. the cardinal number was frequently used instead of the multiplicative (as here), and even of the ordinal. See Kellner, § 265.

Well said, well done: a common Shakespearian usage.

33. For my little cure may mean either 'as for my little *charge*', *i.e.* Anne Bullen, or 'as for my little *remedy*', *i.e.* for preventing the ladies passing away frowning. The latter is the *New English Dictionary* interpretation.

41. beholding, obliged, beholden. See Glossary.

46. if I make my play. This has been variously explained as "if I make my party" (Steevens), "if I may choose my game" (Ritson), and "if I win what I play for" (Wright). But the meaning seems to be 'when I play with spirit, if I "play up"'.

Stage-direction. **chambers**, small pieces of ordnance without a carriage, standing on their breech, and used to fire salutes. The firing of chambers on the arrival of the king is mentioned in Cavendish and Holinshed. See Appendix.

It seems to have been this firing of chambers which caused the burning of the Globe Theatre on 29th June, 1613. See Introduction.

50. Look out there. According to Cavendish, this order was given not by the Chamberlain, but to the Chamberlain and Sir Henry Guildford by Wolsey. This difference helps to prove that the dramatist used Holinshed's account and not Cavendish's, for Holinshed following Stow says "the great chamberleine and the said comptrollor sent to looke", by mistake for "were sent".

75, 76. It was entirely the dramatist's invention to make the first meeting of Henry and Anne Bullen take place at this masque.

86. According to Cavendish and Holinshed, Wolsey mistook Sir Edward Neville for the king. See Appendix.

89. unhappily, unfavourably, not to your credit. Cf. Prologue, 24.

90. pleasant, facetious. Cf. ii. 3. 93.

93. Sir Thomas Bullen was created Viscount Rochford on 18th June, 1525. As this entertainment took place on 3rd January, 1527, there is no anachronism, as is sometimes said, in the mention of "Viscount Rochford".

96. And not to kiss you. It was the custom for a dancer to kiss his partner at the end of a dance, the lady acknowledging the kiss with a curtsy. Staunton quotes from Shirley's *Ball*, Act i., scene 2—

> " if he have privilege
> o kiss another lady, she may say
> He does salute her and return a curtsy,
> To shew her breeding".

Cf. also the *Tempest*, i. 2. 378—

> " Courtsied when you have and kiss'd".

105. Good my lord, a common form of transposition. Cf. iii. 1. 42 and 78, and see Abbott, § 13.

106. measure, dance; usually of a slow stately nature.

108. knock it, strike up. This indefinite *it* is analogous to the cognate accusative. See Kellner, § 283. Cf. ii. 3. 37.

Act II.—Scene I.

This fine scene ends the rôle of Buckingham. It should be re-marked that his introduction, either here or in the first two scenes of Act i., contributes little or nothing to the main action of the drama, and that the chief purpose it serves is to display the power and the unscrupulousness of Wolsey. From the purely æsthetic point of view, however, this scene is one of the most notable in the whole play.

Buckingham was tried on 13th May, 1521, before seventeen of his peers, presided over by the Duke of Norfolk, and he was executed on Tower Hill on 17th May. Holinshed's account is again followed closely, and some of the expressions (even in the stage-direction after l. 54) are copied word for word. See the Appendix.

2. to the hall, Westminster Hall.

8. upon 't, *i.e.* on the verdict.

11. in a little, briefly, in few words.

15. The king's attorney "at this time was John Fitz-James, who was appointed 26 Jan. 1519. He became Chief Baron of the Exchequer 8 Feb. 1522, and Chief Justice of the King's Bench 23 Jan. 1526 (Foss, *Judges of England*, v. 96, 98, 100)" (Wright).

28. learnedly, like one learned in the law.

29. 'Either produced no effect, or only ineffectual pity' (Malone).

40. the end of this, at the bottom of this.

41-44. According to Holinshed, Wolsey saw that the Earl of Surrey, Buckingham's son-in-law, might possibly prevent him bring-ing about the fall of the duke, and he accordingly laid a deep scheme to get him out of the country. In 1520, when Gerald Fitz-Gerald, Earl of Kildare, Deputy of Ireland, came on a visit to England, Wolsey accused him to the king of maladministration, and had him deprived of his office, so as to make room for the Earl of Surrey. In Holinshed's words, "by the cardinals good preferment the earle of Surrie was sent into Ireland as the kings deputie, in lieu of the said earle of Kildare; there to remaine rather as an exile than as lieutenant to the king, euen at the cardinals pleasure, as he himselfe well perceiued" (p. 855). Surrey returned in 1521, after Bucking-ham's execution.

44. father, *i.e.* father-in-law (as in iii. 2. 8, 256), Surrey's second wife being Elizabeth Stafford, Buckingham's eldest daughter.

45. envious, malicious. Cf. *envy* in l. 85. See Glossary.

48. find employment (for). See Abbott, § 201.

50. perniciously, maliciously, to the death.

53. The mirror of all courtesy. Cf. Holinshed (p. 870): "He is tearmed in the books of the law in the said thirteenth yeare of Henrie the eight...to be the floure and mirror of all courtesie".

Stage-direction: **tipstaves**, bailiffs. **with the edge towards him**, a sign that he was condemned to death.

Sir William Sands. Theobald's emendation (from Holinshed) of the Folio reading *Walter* Sands. He was created Lord Sands in 1523, and under this title he has already appeared in scenes 3 and 4 of Act i.

57. lose, forget.

67. their evils. See *2 Kings*, x. 27. The word is used in the same sense in *Measure for Measure*, ii. 2. 172—

> "Shall we desire to raise the sanctuary
> And pitch our evils there?"

74. Is only bitter...dying, the only thing that is bitter to him, and the only thing that is death.

76. divorce, that which causes divorce, here of soul and body. See l. 61, "Even as the axe falls", and ii. 3. 16. Cf. this use of *divorce* with *Timon of Athens*, iv. 3. 382—

> "O thou sweet king-killer, and dear divorce
> 'Twixt natural son and sire!"

79–81. Lovell's remark is to be taken in connection with i. 2. 185, 186.

86. mark my grave. Warburton's emendation of the Folio reading *make my grave*. There is perhaps some confusion with *take* in the preceding line, for *take peace with* does not occur elsewhere in Shakespeare.

89. forsake. The only instance in Shakespeare of this absolute use.

103. Edward Bohun. Buckingham was fifth in descent from Eleanor, daughter of Humphrey de Bohun, Earl of Hereford (see notes on Dramatis Personæ); but the family name of the Buckinghams was Stafford. The mistake is due to Holinshed: see Appendix.

105. I now seal it, 'I now seal my truth, my loyalty, with blood' (Johnson).

107. My noble father. Cf. i. 2. 195, &c. Henry Stafford, Duke of Buckingham, was betrayed by his servant, Humphrey Banaster, in 1483.

108. head, an armed force. Cf. *1 Henry IV.*, i. 3. 284—

> "To save our heads by raising of a head".

In *Hamlet*, iv. 5. 101, it is used not of the army of insurrection, but of the insurrection itself—

> "Laertes in a riotous head
> O'erbears your officers".

This meaning, which is now obsolete, arose, as the present passage may suggest, from a figurative use of the word.

112. Buckingham was restored to the family honours in the first parliament of Henry VII., November, 1485.

127. loose, unrestrained.

129. rub, obstacle, check: a term in the game of bowls for anything hindering a bowl's course. Cf. *King John*, iii. 4. 128—

> "For even the breath of what I mean to speak
> Shall blow each dust, each straw, each little rub,
> Out of the path".

130. ye, which is strictly a nominative, is frequently used by the Elizabethan dramatists instead of the accusative *you*. See in particular iii. 1. 102–111. The distinction is carefully preserved in the authorized version of the Bible. See Abbott, § 236.

132. last hour. The poet makes the execution take place immediately after the sentence, though in point of fact it did not take place till four days later.

133. my long weary life. Buckingham was only forty-three when he was executed.

136. The simple unadorned language of this great speech, and the easy direct verse, bring out admirably Buckingham's calm resignation. Mr. Swinburne remarks, in a fine eulogy, on the naturalness of the emotion, the modesty of effect, the aptness of phrase, and the "prolonged and persistent melody, which if not monotonous is certainly not various".

140, 141. inkling Of an ensuing Evil. This is the first direct hint at the main action of the play. It is exceptional for it to be given so late as the second Act.

148. buzzing, rumour.

152. allay, quell, silence. This rumour arose in the summer of 1527. The confusion of the chronology at the beginning of the play is caused almost entirely by the misplacing of Buckingham's trial; but it was doubtlessly misplaced of set purpose.

155. held, *i.e.* it is held. Cf. i. 3. 45.

156, &c. According to Holinshed, Wolsey desired the divorce so that Henry might marry the French king's sister, the Duchess of Alençon, and thereby strengthen the new French alliance; for he bore Charles V. a grudge for having refused him the Archbishopric of Toledo. But there does not seem to be any historical foundation for this.

160. Campeius (*i.e.* Campeggio) arrived in October, 1528.

Scene 2.

The central incident of the play, the divorce of Katharine, is now approached directly. The rumours mentioned at the end of the preceding scene are confirmed: Henry has determined to proceed with the trial, and Campeius has arrived for the "unpartial judging of this business". The previous events of the play have served to bring out the characters of the three leading actors in the divorce—Katharine, Henry, and Wolsey, and have suggested a motive for it in the king's fascination for Anne Bullen.

1–8. This letter gives further proof of Wolsey's overbearing arrogance and of his utter disregard for the feelings of others. The idea of it may have been taken from Rowley's *When you see me you know me*: see Introduction.

16, 17. It has been pointed out that what Suffolk says is properly an 'aside', and that Norfolk's *'Tis so* answers the remark of the Chamberlain.

19, 20. A double allusion, (1) to Fortune being always represented as blind, and (2) to Fortune's wheel.

24. the emperor…nephew. Cf. i. 1. 176, 177.

35. Will bless the king. Norfolk's prediction comes true. See iv. 2. 163, 164.

40. The French king's sister. See note on ii. 1. 156.

42. bold bad man. This familiar phrase occurs also in the *Faerie Queene*, i. 1. 37.

46. From princes into pages. Holinshed notes that when Wolsey said mass "he made dukes and earles to serue him of wine, …and to hold to him the bason at the lauatorie" (p. 847).

48. pitch, height, dignity.

Stage-direction: **draws the curtain.** "This stage-direction was calculated for and ascertains precisely the state of the theatre in Shakespeare's time. When a person was to be discovered in a different apartment from that in which the original speakers in the scene are exhibited, the artless mode of our author's time was to place such persons in the back part of the stage, behind the curtains, which were occasionally suspended across it. These the person who was to be discovered (as Henry in the present scene) drew back just at the proper time" (Malone).

68. estate, state; as frequently in Shakespeare.

74. Campeius had his first audience of Henry on 22nd October, 1528. The trial did not begin till the following summer.

76, 77. have great care…talker, see that what I have said be not found mere words.

81. sick, *i.e.* sick with pride.

83. have-at-him, thrust, attack. Cf. iii. 2. 309. The First Folio reads *one; haue at him*, and the three others *one heave at him*. The emendation is Dyce's.

92. Have their free voices, are in a position to give an unbiassed judgment, may express their opinions freely. Grant White's reading of *gave* for *have* is not in any way an improvement; for though the learned clerks in Christian kingdoms did pronounce in favour of the divorce, Wolsey is not yet supposed to know their decision. (See iii. 2. 64–67.) He merely means to say that the Spaniards can have no reason to suspect unfairness in the trial now that the case is submitted to the unbiassed judgment of foreigners.

98. the holy conclave, the College of Cardinals.

105. unpartial, impartial. See Abbott, § 442.

106. equal, just, impartial; perhaps also with the idea of 'equal in rank'. See Glossary.

112. "Bicause the king meant nothing but vprightlie therein, and knew well that the queene was somewhat wedded to hir owne opinion, and wished that she should do nothing without counsell, he bad hir choose the best clearks of his realme to be of hir counsell, and licenced them to doo the best on hir part that they could, according to the truth" (Holinshed, p. 907).

120–134. Note the strong dramatic effect of this somewhat grim conversation. After loud protestations of justice, Wolsey unblushingly scoffs at virtue, and shows himself indifferent to having caused the death of one who would not be his tool.

Dr. Richard Pace (1482?–1536, not 1532) was dean of St. Paul's, Exeter, and Salisbury, and held many other posts in recognition of his services to the king. According to Holinshed, Wolsey began to fear that he might become a rival in the king's favour, and accordingly had him sent out of the country on embassies; "the which (*i.e.* Pace) being continuallie abroad in ambassages, and the same oftentimes not much necessarie, by the cardinals appointment, at length he tooke such greefe therewith, that he fell out of his right wits" (p. 907). In 1525 he was forced, on account of mental derangement, to return to England, and in 1526 coadjutors were appointed to his deaneries; but there seems to be little or no ground for the statements as to his ill-treatment by Wolsey.

129. That's Christian care enough, that is as much consideration as a Christian need show.

137. such receipt of learning. See note, iii. 1. 134.

Scene 3.

This scene is essentially a sketch of the character of Anne Bullen. It has no importance in the structure of the play. The part of Anne is a very minor one: so far she has uttered only a few words of no bearing (i. 4), and hereafter she is merely to appear in the marriage procession (iv. 1).

1-11. It is worse than needless to emend the somewhat disjointed grammar of Anne's first speech, for she is plainly supposed to be speaking under strong emotion.

10. To give her the avaunt, to bid her begone. See Glossary.

14. that quarrel, fortune. Dr. Johnson took *quarrel* as an instance of the act used instead of the agent, and this is the most satisfactory interpretation of a reading which may be corrupt: cf. "divorce" in ii. 1. 76. Warburton's explanation was that *quarrel* is used in its old sense of 'arrow' (cf. Fairfax, "twang'd the string, out flew the quarrel long"), and that Fortune is called a *quarrel* "from her striking so deep and suddenly". The Shakespearian references to the 'arrows of fortune' have been urged in support of this view; but, on the other hand, it should be pointed out that in no other passage does Shakespeare use *quarrel* in any but its ordinary sense. Several emendations have been proposed, none of which is convincing.

15. sufferance, suffering, agony. Cf. v. 1. 68.

panging, causing pangs: used as a verb also in *Cymbeline*, iii. 4. 98, "thy memory Will then be pang'd by me".

21. perk'd up, dressed up. See Glossary.

23. having, possession. Cf. iii. 2. 159.

32. cheveril, pliant, elastic. See Glossary. Cf. *Romeo and Juliet*, ii. 4. 87, "O, here's a wit of cheveril, that stretches from an inch narrow to an ell broad!" The word is used most commonly as an epithet to conscience.

36. a three-pence bow'd, a crooked, and hence worthless, three-penny piece. "No three-pences were coined by Henry 8, nor was the coin known in England until the close of the reign of Edward 6. The first large and regular coinage of three-pences took place in the reign of Elizabeth" (Fairholt).

hire; here dissyllabic. See Appendix B.

40. pluck off a little, descend a little in rank: if neither a queen nor a duchess, what of a countess?

44. An allusion to one of Henry's reasons for seeking the divorce.

46. little England. "There is no reason to suppose that more is intended by this than the obvious contrast of 'little England' to 'all the world', but there may have been a secondary reference to the fact that Pembrokeshire was known as 'little England', and that Anne Bullen's first promotion was to be Marchioness of Pembroke. Steevens quotes from Taylor the Water Poet's 'A Short Relation of a Long Journey' [p. 19, Spenser Society's reprint]: 'Concerning Pembrookshire, the people do speak English in it almost generally, and therefore they call it little England beyond Wales, it being the farthest south and west county in the whole Principality'" (Wright).

47. emballing, usually explained as 'investment with the ball', the emblem of royalty. The *New English Dictionary* knows no other instance of this word.

52. Not your demand, *i.e.* the secret of the conversation is not worth your question.

61. Commends, delivers, sends by me; cf. v. 1. 17. See Glossary.

63. Marchioness of Pembroke. "On the first of September [1532], being sundaie, the K., being come to Windsor, created the ladie Anne Bullongne marchionesse of Pembroke, and gaue to hir one thousand pounds land by the yeare" (Holinshed, p. 928).

67, 68. nor...not: one of the commonest forms of the double negative.

70. Beseech, I beseech. See Abbott, § 401. Cf. i. 3. 57.

74. approve, confirm; as commonly in E.E.

78, 79. gem...isle. A reference to the carbuncle, which was supposed to have the power of giving light. Steevens compares *Titus Andronicus*, ii. 3. 226, 227—

> "Upon his bloody finger he doth wear
> A precious ring, that lightens all the hole".

85. suit of pounds, petition for money.

87. compell'd fortune, fortune forced upon you.

89. forty pence, *i.e.* I wager forty pence, a common sum for a small wager. *Forty* is also used for an indefinite number, as in iii. 2. 253.

92. the mud in Egypt, *i.e.* the wealth of Egypt, due to the mud deposited by the annual overflow of the Nile.

97. mo, more. See Glossary.

103. salute my blood, affect, exhilarate my blood. Cf. *Sonnet*, cxxi. 6—

> "For why should others' false adulterate eyes
> Give salutation to my sportive blood".

faints me, makes me faint; the only instance in Shakespeare of this transitive use.

Scene 4.

This scene is of great importance in the development of the drama. It deals directly with the divorce, the matter on which the whole play hinges; it brings out the stronger elements in Katharine's character; and it gives, in Henry's closing remarks, the first hint of Wolsey's fall.

The events which this scene represents happened on 21st June, 1529. Holinshed's account, which has been followed very closely, is given in the Appendix.

Stage-direction: **Archbishop of Canterbury**, William Warham, made primate 1504, died 1532; **the Bishops of Lincoln, Ely, Rochester, and Saint Asaph**, John Longland, Nicholas West, John Fisher, and Henry Standish; see note to line 58. **silver pillars**, part of the insignia of a cardinal.

13, 14. I desire you do me…And to bestow. For the omission of *to* before the former verb, see Abbott, § 350. This speech is largely a versified form of Holinshed's prose. Cf. the first six lines with the following passage: "*Sir* (quoth she) *I desire you* to *doo me iustice and right, and* take some *pitie vpon me, for I am a poore woman, and a stranger, borne out of your dominion; hauing heere no indifferent counsell, and lesse assurance of freendship*". In other passages the identity is no less remarkable: see Appendix.

17. indifferent, impartial.

30. strove. For this participial use of the preterite, cf. *spake*, l. 153, and see Abbott, § 343.

32. had to him derived, had brought upon himself. See Glossary.

33. nay, gave notice, *i.e.* nay, did not give notice. Or perhaps the point of interrogation after *discharged* should be omitted.

36. Upward of twenty years is strictly accurate, for Katharine was married to Henry on 11th June, 1509. She had at least five children, two of whom were sons, but, with the exception of Mary, all had died. See lines 186–193.

41. *I.e.* 'or aught against your sacred person'.

48, 49. one The wisest. This archaic appositional use was still common in E.E. Cf. line 153, and v. 1. 32, 33; and see Abbott, § 18, and Kellner, § 176.

57. Despite Katharine's direct appeal to the king, it is Wolsey who replies, and in a speech of characteristic hypocrisy.

58. of your choice. See note on ii. 2. 112. The "reverend fathers" she chose were "William Warham archbishop of Canturburie, and Nicholas Weast bishop of Elie, doctors of the laws; and Iohn Fisher bishop of Rochester, and Henrie Standish bishop of saint Assaph, doctors of diuinitie, and manie other doctors and well learned men" (Holinshed, p. 907).

62. That longer you desire the court, that you desire the court to delay its proceedings; cf. the legal phrase "to pray for a longer day".

68. Up to this point Katharine has been meek and patient, though dignified; now the cruel insincerity of Wolsey brings out all the latent strength in her character.

77. challenge, a legal word still retained in objecting to jurymen.

80. God's dew, *i.e.* mercy.

81. abhor, protest against; used in the same sense, according to Schmidt, in *The Comedy of Errors*, iii. 2. 164—

" She that doth call me husband, even my soul
    Doth for a wife abhor ".

According to Blackstone *abhor* is a technical term in the canon law = Latin *detestor*. Here the word is taken from Holinshed. See Appendix.

86. stood to, taken the side of.

92. consistory, the College of Cardinals. Cf. ii. 2. 98.

102, 103. the which...in, on which point. The relative is used in E.E. with great freedom, and may refer, not to a special antecedent, but to all the *circumstances* already described.

105. Wolsey has glibly parried Katharine's accusations by appealing to her former charity, denying any act of injustice, and, with great adroitness, referring loyally to the king in the king's presence. Katharine refuses to 'oppose his cunning', and makes further charges against him. Note that these charges are against his character generally; in the former speech she accused him only of duplicity in the divorce proceedings.

113. powers, people of rank and authority. See note on ii. 2. 46. The emendation of *wards* for *words* makes the correspondence of phrase complete, but is somewhat prosaic.

127. Gent. Ush. *i.e.* Griffith. See iv. 2.

133. Though the injustice of the divorce proceedings has lain lightly on the conscience of Henry, he does not venture to speak till after Katharine has left the court.

138. government, self-control.

155. touch of her good person, taint of her reputation.

166. speak, describe (cf. l. 140, iii. 1. 125, and iv. 2. 32); hence ' bear witness to '.

172. Not the Bishop of Bayonne (ambassador in 1529), but Gabriel de Grammont, Bishop of Tarbes (ambassador in 1527). The mistake occurs in Holinshed and Cavendish. " All that was said afterwards officially as to the origin of the king's scruples, and the doubts of Mary's legitimacy, said to have been suggested by the Bishop of Tarbes, is unworthy of serious refutation " (*Dict. Nat. Biog.*).

174. Duke of Orleans, second son of Francis I., afterwards Henry II. The marriage was intended to cement the alliance with France.

178. advertise; accented on the second syllable, as always in Shakespeare.

182. The bosom of my conscience. Holinshed has the phrase, "the secret bottome of my conscience". It is possible that *bosom* may be a misprint; but though the phrase is unusual it presents no difficulty, and corresponds, moreover, with "the region of my breast" in l. 184.

185. mazed considerings, bewildering considerations. Cf. iii. 2. 135.

199. hulling, tossing to and fro like a ship with bare masts in a storm. Holinshed has the phrase, "tossed in the waues of a scrupulous mind". Wright points out that steering is impossible, for the helm of a ship lying 'a-hull' is lashed to the lee side.

204. yet not well, *i.e.* yet do feel not well.

214. consequence of dread, consequences to be dreaded.

222. hands, signature, sign-manual.

230. paragon'd o' the world, considered a paragon by the world.

235-241. This impatient aside brings out with fine dramatic effect Henry's hypocrisy in protesting his willingness to 'wear his mortal state to come' with Katharine, and in praising her as the 'queen of earthly queens', 'the primest creature that's paragon'd o' the world'. It likewise foreshadows Wolsey's fall. In the second scene of this act Henry left the stage saying, "My Wolsey"; he now leaves it saying, "My learn'd and well-beloved servant, Cranmer".

238, 239. Cranmer was abroad collecting the opinions of the continental colleges and universities on the legality of Henry's marriage with Katharine.

Act III.—Scene I.

The sole purpose of this strong scene, which is not in any way essential to the development of the drama, is to depict the character of Katharine. Baffled by her refusal to be tried by any English court, Henry sends the two cardinals to her to persuade her to put her "main cause in the king's protection". She receives them with suspicion and upbraids them for their insincerity, but she ends by asking their forgiveness and telling them to do what they will. The action, it is thus evident, is no further forward at the end of the scene than at the beginning; but the description of Katharine's passionate bearing towards the unscrupulous cardinals is one of the most powerful parts of the play. Note that it is invariably Wolsey who is the foil to Katharine.

The passage in Holinshed which suggested this scene is given in the Appendix.

The Queen's apartments, in the palace of Bridewell. Cavendish, from whom Holinshed's account of this interview is derived, tells how Wolsey and Campeius "went together unto Bridewell, directly to the queen's lodging".

3. Orpheus. The story of Orpheus is told in Ovid's *Metamorphoses*, books x. and xi. Compare this song with the passage in the *Merchant of Venice* (v. 80, &c.) on the power of music.

7. as, as if. Cf. i. 1. 10.

16. An't, if it: printed *and't* in the Folios. See Glossary.

17. presence, presence-chamber.

23. all hoods make not monks, an allusion to the Latin proverb, "cucullus non facit monachum", which is quoted in *Measure for Measure*, v. 1. 263, and *Twelfth Night*, i. 5. 62.

24. part of a housewife. According to Cavendish and Holinshed (see Appendix), Katharine had 'a skein of white thread about her neck' when she received the cardinals. In order to bring out her unaffectedness more clearly, the dramatist makes her receive them in her private room, though the historical authorities say that she went into the "chamber of presence, where the cardinals were attending".

37. so even, (to have been) so consistently pure. Cf. *Julius Cæsar*, ii. 1. 133, "The even virtue of our enterprise".

38. that way I am wife in, *i.e.* has reference to the divorce.

40, 41. 'So great is our integrity of purpose towards thee, most serene queen.' As Cavendish and Holinshed merely state that Wolsey spoke in Latin, the present words are supplied by the dramatist. Wolsey speaks in Latin in order that Katharine's attendants may not understand him, but by so doing he prompts a doubt as to his sincerity.

45. more strange, suspicious. Dyce and Abbott (*Sh. Gr.*, § 2) read *strange-suspicious*, taking this as an instance of compounded adjectives, "the first being a kind of adverb qualifying the second". But this interpretation, as Wright points out, would imply that there had already been some suspicion attaching to Katharine's cause, which is not the case (see line 128). It is better to preserve the punctuation of the Folios, and to interpret the phrase, with Wright, as 'more strange, even suspicious'.

Note the different usage of *strange* at the beginning of the line.

46. here are some will thank you. This construction is frequently explained as 'omission of the relative' (see Abbott, § 244), but it is really a survival of the so-called ἀπὸ κοινοῦ construction of one subject with two predicates, from which the relative clause was developed. See Kellner, §§ 109–111.

51. integrity; repeated from line 40.

64. your late censure. See ii. 4. 74, &c., 105, &c.

74. was set, was sitting; as frequently in Shakespeare.

86. so desperate to be honest, so reckless as honestly to take my part.

87. live a subject; a euphemism for 'not be executed'.

88. weigh out, outweigh, make amends for.

103. cardinal virtues. Katharine's righteous indignation finds vent for the moment in biting sarcasm. The play on the word *cardinal* has been objected to by some critics; but there are occasions, and this is one, when wit, far from being out of keeping with passion, is its best expression. "On a death-bed there is a feeling which may make all things appear but as puns and equivocations. And a passion there is that carries off its own excess by plays on words as naturally, and, therefore, as appropriately to drama, as by gesticulations, looks, or tones" (Coleridge, on *Richard II.*).

117. churchmen's habits. Cf. line 23.

119. already. Since 1525 or 1526.

120. I am old. She was at this time in her forty-fourth year.

125. speak myself. See note on ii. 4. 166.

134. a constant woman to her husband, *i.e.* a woman constant to her husband. This bold transposition is a characteristic idiom of E.E., but uncommon in M.E. See Kellner, § 466, and Abbott, § 419 a.

145. angels' faces; probably an allusion to the famous 'non Angli sed angeli' of Gregory the Great.

161. carriage. Cf. iv. 2. 145, and *carried* in ii. 4. 143.

176. used myself, behaved myself.
Katharine's passion has now passed; the strain of the struggle has been too great for her. The apparent sincerity of the cardinals makes her fear that she may have wronged them.

Scene 2.

This great scene may be divided roughly into three parts: (1) the final interview of Henry and Wolsey, (2) the triumph of the nobles whom Wolsey has hitherto cowed, and (3) the farewell of Wolsey to his greatness. The first and third parts are essentially the dramatist's invention, for the details furnished by Holinshed are worked in incidentally, and are only subservient to the depiction of Wolsey's character; the second part is founded more directly on Holinshed. Though in a sense the most important scene, it defeats the possibility of a dramatic climax. With the fall of Wolsey, most of the preceding action is brought to an abrupt conclusion; and his fall, despite the part he has so far played, has little or no bearing on the succeeding acts. There is no central and decisive moment in the story, and accordingly no unity.

The chronology of the scene is very confused. The king's displeasure was not so sudden as it is made to appear, and there was an interval of four years between some of the events referred to as contemporaneous (*e.g.* the appointment of Sir Thomas More as Lord Chancellor, and of Cranmer as Archbishop of Canterbury). But this condensation increases the dramatic intensity.

The Duke of Norfolk died in 1524, and his appearance here is therefore an anachronism. As he was succeeded by his son the Earl of Surrey, the dramatic Norfolk and Surrey are historically the same person.

2. force, urge: as occasionally in Shakespeare. Cf. *Coriolanus*, iii. 2. 51, "Why force you this?"

8. my father-in-law, the Duke of Buckingham. See note on ii. 1. 44.

11. Strangely neglected, *i.e.* not strangely neglected. The negative has to be supplied from the prefix in '*un*contemned'.

13. Out of, other than, except.

14, &c. The Chamberlain's attitude to Wolsey has altered since i. 3. 55, 56.

16. Gives way to us, makes a way for us, favours us. Cf. v. 1. 143.

23. to come off, to escape. *He* may possibly refer to the king, in which case the meaning of *to come off* would be 'to change'; but it is better to take it as referring to Wolsey.

26. contrary proceedings. Wolsey posed to Henry as favouring the divorce, but at the same time he was doing all he could to delay it. He saw that if it was granted the king would immediately marry Anne Bullen, and as this would defeat the projected marriage to the French king's sister (see note, ii. 1. 156), he "required the pope by letters and secret messengers, that in anie wise he should defer the iudgement of the diuorse, till he might frame the kings mind to his purpose" (Holinshed, p. 909).

38. him now seems redundant; but this was a regular idiom in E.E. See Kellner, §§ 104–106.

39. hedges, creeps along by hedgerows. The nautical metaphor in *coasts* is continued in *founder*.

41, 42. The date of the marriage cannot be definitely ascertained, but the weight of evidence seems to favour 25th January, 1533. Hall and Holinshed give 14th November, 1532.

45. Trace, follow.

50–52. Cf. the remark of the Chamberlain, ii. 3. 77–79.

52. memorized, made memorable.

57, 58. Campeggio took leave of Henry at Grafton Regis on 20th September, 1529. The dramatist here departs from Holinshed, who says expressly that "Campeius tooke his leaue of the king and nobilitie" (p. 908). Mr. Boswell-Stone suggests that the legate's clandestine departure was probably inferred from a misleading statement in Foxe's *Actes and Monumentes of the Churche*: Campeggio "craftily shifted hym self out of the realme before the day came appoynted for determination, leauing his suttle felow behynd hym to wey with the king in the meane time".

61. Ha! Cf. i. 2. 186; ii. 2. 62, 65, 71; v. 1. 66, 81, 86; and v. 2. 25. In Rowley's *When you see me you know me* (see note, Prologue, 14–16) there is an interesting reference to this favourite ejaculation of Henry—

"*King.* Am I not Harry? am I not England's king? Ha!

Will Summers. So la! Now the watchword's given: nay, an he once cry Ha! ne'er a man in the court dare for his head speak again" (Ed. Elze, 1874, p. 19).

64. He is return'd in his opinions, *i.e.* 'having sent in advance the opinions he has gathered'.

70, 71. In 1533 it was enacted by Parliament that "queene Katharine should no more be called queene, but princesse Dowager, as the widow of prince Arthur" (Holinshed, p. 929).

85, 86. the Duchess of Alençon, The French king's sister. See note on ii. 1. 156. This is another anachronism; for Margaret, Duchess of Alençon, had married Henry of Navarre, by January, 1527. Moreover, it is doubtful if Wolsey ever endeavoured to arrange this marriage.

90. The Marchioness of Pembroke. See ii. 3. 63.

96. candle. Staunton suggests that "there may be a play intended on the word *Bullen*, which is said to have been an ancient provincial name for a candle". This lacks confirmation, though, according to the *New English Dictionary*, *bullen* is defined in several dictionaries of provincial words as 'hemp-stalks peeled'; and, as Wright remarks, "if these were used for wicks, as rushes were, they might give their name to a candle".

99. spleeny, headstrong, hot-headed. According to Mr. Boswell-Stone, there is no mention in Hall or Holinshed of Anne's Lutheranism, but it is alluded to by Foxe: "The Cardinall of Yorke perceaued the kyng to cast fauour to the Lady Anne, whom he knew to be a Lutheran ". There are frequent references to Luther and the 'sect of Lutherans' in Rowley's *When you see me you know me*: see Introduction.

101. hard-ruled, *i.e.* hard to be ruled, not easily managed.

102, 103. one Hath crawl'd. See note on iii. 1. 46.

124. thus importing, to this effect.

There is no historical truth in this incident of the inventory; but, as Steevens pointed out, Holinshed tells how a similar mischance befell Thomas Ruthall, Bishop of Durham, and how Wolsey snatched the opportunity to bring the bishop into disfavour. Accordingly the dramatist "has represented the fall of that great man as owing to an incident which he had once improved to the destruction of another".

127, 128. *I.e.* describes more than what a subject should possess. Cf. ii. 4. 140, "speak thee out", where *out* is used in the sense of 'fully'. *Out* connected with a verb has one or other of these two senses in E.E. Cf. *Outworths*, i. 1. 123.

134. below the moon: referring to line 118.

137, &c. Henry makes full use of his knowledge of the inventory, while Wolsey, unconscious of Henry's irony, plies him as usual with "the honey of his language".

140. leisure, time at one's own disposal, implying work that is not obligatory. Cf. *Measure for Measure*, iii. 2. 261 : "Yet had he framed to himself...many deceiving promises of life; which I by my good leisure have discredited to him ".

142. husband, manager, economist. See Glossary.

149. tendance, attention.

154–156. Wolsey was appointed by Henry VII. to the deanery of Lincoln.

166–171. A certain amount of difficulty has been read into this passage somewhat unnecessarily. *Studied purposes* is plainly the subject (not the object) of *requite*, and *which* plainly refers to *studied purposes* (not to *royal graces*): "Your royal graces", says Wolsey, "have been more than my studied purposes could requite, even though my purposes went beyond all human endeavour; my endeavours have ever come short of my purposes, but they have kept pace with my abilities." In simpler form: "Your royal graces cannot be requited even by superhuman efforts; I have not done what I should have liked, but I have done all I could."

176. allegiant, loyal; according to the *New English Dictionary*, this is the only instance of the word before the present century.

178. has, *i.e.* has been. Cf. line 192.

181-183. the honour of it, &c. The honour of being loyal is its own reward, as, on the other hand, the foulness of disloyalty is its own punishment.

189. in love's particular, from the special reason of love.

192. that am, have, and will be. This is the reading of the Folios. If it is correct, *have* stands for 'have been' (cf. l. 178), and the whole sentence is an instance of anacoluthon, the construction being changed in l. 196 after the parenthesis. The Cambridge edition notes more than twenty emendations, the best of which are "that am true and will be", and "that am your slave and will be". The text as it stands is, however, probably correct. If the construction is faulty, the meaning is clear.

197. chiding, resounding. Cf. *1 Henry IV.*, iii. 1. 45, "the sea That chides the banks of England".

200-203. The honey of Wolsey's language has indeed been marred. His unctuous protestations have only increased the king's resentment.

210-213. Wolsey's candidature for the papacy was really supported by Henry, who hoped, in the event of Wolsey's election, to get papal sanction for the divorce.

214. cross, perverse. Cf. l. 234.

226. exhalation, meteor. Cf. *1 Henry IV.*, ii. 4. 352, "Do you see these meteors? do you behold these exhalations?" It was believed that meteors were 'exhaled' from the earth by the heat of the sun; thus *Romeo and Juliet*, iii. 5. 13, "It is some meteor that the sun exhales".

228-349. The taunts of the nobles follow hard on the frowns of the king. Wolsey's annoyance at the triumph of those whom he has so long kept under foot vents itself in scornful reproaches, while the nobles now speak with a freedom which they could never allow themselves before, and their hatred is all the more virulent from having been so long restrained.

229. Wolsey surrendered the great seal to the Dukes of Norfolk and Suffolk on 17th October, 1529.

231. Asher House, near Hampton Court, was a residence of the Bishop of Winchester. Wolsey himself was at this time Bishop of Winchester; but the dramatist's "Lord of Winchester" was probably Gardiner, Wolsey's successor in the see. Asher was the old form of Esher.

236, 237. Till I find...malice, till I find more reason for rendering up the great seal than a mere statement of the king's will, till I find more reason than your malice. *Will* and *words* refer to *king's will* in l. 235 and *words* in l. 233.

238. deny, refuse.

250. letters-patents. The plural termination of the adjective is a survival of the original French form.

253. forty, often used as an indefinite number. Cf. ii. 3. 89.

255. scarlet, alluding to the red robe and hat of the cardinal.

260. deputy for Ireland. See note on ii. 1. 41–44.

262. gavest him, didst impute to him.

272. That. The antecedent is *I* in l. 270, "I, that...dare".

280. jaded, treated like jades, spurned.

282. dare us with his cap like larks, an allusion to the method of snaring larks by attracting their attention with scarlet cloth or small mirrors. *Dare* is used in the sense of 'dazing', 'making to crouch with fear', as in *Henry V.*, iv. 2. 36—

> "For our approach shall so much dare the field
> That England shall crouch down in fear and yield".

See Glossary. The cardinal's cap or biretta was scarlet.

295. sacring bell, the bell rung at mass at the elevation of the Host, or before the Sacrament when carried to the sick. There does not seem to be any historical ground for this special taunt, though Wolsey's private life was not irreproachable.

300. thus much, I can say thus much.

According to Holinshed (p. 909), "When the nobles of the realme perceiued the cardinall to be in displeasure, they began to accuse him of such offenses as they knew might be proued against him, and thereof they made a booke conteining certeine articles, to which diuerse of the kings councell set their hands". It is in keeping with the general condensation of the events of this act that these articles are represented as having been drawn up before Wolsey fell into disfavour.

307. objections, charges, accusations, as commonly in E.E.

309. Have at you! an exclamation of warning in attacking. Cf. v. 3. 113, and ii. 2. 83.

310–332. The account of the articles is taken from Holinshed (p. 912). In December, 1529, "was brought downe to the commons the booke of articles, which the lords had put to the king against the cardinall, the chief wherof were these:

1. First, that he without the kings assent had procured to be a legat, by reason whereof he tooke awaie the right of all bishops and spirituall persons.

2. Item, in all writings which he wrote to Rome, or anie other foreign prince, he wrote *Ego & rex meus*, I and my king: as who would saie that the king were his seruant. . . .

4. Item, he without the kings assent carried the kings great

seale with him into Flanders, when he was sent ambassador to the emperour.

5. Item, he, without the kings assent, sent a commission to sir Gregorie de Cassado, knight, to conclude a league betweene the king & the duke of Ferrar, without the kings knowledge. . . .

7. Item, that he caused the cardinals hat to be put on the kings coine. . . .

9. Item, that he had sent innumerable substance to Rome, for the obteining of his dignities; to the great impouerishment of the realme."

314. Ego et Rex meus. This famous 'article' is not historically accurate. Wolsey was accused, not of 'bringing the king to be his servant', but, by the use of the expression 'the king and I' (not *ego et rex meus*), of 'using himself more like a fellow of the king than a subject' (*Calendar, Henry VIII.*, iv. iii. p. 2712).

321. Gregory de Cassado, properly Sir Gregory Casale or Casalis, sometime English agent at Rome. The mistake is due to Holinshed.

323. Ferrara, the Duke of Ferrara.

325. Your holy hat...coin. The charge brought against Wolsey was that he had stamped "the cardinal's hat under the king's arms on the coin of groats made at York" (*Calendar, Henry VIII.*, iv. iii. p. 2713). Douce calls this an "absurd and frivolous allegation", because the episcopal privilege of coining money had been long established, and was conceded in this reign to other archbishops, "nor could there be any substantial reason for regarding the cardinal's hat as more offensive than the bishop's mitre, which had already appeared on the coins of Durham". But Wright points out that the cardinal's hat was "the emblem of a foreign title".

329. mere, utter, absolute. Cf. *Othello*, ii. 2. 3, "the mere perdition of the Turkish fleet".

337-341. "The king, being informed that all those things that the cardinall had doone by his power legatine within this realme, were in the case of the præmunire and prouision, caused his atturneie Christopher Hales to sue out a writ of praemunire against him" (Holinshed, p. 909). This was in October, 1529.

340. præmunire. Statutes of *præmunire* (so called from the first words, *praemunire fac*) were passed by Edward III., Richard II., and Henry IV., making it illegal to refer any matter properly belonging to the king's court to any authority outside the realm. They were specially aimed against papal encroachments. The statute usually referred to is that passed by Richard II. in 1393.

342-344. After Wolsey's retirement to Esher, "in the kings bench, his matter for the praemunire being called vpon, two atturneis, which he had authorised by his warrant signed with his owne hand, confessed the action; and so had iudgement to forfeit all his lands, tenements, goods, and cattels, and to be out of the kings protection" (Holinshed, p. 909).

343. Chattels. Theobald's emendation, suggested by Holinshed, of the Folio reading *castles*. See Glossary.

350, &c. When Wolsey recognizes that the king's favour is lost irreparably, he throws aside all his haughty pride and all the hypocrisy on which his power has hitherto rested, and becomes simply sincere. The pathos and the genuine nobility of his farewell to worldly greatness win him, for the first time, our sympathy.

350. little good. Note the play on the words.

368. aspire, rise, mount up. Cf. *Merry Wives*, v. 5. 101, "whose flames aspire As thoughts do blow them".

369. aspect; accented on the second syllable, as always in Shakespeare.

their ruin, the ruin they cause.

371. Lucifer. Cf. *Isaiah*, xiv. 12, "How art thou fallen from heaven, O Lucifer, son of the morning!"

393. Sir Thomas More was made Lord Chancellor on 25th October, 1529.

399. Steevens compares a similar conceit in Drummond of Hawthornden's *Teares for the Death of Moeliades*:

"The Muses, Phœbus, Love, have raised of their teares
A crystal tomb to him, through which his worth appears".

The Chancellor, as Johnson points out, is the general guardian of orphans.

400. Cranmer was consecrated Archbishop of Canterbury, in succession to William Warham, on 30th March, 1533, more than two years after Wolsey's death.

402–406. On 12th April (Easter Eve), 1533, Anne Bullen "went to hir closet openlie as queene; and then the king appointed the daie of hir coronation to be kept on Whitsundaie next following" (Holinshed, p. 929).

405. voice, rumour. Cf. iv. 2. 11.

408. gone beyond, overreached.

411. noble troops. Wolsey's retinue seems to have consisted of about five hundred persons. Cavendish states in his careful account of Wolsey's household that "he had a great number daily attending upon him, both of noblemen and worthy gentlemen, of great estimation and possessions, with no small number of the tallest yeomen". The whole passage is repeated in Holinshed.

415. Like Buckingham (ii. 1. 86–94) and Katharine (iv. 2. 125–127, 163, 164), Wolsey, far from bearing the king any malice, devoutly hopes for his prosperity.

420. make use now, avail yourself of your opportunities.

430. to play the woman. Cf. *Macbeth*, iv. 3. 230—

> " O, I could play the woman with mine eyes ".

441. Cf. *Paradise Lost*, i. 36–40—

> " his pride
> Had cast him out from Heaven, with all his host
> Of rebel Angels, by whose aid, aspiring
> To set himself in glory above his peers,
> He trusted to have equalled the Most High ".

451. an inventory. " There was shewed a writing sealed with his seale, by the which he gaue to the king all his mooueables and vnmooueables " (Holinshed, p. 912). The details of the inventory are given in Stow's *Chronicle*.

455–457. " If I had serued God as diligentlie as I haue doone the king, he would not haue giuen me ouer in my greie haires " (Holinshed, p. 917: taken from Cavendish). These historic words were in reality addressed not to Cromwell, who had by this time entered the king's service, but to Sir William Kingston, Constable of the Tower. The dramatic purpose of the change is evident.

Act IV.—Scene I.

Like the fourth scene of the first Act, this scene is in great part a pageant. Otherwise it is entirely *narrative*. In the absence of *dramatic* force it is in contrast to the great scene which follows.

The coronation of Anne Bullen took place on 1st June, 1533.

1. once again. See the beginning of ii. 1.

12. better taken, better received. A long account of these pageants will be found in Holinshed.

24–33. " The archbishop of Canturburie, accompanied with the bishops of London, Winchester, Bath, Lincolne, and diuers other learned men in great number, rode to Dunstable, which is six miles from Ampthill, where the princesse Dowager laie; and there by one Doctor Lee she was cited to appeare before the said archbishop in cause of matrimonie in the said towne of Dunstable, and at the daie of appearance she appeared not, but made default; and so she was called peremptorie euerie daie fifteen daies togither; and, at the last, for lacke of appearance, by the assent of all the learned men there present, she was diuorsed from the king, and the marriage declared to be void and of none effect" (Holinshed, pp. 929, 930). This happened on 23rd May, 1533.

28. Ampthill. Ampthill Castle, in Bedfordshire, made part of the crown property under Henry VII.

34. Kimbolton. Kimbolton Castle, in Huntingdonshire; in Katharine's time the property of the Wingfields, now the seat of the Duke of Manchester.

Stage-direction: **The Order of the Coronation.** The details are taken from Holinshed, but are altered in two important points, viz. the Earl of Surrey and the Duke of Norfolk take the place of the Earl of Arundel and Lord William Howard, Norfolk's brother and deputy. This change was probably made to avoid the introduction of two new characters. **Collars of SS** (spelt *esses* in the Folios, and so pronounced) were so called from their S-shaped links; an illustration will be found in Gardiner's *Student's History of England*, p. 387. **the Cinque-ports** (Dover, Hastings, Romney, Hythe, and Sandwich, to which Rye and Winchelsea were added) enjoyed the special privilege of sending representatives to hold the canopy over the sovereign's head at coronations: see William Boys's *Collections for an History of Sandwich in Kent with Notices of the other Cinque Ports*, 1792, pp. 399, 414. **the old Duchess of Norfolk** was the widow of the second duke, the character represented throughout the play: for the anachronism see note, iii. 2. *init.*

47. Conscience. Cf. ii. 2. 15, 16.

59. rankness, exuberance.

62-94. The description of the coronation is founded on Holinshed. See Appendix.

67. opposing. Cf. *2 Henry VI.*, iv. 10. 48, "Oppose thy steadfast-gazing eyes to mine".

71, 72. Hazlitt draws special attention to the 'great individual beauty' of this image.

77. rams, battering-rams.

78. press, crowd. Cf. v. 4. 75.

85. bow'd her. Cf. iii. 1. 5. *Bow* is used both reflexively and intransitively in Shakespeare. On the tendency to drop the reflexive pronoun, see Kellner, § 345.

89. bird of peace, the rod of ivory surmounted with the dove.

94-97. After Wolsey's fall, York Place, hitherto the residence of the archbishops of York, was annexed to the king's palace at Westminster. Mention of the name being changed to Whitehall is made in Hall, but not in Holinshed.

The coronation feast was in reality held in Westminster Hall.

101–103. **Stokesly, John**, was made Bishop of London in November, 1530. For **Gardiner**, see notes on Dramatis Personæ.

102. **preferr'd**, promoted.

104. A hint of Act v. scene 3.

107. **a friend will.** See note on iii. 1. 46.

111. **jewel house.** Cromwell was made Master of the Jewel House on 14th April, 1532, and a member of the Privy Council in 1531.

116. **Something I can command**, I can provide some entertainment.

Scene 2.

This fine scene is called by Mr. Swinburne "the crowning glory of the whole poem"; and a critic of so different a stamp as Dr. Johnson, declares it to be "above any other part of Shakespeare's tragedies, and perhaps above any scene of any other poet, tender and pathetic, without gods, or furies, or poisons, or precipices, without the help of romantic circumstances, without improbable sallies of poetical lamentation, and without any throes of tumultuous misery". Some of the details are borrowed from Holinshed, but the general idea of the scene is entirely the dramatist's own. Wolsey died actually more than five years before Katharine, but there is something poetically fitting in making her hear of the death of her old enemy only when she is dying herself; while the representation of her charitable bearing to him, and of her readiness to do him honour, adds the crowning touch to a magnificent characterization.

Kimbolton. See iv. 1. 34, and *Katharine* and *Capucius* in notes on Dramatis Personæ.

2. **loaden.** This strong participle is common in E.E.

10. **happily**, haply: Shakespeare uses the two words interchangeably.

11. **voice**, rumour. Cf. iii. 2. 405.

12. **Earl Northumberland**, Henry Percy, sixth Earl. He was said by the enemies of Anne Bullen to have been married to her in his youth, but he denied it on oath.

Wolsey was arrested at Cawood, not at York, on 4th November, 1530. On the 6th he left Cawood, under arrest, on the way to his trial in London. That night he lodged at Pomfret Abbey, and next day proceeded to Doncaster, and thence to Sheffield Park, a seat of George Talbot, Earl of Shrewsbury, whose hospitality he enjoyed for a fortnight. On the 22nd, "he fell sick suddenly", but he had to continue his journey. On the 24th he moved to Hardwick Hall in Nottinghamshire, another residence of the Earl of Shrewsbury, and, after passing the following night at Nottingham.

arrived at Leicester Abbey on the 26th. There, on the 29th, "three nights after this", he died.

"The next daie he rode to Leicester abbeie, and by the waie waxed so sicke that he was almost fallen from his mule ; so that it was night before he came to the abbeie of Leicester, where at his comming in at the gates, the abbat with all his conuent met him with diuerse torches light, whom they honorablie receiued and welcomed. To whom the cardinall said : Father abbat, I am come hither to lay my bones among you" (Holinshed, p. 917).

17. **with easy roads,** by easy stages.

19. **covent,** an early form of *convent.* See Glossary.

32. **speak.** See note on ii. 4. 166.

34. **stomach,** pride, arrogance.

35. **suggestion.** See Glossary, s.v. *suggests.*

36. **Tied,** brought into a state of bondage. Several editors follow Hanmer in reading *tith'd.*

37. **i' the presence,** *i.e.* of the king.

39, 40. This was Katharine's own experience : Act iii. scene i.

43, 44. See iii. 2. 294–296.

45, 46. Cf. *Julius Cæsar*, iii. 2. 80, 81—

> "The evil that men do lives after them ;
> The good is oft interred with their bones".

Steevens points out a very similar expression in Beaumont and Fletcher's *Philaster*, v. 3—

> "all your better deeds
> Shall be in water writ, but this in marble".

50. The Folios have a full stop after *honour,* and omit the full stop after *cradle.* The emendation, which was made by Theobald, is not invariably adopted, but it is supported by Holinshed (see Appendix), and by common sense.

52. **fair-spoken.** For this active sense of the past participle, see Kellner, § 408.

58. **you,** apostrophizing Ipswich and Oxford.

59. All that now remains of the college Wolsey founded at Ipswich is the brick gateway. The Oxford college is Christ Church, originally called Cardinal College ; his connection with it is commemorated in its crest, a cardinal's hat.

60. **the good that did it,** the goodness (or good man) that founded it. Various emendations have been proposed, *e.g.* "the good he did it" (Pope), "the good that rear'd it" (Staunton). Wright takes *good* to mean "wealth and munificence".

64. See iii. 2. 377–380.

74. modesty, moderation.

78. Cause is commonly followed by the infinitive without *to* in E.E. Cf. l. 128.

82. The vision represents what Katharine is supposed to see in a dream (l. 93), the attendants being ignorant of it (l. 86).

92. I shall, *i.e.* 'I shall wear them', or possibly, 'I shall be worthy to wear them'.

94. music, musicians, cf. iv. 1. 91; **leave,** leave off, cease, cf. v. 4. 1.

100. The rude intrusion of the messenger makes Katharine recover something of her old spirit.

107. Admit, allow, grant; as frequently in Shakespeare.

110. My royal nephew. See note on i. 1. 176.

132. model in E.E. has the two distinct meanings of (1) pattern, and (2) copy, image (as here).

his young daughter, Mary, afterwards queen.

141. both my fortunes, in prosperity and adversity, as queen and "princess dowager".

146. let him be a noble. The usual explanation is 'even though he should be a noble', or something to that effect (Rolfe, Wright, &c.): but this seems to imply satire, where anything but satire is intended. It was the general custom for the ladies of a queen to be married to noblemen, and Katharine hopes that her unjust divorce will not affect their prospects.

159. fashion, character, nature. Cf. *Hamlet*, iii. 1. 183, "puts him thus From fashion of himself".

169. maiden flowers. Cf. *Hamlet*, v. 1. 255, 256—

"Yet here she is allow'd her virgin crants (*chaplets*),
Her maiden strewments".

173. I can no more, a phrase of frequent occurrence in Shakespeare. See Glossary.

Act V.

"The interest, instead of rising towards the end, falls away utterly, and leaves us in the last act among persons whom we scarcely know, and events for which we do not care" (Spedding). Far from containing the denouement, the fifth act is barely connected with the preceding events of the drama: and though the deaths of Katharine and Wolsey have rendered a denouement impossible, still the two leading characters of the earlier portions of the play would naturally be expected to have some direct bearing on the closing act. As it is, they are entirely forgotten, and their places are taken by Cranmer, who has not yet appeared, and Gardiner, who so far has spoken only an 'aside' (ii. 2). In addition to the absence of unity in the action, there is a break in the spirit, for the joyous celebration of the final act is at variance with the "sad, high, and working" nature of the rest of the drama.

The historical details are taken mostly from Foxe's *Acts and Monuments of the Church*; those dealing with the christening of Elizabeth are from Holinshed.

Scene I.

The chronology is very confused. Anne Bullen gave birth to Elizabeth on 7th September, 1533; but Sir Thomas Lovell had died in 1524, and it was in 1544 or 1545 that Cranmer was summoned before the council.

3. times to repair our nature. Cf. Wolsey's remark to Henry, iii. 2. 146, 147.

7. primero, a game of cards: referred to also in *Merry Wives*, iv. 5. 104. It was introduced from Spain or Italy, and seems to have fallen out of fashion in the seventeenth century on the introduction of ombre.

8. I must to him. See note on i. 3. 62.

13. touch, hint.

19. and fear'd, and it is feared: a common ellipsis.

22. Good time, good fortune. Cf. *Winter's Tale*, ii. 1. 20, "good time encounter her!"

28. way, religious belief. Like Wolsey, Gardiner disliked Anne Bullen as a "spleeny Lutheran" (iii. 2. 99).

32, 33. two The most remark'd. See note on ii. 4, 48, 49.

34. jewel house. See iv. 1. 111, 112. Cromwell was made Master of the Rolls on 8th October, 1534, and Secretary in or before April of the same year.

36. gap, "the opening through which preferments pass" (Wright).

    trade, beaten track. See Glossary.

37. the time, the present state of affairs. Cf. *Hamlet*, i. 5. 189, "the time is out of joint".

43. Incensed, made to believe, incited. Nares plausibly suggested *insensed*, instructed, informed, "a provincial expression still quite current in Staffordshire, and probably Warwickshire, whence we may suppose Shakespeare had it".

47. **broken with,** communicated with. Cf. *Two Gentlemen of Verona,* iii. 1. 59, "I am to break with thee of some affairs".

56–60. Henry has lost at primero; but Suffolk's endeavour to console him is amusingly successful.

68. **sufferance.** Cf. ii. 3. 15.

75, 76. The king refers to the coming interview with Cranmer. He has commanded him, as Gardiner has said, to appear before the council in the morning; but before this he wishes, for reasons which will soon appear, to have a private meeting with him.

86. **Avoid,** quit, leave. See Glossary.

87. Cf. iii. 2. 205, where Wolsey is suspicious of the king's frown, but with better reason.

106. **a brother of us,** *i.e.* a Privy Councillor.

116. **holidame.** See Glossary.

117. The following forty lines reproduce many of Foxe's phrases. See Appendix.

Henry is surprised at Cranmer's humility and submissiveness. He had expected him to beg to be brought face to face with his accusers before being committed to the Tower.

121. **indurance,** durance, confinement; the word is borrowed from Foxe. Johnson defines it (in his *Dictionary*) as 'delay, procrastination', and Schmidt as 'suffering'. Murray *suggests* 'protraction of an existing condition', but gives a contemporary instance in the sense of 'durance', viz. Knolles, *Hist. Turks* (1603), "which …composition…made in the absence and indurance of their Generall, was by the Turkes faithfully kept".

122. **The good I stand on,** *i.e.* my defence, the goodness on which I rely.

125. **Being of those virtues vacant,** if it is devoid of truth and honesty.

129. **ever,** always.

137. **whiles,** strictly the genitive of *while,* 'time', used adverbially. See Abbott, § 137.

143. **give way to,** allow. Cf. iii. 2. 16.

152–157. Cranmer offers an interesting contrast to Wolsey and Buckingham, and even to Katharine.

158–176. The humorous old lady—the old cat, as Steevens calls her—again relieves for the moment the seriousness of the play: cf. ii. 3.

166–168. A loose construction: "desires your visitation and you to be, &c.".

170. **mark,** worth 13*s.* 4*d.*

171. **By this light,** a gentle oath.

172. **is for,** is fit for.   See Abbott, § 405.

Scene 2.

This is a direct continuation of the preceding scene. It is a characteristic of the act that each scene is evolved more or less directly out of the preceding one, and follows without any interval of time.

There is no division in the Folios between scenes two and three. It was introduced by the Cambridge editors, acting on a suggestion of Grant White.

9. **happily,** fortunately.   Contrast iv. 2. 10.

13. **sound,** proclaim: a common Shakespearian usage. Schmidt takes it in the sense of "to search with a plummet, to try, to examine"; but the simpler explanation seems the preferable.

17. **at door.**   Cf. v. 3. 140, and see Abbott, § 90.

Stage-direction: **at a window above.** "The suspicious vigilance of our ancestors contrived windows which overlooked the insides of chapels, halls, kitchens, passages, &c. Some of these convenient peep-holes may still be found in colleges, and such ancient houses as have not suffered from the reformations of modern architecture" (Steevens).

21. **saw,** has seen.   Butts's remark is broken by the king's question.

22. **Body o' me,** another characteristic exclamation of Henry (cf. iii. 2. 61).   It likewise appears in Rowley's *When you see me you know me.*

28. **parted,** shared.   Contrast iv. 1. 92.

Scene 3.

Lord Chancellor: see notes on Dramatis Personæ. Cromwell was beheaded in 1540, at least four years earlier than Cranmer's appearance before the Council.

9. **present,** present time.

10-15. These lines were apparently suggested by a sentence in Hall: "My frendes all, you knowe well that wee bee men frayle of condicion and no Angels, and by frayltie and lacke of wysedome wee haue misdemeaned our selfe toward the kyng our Soueraygne Lord and his lawes, so that all wee of the Cleargy were in the Premunire". (See Mr. Boswell-Stone's *Shakspere's Holinshed,* p. xxiv.)

11, 12. capable Of our flesh, susceptible to the weaknesses of our flesh.

24. manage, training or handling of a horse. Cf. *1 Henry IV.*, ii. 3. 52, "Speak terms of manage to thy bounding steed".

30. The upper Germany. This refers to the troubles caused by the Anabaptists from about 1525 to 1535. There is a similar but more explicit statement in Rowley's *When you see me you know me* (see Introduction); it may have suggested the present reference, as Foxe (see Appendix) speaks only of 'diuers partes of Germany'.

38. with a single heart, in all sincerity. Cf. the Biblical phrase "singleness of heart".

40. conscience and...place, the same antithesis as 'life and office' in l. 33.

49, 50. Henry had already pointed this out to Cranmer. See v. 1. 104–108.

50. by that virtue, by virtue of that.

51. Note how Gardiner becomes more and more contemptuous, thinking he has Cranmer quite at his mercy. He is one of those ambitious, unscrupulous men who "make envy and crooked malice nourishment".

58, &c. Cranmer's resentment at Gardiner's open malice is vented in bitter irony. In his references to meekness, modesty, and conscience, he really, though unintentionally, contrasts his own character with Gardiner's.

60. Note the transposition of *both*; cf. *only* in l. 112.

69. modest, moderate. Cf. *modesty*, iv. 2. 74.

71. painted gloss, embellished comments, rhetorical remarks. *Gloss* is used in the sense of 'explanation, comment' rather than in that of 'lustre, polish'.

　　discovers, reveals.

72. words and weakness, a hendiadys.

77. To load a falling man. Cf. iii. 2. 333, "Press not a falling man too far".

78. I cry your honour mercy, I beg your honour's pardon: said ironically. Gardiner had already (v. 1. 31) classed Cranmer and Cromwell together.

85. This is too much. The Folios give this speech, as well as that beginning *Then thus for you* (l. 87), to the Lord Chamberlain (*Cham.*). The alteration, which is warranted by the nature of the speeches, was made by Capell.

103–107. The remarks here made by Suffolk and Norfolk were really uttered by the Earl of Bedford: see Appendix. This is another case (see note on the *Order of the Coronation*, iv. 1) in which the dramatist has consciously departed from historical accuracy in order to avoid the introduction of a new character.

109. My mind gave me, I suspected, I had a misgiving.

113. have at ye! See note on iii. 2. 309.

114–121. Gardiner's fulsome flattery of the king recalls Wolsey's (iii. 2). There is, indeed, a certain similarity between the two ecclesiastics; but Gardiner has nothing of the strength and grandeur of Wolsey.

119. dear, earnest: used regularly in E.E. as an intensive; thus, 'my dearest foe' = 'my greatest foe'.

125. They, referring to 'commendations'; or perhaps "*they*... may be inherent in *flattery* = flattering terms" (Deighton).

bare, Malone's emendation of the Folio reading *base*.

130, 131. proudest He. Abbott (*Sh. Gr.*, § 216) objects to this punctuation as "intolerably harsh", and would read with Collier "the proudest, He that dares most". The punctuation in the text, however, is that of the Folios, and it is supported by *3 Henry VI.*, i. 1. 46, "The proudest he that holds up Lancaster".

146. mean, means: the singular form is common in Shakespeare.

166–168. Abbott follows Capell in taking this as three lines of verse, ending respectively with *have, Norfolk,* and *please you*. "To write these lines in prose, as in the Folio and Globe, makes an extraordinary and inexplicable break in a scene which is wholly verse" (*Sh. Gr.*, § 456). But such a line as "Two noble partners with you; the old Duchess of Norfolk" seems extraordinary if not inexplicable verse. Pope arranged the passage in lines ending *have, duchess,* and *Dorset.*

166. you 'ld spare your spoons, *i.e.* you wish to save your spoons. "It seems to have been an old custom for sponsors at christenings to give one or more such spoons (i.e. *Apostle spoons*) to the child for whom they answered; usually the spoon would bear the figure of the saint in honour of whom the child was named, or the patron saint of the donor, each apostle being distinguished by his own particular emblem" (Cripps, *College and Corporation Plate*, quoted by Wright). The custom survives in Germany.

167, 168. the old Duchess of Norfolk. See note on iv. 1, *Order of Coronation.*

168. Lady Marquess Dorset, "Margaret, widow of Thomas Grey, second marquess, who died in 1530. She was daughter of Sir Robert Wotton, and her first husband was William Medley" (Wright). *Marquess,* 'marchioness', which is used in the stage-direction of scene 5. Holinshed likewise has the two forms

'marchioness' and 'marquesse', the latter probably by analogy
with duchess, countess, &c.

172. **confirmation**, assurance.

175, 176. Foxe tells how Cranmer was so well known to be of a
forgiving disposition that "it came into a common prouerbe, Do vnto
my Lord of Canterbury displeasure or a shrewed turne, and then you
may be sure to haue him your frend whiles he lyueth" (Ed. 1570,
p. 2036).

176. **shrewd**, ill-natured, bad.   See Glossary.

Scene 4.

2. **Parish-garden**, a celebrated bear-garden on Bankside, Southwark, near the Globe Theatre: the name is derived from Robert
de Paris, who had a house there in Richard the Second's time.
It is usually, and more correctly, called *Paris-garden*; but there
are other contemporary instances of *Parish-garden*, the reading of
the first three Folios.

2. **gaping**, bawling, shouting: an occasional meaning of the word
in E.E., now only dialectal.

8. **ale and cakes**, the usual fare at weddings, christenings, &c.

9. **much impossible**. In E.E. *much* is commonly used as
an adverb with adjectives, not merely with participles.

13. **Powle's**, St. Paul's Cathedral.

18. **spare;** the only instance in Shakespeare of this substantival
use.

19. **Sir Guy** of Warwick, another hero (cf. i. 1. 38) of mediæval
romance.   His great exploit was the slaying of the giant Colbrand,
the Danish champion, in a duel fought at Winchester in the presence
of Athelstan.

24. **for a cow**, a proverbial expression still in use in the South
of England.   "A phrase evidently identical with that used by
Shakespeare (or Fletcher)...exists and is in use to this day in the
South of England.   'Oh! I would not do that for a cow, save her
tail', may still be heard in the mouths of the vulgar in Devonshire"
(*Literary Gazette*, 25th Jan., 1862, quoted by Dyce).

30. **Moorfields**, where the train-bands of the city were exercised.

34. **brazier;** with the double reference, as Johnson points out,
to (1) a worker in brass, and (2) a portable fireplace.

36. **the line**, the equator.

37. **fire-drake**, strictly a 'fiery-dragon'; also a 'meteor', a 'will
o' the wisp', and an 'artificial firework'.   It is here used in the
second of these four senses, as is shown by l. 42.

39. to blow us, *i.e.* to blow us up.

40. a haberdasher's wife of small wit. Wright explains this as "who dealt in small wit, and had a ready tongue", comparing the phrase, "all haberdashers of small wit", in Ben Jonson's *Magnetic Lady*. But this explanation seems forced. The simple meaning tallies better with the "pinked porringer" of the following line.

41. pinked porringer, a cap shaped like a porringer, and pierced or worked with small holes. Cf. *Taming of the Shrew*, iv. 3. 64, "Why, this was moulded on a porringer", the reference being like-wise to a cap.

43. Clubs! The rallying cry of the London prentices; they carried clubs ostensibly to stop fights. See the *Fortunes of Nigel*, chap. i.

47. to the broomstaff to me, within a broomstaff's length of me.

48. loose shot, random shooters.

50. win the work, carry the fortification.

53, 54. the tribulation of Tower-hill, or the limbs of Limehouse. No satisfactory explanation of this has been given. Johnson thought that reference was made to certain Puritan congre-gations, but his suggestion, though expanded by subsequent editors, is unsubstantiated by direct evidence. Others hold that the phrases have no special reference, being "coined for the occasion", and having their origin in "the love of alliteration".

54. limbs, *i.e.* 'limbs of the devil'.

55, 56. Limbo Patrum, prison. See Glossary. Note the play on *limbs*.

57. running banquet. Cf. i. 4. 12. The whipping the rioters are to get from the two beadles will be a 'dessert' after the three days of prison.

69, 70. lay ye all By the heels, put you all in the stocks.

72. baiting, drinking heavily. See Glossary.

bombards, large leather jugs or bottles for liquor. Cf. *1 Henry IV.*, ii. 4. 497, where the Prince calls Falstaff "that huge bombard of sack". The word occurs also in the *Tempest*, ii. 2. 21. Dr. Murray suggests that *bombards* were probably so called "from some resemblance to the early cannons", *bombard* being the name of the largest piece of ordnance.

77. Marshalsea, a prison in Southwark, latterly used for debtors (see Dickens's *Little Dorrit*), and now demolished.

80. **camlet**, a light stuff, usually made mostly of wool or hair. See Glossary.

o', off from.

81. **peck**, pitch.   See Glossary.

pales, palings.

Scene 5.

Elizabeth was christened on 10th September, 1533, at Greenwich; but the scene appears to be laid at Westminster (cf. i. 2. *init.*).

1–3. "When the ceremonies and christening were ended, Garter, cheefe king of armes, cried alowd, God of his infinite goodnesse send prosperous life & long to the high and mightie princesse of England, Elizabeth: & then the trumpets blew" (Holinshed, p. 934).

5. **My noble partners**, the other sponsors.   See v. 3. 167.

12. **gossips**, sponsors.   See Glossary.

prodigal.   According to Holinshed (p. 934), "the archbishop of Canturburie gaue to the princesse a standing cup of gold: the dutches of Norffolke gaue to hir a standing cup of gold, fretted with pearle: the marchionesse of Dorset gaue three gilt bolles, pounced with a couer: and the marchioness of Excester gaue three standing bolles grauen, all gilt with a couer".

23. **Saba**, the queen of Sheba: see *1 Kings*, x., and *2 Chronicles*, ix. The form *Saba* is taken from the Vulgate, *Regina Saba*.

34. **Under his own vine.**   See *1 Kings*, iv. 25, *Micah*, iv. 4, *Zechariah*, iii. 10, &c.   There are several echoes of Biblical phrases in this scene: cf. lines 52–55.

37. **read**, learn.

38. The sentiment of Tennyson's *Lady Clara Vere de Vere.*

40. **the maiden phœnix**, the fabulous Arabian bird which reproduced itself from its own ashes.   Cf. *Samson Agonistes*, 1699–1702—

> "that self-begotten bird,
> In the Arabian woods embost,
> That no second knows nor third,
> And lay erewhile a holocaust", &c.

43. **one**, *i.e.* James I., the reigning sovereign.

52. **new nations.**   This probably alludes to the first settlement of Virginia in 1607.   Malone suggests that there may be a reference to the settlements contemplated in 1612, when there was a lottery for the plantation of Virginia.

57. **An aged princess.**   Elizabeth died in 1603, aged sixty-nine, having reigned forty-six years.

69. **my good lord mayor,** Sir Stephen Pecocke or Peacock. He was lord mayor also on the occasion of the coronation (iv. 1).

70. **your good brethren,** the aldermen and councillors.

74. **no man think,** let no man think.

75. **Has,** he has; the Folios read '*Has.*   Cf. i. 3. 57.

Epilogue.

Most of what was said of the Prologue is equally applicable to the Epilogue.   It is undoubtedly not by Shakespeare.

7. **that,** so that: cf. i. 1. 25.

10. **construction,** interpretation.

APPENDIX A.

THE HISTORICAL AUTHORITIES.

The chief sources of the incidents of *Henry VIII.* are the second edition (1587) of Holinshed's *Chronicle* and Foxe's *Actes and Monumentes of the Churche* (first edition, 1563). The following are the longer passages which have been followed in the play.

Act I. Scenes 1 and 2. Holinshed, pp. 862-864.

The cardinall, boiling in hatred against the duke of Buckingham, & thirsting for his bloud, deuised to make Charles Kneuet, that had beene the dukes surueior, and put from him . . . an instrument to bring the duke to destruction. This Kneuet being had in examination before the cardinall, disclosed all the dukes life. And first he vttered, that the duke was accustomed by waie of talke, to saie, how he meant so to vse the matter, that he would atteine to the crowne, if king Henrie chanced to die without issue: & that he had talke and conference of that matter on a time with George Neuill, lord of Aburgauennie, vnto whome he had giuen his daughter in marriage; and also that he threatened to punish the cardinall for his manifold misdooings, being without cause his mortall enimie.

The cardinall hauing gotten that which he sought for, incouraged, comforted, and procured Kneuet, with manie comfortable words and great promises, that he should with a bold spirit and countenance obiect and laie these things to the dukes charge, with more if he knew it when time required. Then Kneuet partlie prouoked with desire to be reuenged, and partlie mooued with hope of reward, openlie confessed, that the duke had once fullie determined to deuise meanes how to make the king away, being brought into a full hope that he should be king, by a vain prophesie which one Nicholas Hopkins, a monke of an house of the Chartreux order beside Bristow, called Henton, sometime his confessor had opened vnto him.

The cardinall hauing thus taken the examination of Kneuet, went vnto the King, and declared vnto him, that his person was in danger by such traitorous purpose, as the duke of Buckingham had conceiued in his heart, and shewed how that now there is manifest tokens of his wicked pretense: wherefore, he exhorted the king to prouide for his own suertie with speed. The king hearing the accusation, inforced to the vttermost by the cardinall, made this answer; If the duke haue deserued to be punished, let him haue according to his deserts. The duke herupon was sent for vp to London, & at his coming thither, was streightwaies attached, and brought to the Tower by sir Henrie Marneie, capteine of the gard, the sixteenth of Aprill. There was also attached the foresaid Chartreux monke, maister Iohn de la Car alias de la Court, the dukes confessor, and sir Gilbert Perke priest, the dukes chancellor.

After the apprehension of the duke, inquisitions were taken in diuerse shires of England of him; so that, by the knights and gentlemen, he was indicted of high treason, for certeine words spoken . . . by the same duke at Blechinglie, to the lord of Aburgauennie; and therewith was the same lord attached for concelement, and so likewise was the lord Montacute, and both led to the Tower.

.   .   .   .

And furthermore, the same duke on the fourth of Nouember, in the eleuenth yere of the kings reigne, at east Greenwich in the countie of Kent, said vnto one Charles Kneuet esquier, after that the king had reprooued the duke for reteining William Bulmer knight into his seruice, that if he had perceiued that he should haue beene committed to the Tower (as he doubted hee should haue beene) hee would haue so wrought, that the principall dooers therein should not haue had cause of great reioising: for he would haue plaied the part which his father intended to haue put in practise against king Richard the third at Salisburie, who made earnest sute to haue come vnto the presence of the same king Richard: which sute if he might haue obteined, he hauing a knife secretlie about him, would haue thrust it into the bodie of king Richard, as he had made semblance to kneele downe before him. And in speaking these words, he maliciouslie laid his hand vpon his dagger, and said, that if he were so euill vsed, he would doo his best to accomplish his pretensed purpose, swearing to confirme his word by the bloud of our Lord.

Beside all this, the same duke the tenth of Maie, in the twelfe yeare of the kings reigne, at London in a place called the Rose, within the parish of saint Laurence Poultnie in Canwike street ward, demanded of the said Charles Kneuet esquier, what was the talke amongest the Londoners concerning the kings iournie beyond the seas? And the said Charles told him, that manie stood in doubt of that iourneie, least the Frenchmen meant some deceit towards the king. Wherto the duke answered, that it was to be feared, least it would come to passe, according to the words of a certeine holie moonke. For there is (saith he) a Chartreux moonke, that diuerse times hath sent to me, willing me to send vnto him my chancellor: and I did send vnto him Iohn de la Court my chapleine, vnto whome he would not declare anie thing, till de la Court had sworne vnto him to keepe all things secret, and to tell no creature liuing what hee should heare of him, except it were to me.

And then the said moonke told de la Court, that neither the king nor his heires should prosper, and that I should indeuour my selfe to purchase the good wils of the communaltie of England; for I the same duke and my bloud should prosper, and haue the rule of the realme of England. Then said Charles Kneuet; The moonke maie be deceiued through the diuels illusion: and that it was euill to meddle with such matters. Well (said the duke) it cannot hurt me, and so (saith the indictment) the duke seemed to reioise in the moonks words. And further, at the same time, the duke told the said Charles, that if the king had miscarried now in his last sick-nesse, he would haue chopped off the heads of the cardinall, of sir Thomas Louell knight, and of others; and also said, that he had rather die for it, than to be vsed as he had beene.

Act I. Scene 4. Holinshed, pp. 921, 922.

And when it pleased the king for his recreation to repaire to the cardinals house (as he did diuerse times in the yeare) there wanted no preparations or furniture: bankets were set foorth with maskes and mummeries, in so gorgeous a sort and costlie maner, that it was an heauen to behold. There wanted no dames or damosels meet or apt to danse with the maskers, or to garnish the place for the time: then was there all kind of musike and harmonie, with fine voices both of men and children.

On a time the king came suddenlie thither in a maske with a dozen maskers all in garments like sheepheards, made of fine cloth of gold, and crimosin sattin paned, & caps of the same, with visards of good physnomie, their hairs & beards either of fine gold-wire silke, or blacke silke, hauing sixteene torch-bearers, besides their drums and other persons with visards, all clothed in sattin of the same color. And before his entring into the hall, he came by water to the water gate without anie noise, where were laid diuerse chambers and guns charged with shot, and at his landing they were shot off, which made such a rumble in the aire, that it was like thunder: it made all the noblemen, gentlemen, ladies, and gentlewomen, to muse what it should meane, comming so suddenlie, they sitting quiet at a solemne banket, after this sort.

First yee shall vnderstand that the tables were set in the chamber of presence iust couered, & the lord cardinall sitting vnder the cloth of estate, there hauing all his seruice alone; and then was there set a ladie with a noble man, or a gentleman and a gentlewoman, through-out all the tables in the chamber on the one side, which were made and ioined as it were but one table: all which order and deuise was doone by the lord Sandes, then lord chamberleine to the king, and by sir Henrie Gilford, comptroller of the kings maiesties house. Then immediatlie after the great chamberleine and the said comp-trollor [were] sent to looke what it should mean (as though they knew nothing of the matter), who looking out of the windowes into the Thames, returned againe and shewed him, that it seemed they were noblemen and strangers that arriued at his bridge, comming as ambassadours from some forren prince.

With that (quoth the cardinall) I desire you, bicause you can speake French, to take the paines to go into the hall, there to receiue them according to their estates, and to conduct them into this chamber, where they shall see vs, and all these noble personages being merie at our banket, desiring them to sit downe with vs, and to take part of our fare. Then went he incontinent downe into the hall, whereas they receiued them with twentie new torches, and conueied them vp into the chamber, with such a noise of drums and flutes, as seldome had beene heard the like. At their entring into the chamber, two and two togither, they went directlie before the cardinall where he sate and saluted him reuerentlie.

To whom the lord chamberleine for them said: Sir, for as much as they be strangers, and can not speake English, they haue desired me to declare vnto you, that they, hauing vnderstanding of this your triumphant banket, where was assembled such a number of excellent dames, they could doo no lesse, vnder support of your grace, but to repaire hither, to view as well their incomparable beautie, as for to accompanie them at mum-chance, and then to danse with them: and, sir, they require of your grace licence to accomplish the said cause of their comming. To whom the cardinall said he was verie well content they should so doo. Then went the maskers and first saluted all the dames, and returned to the most worthie, and there opened their great cup of gold filled with crownes and other peeces of gold, to whom they set certeine peeces of gold to cast at.

Thus perusing all the ladies and gentlewomen, to some they lost, and of some they woone: and marking after this maner all the ladies, they returned to the cardinall with great reuerence, powring downe all their gold so left in their cup, which was aboue two hundred crownes: At all (quoth the cardinall) and so cast the dice and wan them, whereat was made a great noise and ioy. Then quoth the cardinall to the lord chamberleine, I pray you (quoth he) that you would shew them, that me seemeth there should be a nobleman amongst them who is more meet to occupie this seat and place than I am; to whom I would most gladlie surrender the same according to my dutie, if I knew him.

Then spake the lord chamberleine to them in French, and they rounding him in the eare, the lord chamberlein said to my lord cardinall: Sir (quoth he) they confesse that among them there is such a noble personage, whome, if your grace can appoint him out from the rest, he is content to disclose himselfe, and to accept your place. With that the cardinall, taking good aduisement among them, at the last (quoth he) me seemeth the gentleman with the blacke beard should be euen he: and with that he arose out of his chaire, and offered the same to the gentleman in the blacke beard, with his cap in his hand. The person to whom he offered the chaire was sir Edward Neuill, a comelie knight, that much more resembled the kings person in that maske than anie other.

The king, perceiuing the cardinall so deceiued, could not forbeare laughing, but pulled downe his visar and master Neuils also, and dashed out such a pleasant countenance and cheere, that all the noble estates there assembled, perceiuing the king to be there among them, reioised verie much. The cardinall eftsoons desired his highnesse to take the place of estate. To whom the king answered, that he would go first and shift his apparell, and so departed into my lord cardinals chamber, and there new apparelled him: in which time the dishes of the banket were cleane taken vp, and the tables spred againe with new cleane perfumed cloths; euerie man and woman sitting still vntill the king with all his maskers came among them againe all new apparelled.

Then the king tooke his seat vnder the cloth of estate, commanding euerie person to sit still as they did before: in came a new banket before the king, and to all the rest throughout all the tables, wherein were serued two hundred diuerse dishes, of costlie deuises and subtilties. Thus passed the night with banketting, dansing, and other triumphs, to the great comfort of the king, and pleasant regard of the nobilitie there assembled.

Act II. Scene 1. Holinshed, p. 865.

There were also appointed to sit as peeres and iudges vpon the said duke of Buckingham, the duke of Suffolke, the marques Dorset, the earles of Worcester, Deuonshire, Essex, Shrewesburie, Kent, Oxford, and Derbie, the lord of saint Iohns, the lord de la Ware, the lord Fitz Warren, the lord Willoughbie, the lord Brooke, the lord Cobham, the lord Herbert, and the lord Morleie. There was made within the hall at Westminster a scaffold for these lords, and a presence for a iudge, railed and counterrailed about, and barred with degrees. When the lords had taken their place, the duke was brought to the barre, and vpon his arreignement pleaded not guiltie, and put himselfe vpon his peeres. Then was his indictment read, which the duke denied to be true, and (as he was an eloquent man) alledged reasons to falsifie the indictment; pleading the matter for his owne iustification verie pithilie and earnestlie. The kings attourneie against the dukes reasons alledged the examinations, confessions, and proofes of witnesses.

The duke desired that the witnesses might bee brought foorth. And then came before him Charles Kneuet, Perke, de la Court, & Hopkins the monke of the priorie of the Charterhouse beside Bath, which like a false hypocrite had induced the duke to the treason with his false forged prophesies. Diuerse presumptions and accusations were laid vnto him by Charles Kneuet, which he would faine haue couered. The depositions were read, & the deponents deliuered as prisoners to the officers of the Tower. Then spake the Duke of Norffolke, and said: My lord, the king our souereigne lord hath commanded that you shall haue his lawes ministred with fauour and right to you. Wherefore if you haue anie other thing to say for

your selfe, you shall be heard. Then he was commanded to withdraw
him, and so was led into Paradise, a house so named. The lords
went to councell a great while, and after tooke their places.

Then said the duke of Norffolke to the duke of Suffolke: What
say you of sir Edward duke of Buckingham touching the high treasons? The duke of Suffolke answered: He is giltie; & so said the
marques and all the other earles and lords. Thus was this prince
duke of Buckingham found giltie of high treason, by a duke, a
marques, seuen earles, & twelue barons. The duke was brought to
the barre sore chafing, and swet maruellouslie; & after he had made
his reuerence, he paused a while. The duke of Norffolke as iudge
said: Sir Edward, you haue heard how you be indicted of high
treason, you pleaded thereto not giltie, putting your selfe to the
peeres of the realme, which haue found you giltie. . . .

The duke of Buckingham said, My lord of Norffolke, you haue
said as a traitor should be said vnto, but I was neuer anie: but my
lords I nothing maligne for that you have doone to me, but the
eternall God forgiue you my death, and I doo: I shall neuer sue to
the king for life, howbeit he is a gratious prince, and more grace
may come from him than I desire. I desire you my lords and all
my fellowes to pray for me. Then was the edge of the axe turned
towards him, and he led into a barge. Sir Thomas Louell desired
him to sit on the cushins and carpet ordeined for him. He said nay;
for when I went to Westminster I was duke of Buckingham, now I
am but Edward Bohune the most caitife of the world. Thus they
landed at the Temple, where receiued him sir Nicholas Vawse &
sir William Sands baronets, and led him through the citie, who
desired euer the people to pray for him.

Act II. Scene 4.   Holinshed, pp. 907, 908.

The place where the cardinals should sit to heare the cause of
matrimonie betwixt the king and the queene, was ordeined to be at
the Blacke friers in London, where in the great hall was prepara-
tion made of seats, tables, and other furniture, according to such a
solemne session and roiall apparance. The court was platted in
tables and benches in manner of a consistorie, one seat raised higher
for the iudges to sit in. Then as it were in the midst of the said
iudges aloft aboue them three degrees high, was a cloth of estate
hanged, with a chaire roiall vnder the same, wherein sat the king;
and besides him, some distance from him sat the queene, and vnder
the iudges feet sat the scribes and other officers: the cheefe scribe
was doctor Steeuens, and the caller of the court was one Cooke of
Winchester.

Then before the king and iudges within the court sat the archbishop of Canturburie, Warham, and all the other bishops. Then
stood at both ends within, the counsellors learned in the spirituall
laws, as well the kings as the queenes. The doctors of laws for
the king . . . had their conuenient roomes. Thus was the court

furnished. The iudges commanded silence whilest their commission was read, both to the court and to the people assembled. That doone the scribes commanded the crier to call the king by the name of king Henrie of England, come into the court, &c. With that the king answered and said, Heere. Then called he the queene by the name of Katharine queene of England come into the court, &c. Who made no answer, but rose out of hir chaire.

And bicause shee could not come to the king directlie, for the distance seuered betweene them, shee went about by the court, and came to the king, kneeling downe at his feet, to whome she said in effect as followeth: Sir (quoth she) I desire you to doo me iustice and right, and take some pitie vpon me, for I am a poore woman, and a stranger, borne out of your dominion, hauing heere no indifferent counsell, & lesse assurance of freendship. Alas sir, what haue I offended you, or what occasion of displeasure haue I shewed you, intending thus to put me from you after this sort? I take God to my iudge, I haue beene to you a true & humble wife, euer conformable to your will and pleasure, that neuer contraried or gainesaid any thing thereof, and being alwaies contented with all things wherein you had any delight, whether little or much, without grudge or displeasure, I loued for your sake all them whome you loued, whether they were my freends or enimies.

I haue beene your wife these twentie yeares and more, & you haue had by me diuerse children. If there be anie iust cause that you can alleage against me, either of dishonestie, or matter lawfull to put me from you; I am content to depart to my shame and rebuke: and if there be none, then I praie you to let me haue iustice at your hand. The king your father was in his time of excellent wit, and the king of Spaine my father Ferdinando was reckoned one of the wisest princes that reigned in Spaine manie yeares before. It is not to be doubted, but that they had gathered as wise counsellors vnto them of euerie realme, as to their wisedoms they thought meet, who deemed the marriage betweene you and me good and lawfull &c. Wherefore, I humblie desire you to spare me, vntill I may know what counsell my freends in Spaine will aduertise me to take, and if you will not, then your pleasure be fulfilled. With that she arose vp, making a lowe curtesie to the king, and departed from thence.

The king being aduertised that shee was readie to go out of the house, commanded the crier to call hir againe, who called hir by these words; Katherine queene of England, come into the court. With that (quoth maister Griffith) Madame, you be called againe. On on (quoth she) it maketh no matter, I will not tarrie, go on your waies. And thus she departed, without anie further answer at that time, or anie other, and neuer would appeare after in anie court. The king perceiuing she was departed, said these words in effect: For as much (quoth he) as the queene is gone, I will in hir absence declare to you all, that shee hath beene to me as true, as obedient, and as conformable a wife, as I would wish or desire. She hath all the vertuous qualities that ought to be in a woman of hir dignitie, or in anie other of a baser estate, she is also surelie a noble woman borne, hir conditions will well declare the same.

With that quoth Wolseie the cardinall: Sir, I most humblie require your highnesse, to declare before all this audience, whether I haue beene the cheefe and first moouer of this matter vnto your maiestie or no, for I am greatlie suspected heerein. My lord cardinall (quoth the king) I can well excuse you in this matter, marrie (quoth he) you haue beene rather against me in the tempting heereof, than a setter forward or moouer of the same. The speciall cause that mooued me vnto this matter, was a certeine scrupulositie that pricked my conscience, vpon certeine words spoken at a time when it was, by the bishop of Baion the French ambassador, who had beene hither sent, vpon the debating of a marriage to be concluded betweene our daughter the ladie Marie, and the duke of Orleance, second son to the king of France.

Vpon the resolution and determination whereof, he desired respit to aduertise the king his maister thereof, whether our daughter Marie should be legitimate in respect of this my marriage with this woman, being sometimes my brothers wife. Which words once conceiued within the secret bottome of my conscience, ingendered such a scrupulous doubt, that my conscience was incontinentlie accombred, vexed, and disquieted; whereby I thought my selfe to be greatlie in danger of Gods indignation. Which appeared to be (as me seemed) the rather, for that he sent vs no issue male : and all such issues male as my said wife had by me, died incontinent after they came into the world, so that I doubted the great displeasure of God in that behalfe.

Thus my conscience being tossed in the waues of a scrupulous mind, and partlie in despaire to haue anie other issue than I had alredie by this ladie now my wife, it behooued me further to consider the state of this realme, and the danger it stood in for lacke of a prince to succeed me, I thought it good in release of the weightie burthen of my weake conscience, & also the quiet estate of this worthie relme, to attempt the law therin, whether I may lawfullie take another wife more lawfullie, by whome God may send me more issue, in case this my first copulation was not good, without anie carnall concupiscence, and not for anie displeasure or misliking of the queenes person and age, with whome I would be as well contented to continue, if our marriage may stand with the laws of God, as with anie woman aliue.

In this point consisteth all this doubt that we go about now to trie, by the learning, wisedome, and iudgement of you our prelats and pastors of all this our realme and dominions now heere assembled for that purpose; to whose conscience & learning I haue committed the charge and iudgement : according to the which I will (God willing) be right well content to submit my selfe, and for my part obeie the same. Wherein, after that I perceiued my conscience so doubtfull, I mooued it in confession to you my lord of Lincolne then ghostlie father. And for so much as then you your selfe were in some doubt, you mooued me to aske the counsell of all these my lords: wherevpon, I mooued you my lord of Canturburie, first to haue your licence, in as much as you were metropolitane, to put this matter in question, and so I did of all you my lords: to which you granted vnder your seales, heere to be shewed. That is truth, quoth the archbishop of Canturburie. After that the king rose vp, and the court was adiorned vntill another daie.

Heere is to be noted, that the queene in presence of the whole court most greeuouslie accused the cardinall of vntruth, deceit, wickednesse, & malice, which had sowne dissention betwixt hir and the king hir husband; and therefore openlie protested, that she did vtterlie abhorre, refuse, and forsake such a iudge, as was not onelie a most malicious enimie to hir, but also a manifest aduersarie to all right and iustice, and therewith did she appeale vnto the pope, committing hir whole cause to be iudged of him. But notwithstanding this appeale, the legats sat weekelie, and euerie daie were arguments brought in on both parts, and proofes alleaged for the vnderstanding of the case, and still they assaied if they could by anie meanes procure the queene to call backe hir appeale, which she vtterlie refused to doo. The king would gladlie haue had an end in the matter, but when the legats draue time, and determined vpon no certeine point, he conceiued a suspicion, that this was doone of purpose, that their doings might draw to none effect or conclusion.

Act III. Scene 1.   Holinshed, p. 908.

And thus this court passed from sessions to sessions, and daie to daie, till at certeine of their sessions the king sent the two cardinals to the queene (who was then in Bridewell) to persuade with hir by their wisdoms, and to aduise hir to surrender the whole matter into the kings hands by hir owne consent & will, which should be much better to hir honour, than to stand to the triall of law, and thereby to be condemned, which should seeme much to hir dishonour.

The cardinals being in the queenes chamber of presence, the gentlemen vsher aduertised the queene that the cardinals were come to speake with hir. With that she rose vp, & with a skeine of white thred about hir necke, came into hir chamber of presence, where the cardinals were attending. At whose comming, quoth she, What is your plesure with me? If it please your grace (quoth cardinall Wolseie) to go into your priuie chamber, we will shew you the cause of our comming. My lord (quoth she) if yee haue anie thing to saie, speake it openlie before all these folke, for I feare nothing that yee can saie against me, but that I would all the world should heare and see it, and therefore speake your mind. Then began the cardinall to speake to hir in Latine. Naie good my lord (quoth she) speake to me in English.

Forsooth (quoth the cardinall) good madame, if it please you, we come both to know your mind how you are disposed to doo in this matter betweene the king and you, and also to declare secretlie our opinions and counsell vnto you: which we doo onelie for verie zeale and obedience we beare vnto your grace. My lord (quoth she) I thanke you for your good will, but to make you answer in your request I cannot so suddenlie, for I was set among my maids at worke, thinking full little of anie such matter, wherein there needeth a longer deliberation, and a better head than mine to make answer, for I need counsell in this case which toucheth me so neere, & for anie counsell or freendship that I can find in England, they are not for my profit. What thinke you my lords, will anie Englishman counsell me, or be freend to me against the K. pleasure that is his subiect? Naie forsooth. And as for my counsell in whom I will put my trust, they be not here, they be in Spaine in my owne countrie.

And my lords, I am a poore woman, lacking wit, to answer to anie such noble persons of wisedome as you be, in so weightie a matter, therefore I praie you be good to me poore woman, destitute of freends here in a forren region, and your counsell also I will be glad to heare. And therewith she tooke the cardinall by the hand, and led him into hir priuie chamber with the other cardinall, where they tarried a season talking with the queene. Which communication ended, they departed to the king, making to him relation of hir talke.

Act IV. Scene 1. Holinshed, p. 933.

First went gentlemen, then esquiers, then knights, then the aldermen of the citie in their cloks of scarlet, after them the iudges in their mantels of scarlet and coiffes. Then followed the knights of the bath being no lords, euerie man hauing a white lace on his left sleeue, then followed barons and vicounts in their parlement robes of scarlet. After them came earls, marquesses and dukes in their robes of estate of crimsin veluet furred with ermine poudered according to their degrees. After them came the lord chancellor in a robe of scarlet open before, bordered with lettise: after him came the kings chapell and the moonks solemnelie singing with procession, then came abbats and bishops mitered, then sargeants and officers of armes, then after them went the maior of London with his mace and garter in his cote of armes, then went the marquesse Dorset in a robe of estate which bare the scepter of gold, and the earle of Arundell which bare the rod of iuorie with the doue both togither.

Then went alone the earle of Oxford high chamberleine of England which bare the crowne, after him went the duke of Suffolke in his robe of estate also for that daie being high steward of England, hauing a long white rod in his hand, and the lord William Howard with the rod of the marshalship, and euerie knight of the garter had. on his collar of the order. Then proceeded foorth the queene in a circot and robe of purple veluet furred with ermine, in hir here coiffe and circlet . . . and ouer hir was borne the canopie by foure of the fiue ports, all crimsin with points of blue and red hanging on

their sleeues, and the bishops of London and Winchester bare vp
the laps of the queenes robe. The queenes train which was verie
long was borne by the old duches of Norffolke: after hir folowed
ladies. . . .

When she was thus brought to the high place made in the middest
of the church, betweene the queere and the high altar, she was set
in a rich chaire. And after that she had rested a while, she descended downe to the high altar and there prostrate hir selfe while
the archbishop of Canturburie said certeine collects: then she rose,
and the bishop annointed hir on the head and on the brest, and then
she was led vp againe, where after diuerse orisons said, the archbishop set the crowne of saint Edward on hir head, and then deliuered hir the scepter of gold in hir right hand, and the rod of
iuorie with the doue in the left hand, and then all the queere soong
Te Deum, &c. Which doone, the bishop tooke off the crowne of
saint Edward being heauie and set on the crowne made for hir. . . .

Now in the meane season euerie duches had put on their bonets a
coronall of gold wrought with flowers, and euerie marquesse put on
a demie coronall of gold, euerie countesse a plaine circlet of gold
without flowers, and euerie king of armes put on a crowne of coper
and guilt, all which were worne till night. When the queene had
a little reposed hir, the companie returned in the same order that
they set foorth, and the queene went crowned and so did the ladies
aforesaid. . . . Now when she was out of the sanctuarie and ap-
peered within the palace, the trumpets plaied maruellous freshlie,
then she was brought to Westminster hall.

Act IV. Scene 2. Holinshed, pp. 917 and 922.

This cardinall (as Edmund Campian in his historie of Ireland
describeth him) was a man vndoubtedly borne to honor: I thinke
(saith he) some princes bastard, no butchers sonne, exceeding wise,
faire spoken, high minded, full of reuenge, vitious of his bodie,
loftie to his enimies, were they neuer so big, to those that accepted
and sought his freendship woonderfull courteous, a ripe schooleman,
thrall to affections, brought a bed with flatterie, insatiable to get,
and more princelie in bestowing, as appeareth by his two colleges at
Ipswich and Oxenford, the one ouerthrowne with his fall, the other
vnfinished, and yet as it lieth for an house of students, considering
all the appurtenances incomparable thorough Christendome, whereof
Henrie the eight is now called founder, bicause he let it stand. He
held and inioied at once the bishopriks of Yorke, Duresme, &
Winchester, the dignities of lord cardinall, legat, & chancellor, the
abbeie of saint Albons, diuerse priories, sundrie fat benefices In
commendam, a great preferrer of his seruants, an aduancer of learning, stout in euerie quarell, neuer happie till this his ouerthrow.
Wherein he shewed such moderation, and ended so perfectlie, that
the houre of his death did him more honor, than all the pompe of
his life passed. . . . .

This cardinall . . . was of a great stomach, for he compted himselfe equall with princes, & by craftie suggestion gat into his hands innumerable treasure: he forced little on simonie, and was not pittifull, and stood affectionate in his owne opinion: in open presence he would lie and saie vntruth, and was double both in speech and meaning: he would promise much & performe little: he was vicious of his bodie, and gaue the clergie euill example.

Act V. Scenes 1-3. Foxe, pp. 2040, 2041 (ed. 1570).

Notwithstanding not long after that, certayn of the Counsayl, whose names neede not to bee repeated, by the entisement and pro-uocation of his [Cranmer's] auncient enemy the bishop of Winchester and other of the same sect, attempted the kyng agaynst hym, declaryng plainly, that the realme was so infected with heresies and hereticks, that it was daungerous for his hyghnes farther to permyt it vnreformed, lest peraduenture by long sufferyng, such contention should aryse and ensue in the realme among hys subiectes, that thereby might spring horrible commotions and vprores, lyke as in some partes of Germany it dyd not long ago: the enormity whereof they could not impute to any so much, as to the Archbishop of Canterbury, who by hys own preachyng and hys Chapleins, had filled the whole Realme full of diuers pernitious heresies. The kyng woulde needes know hys accusers. They answered, that forasmuch as he was a Counseller, no man durst take vp on hym to accuse hym: but if it would please his hyghnes to commit hym to the Tower for a tyme, there would be accusations and proufes inough against him, for otherwyse iust testimonye and wytnes agaynst hym would not appeare, and therefore your highnes (sayd they) must needes geue vs the Counsail libertie and leaue to commit hym to durance.

The king perceyuing their importune sute against the Archbishop (but yet meaning not to haue hym wronged and vtterly geuen ouer vnto their handes) graunted to them, that they should the next day commit hym to the Tower for his tryall. When night came, the king sent sir Antony Deny about midnight to Lambeth to the Archbishop, willing him forthwith to resort vnto hym at the Court. The message done, the Archbishop speedely addressed hymselfe to the Court, and commyng into the Galery where the king walked and taryed for him, his hyghnes sayd: Ah, my Lorde of Caunterbury, I can tell you Newes. For dyuers waighty considerations it is determined by mee and the Counsaile, that you to morrow at ix. of the clocke shal be committed to the Tower, for that you and your Chaplaynes (as information is geuen vs) haue taught and preached, and thereby sowen within the Realme, such a number of execrable heresies, that it is feared, the whole Realme being infected with them, no small contentions and commotions will ryse thereby amongst my subiectes, as of late dayes the lyke was in diuers partes of Germany: and therefore the Counsail haue requested me for the trial of this matter, to suffer them to commit you to the Tower, or els no man dare come forth as witnes in these matters, you being a Counsellour.

When the king had sayd his mynd, the Archbishop kneeled downe, and sayd : I am content if it please your grace, with all my hart, to go thether at your hyghnes commaundement, and I most humbly thanke your maiesty, that I may come to my triall, for there bee that haue many wayes sclaundered me, and now this way I hope to try my selfe not worthy of such a report.

The king perceyuing the mans vprightnes, ioyned with such simplicity, sayd : Oh Lord, what maner a man be you? What simplicity is in you? I had thought that you would rather haue sued to vs to haue taken the paynes to haue heard you and your accusers together for your triall without any such indurance. Do not you know what state you be in with the whole world, & how many great enemies you haue? Do you not consider what an easye thing it is to procure three or foure false knaues to wytnes against you? Thinke you to haue better lucke that way, then your master Christ had? I see by it, you wyll runne headlong to your vndoing, if I would suffer you. Your enemies shal not so preuayle agaynst you, for I haue otherwyse deuised with my selfe to keepe you out of their handes. Yet notwithstanding, to morrow when the Counsaile shall sit and send for you, resorte vnto them, and if in charging you with this matter, they do commit you to the Tower : require of them, because you are one of them a Counseller, that you may haue your accusers brought before them, and that you may aunswere their accusations before them, without any further indurance, and vse for your selfe as good persuasions that way as you may deuise, and if no intreaty or reasonable request wil serue, then deliuer vnto them this my ryng (which then the kyng deliuered vnto the Archbyshop) and say vnto them, if there be no remedy my Lordes, but that I must needes go to the Tower, then I reuoke my cause from you and appeale to the kynges own person by this hys token vnto you all, for (sayd the king then vnto the Archbyshop) so soone as they shal see this my ryng, they know it so well, that they shall vnderstand, that I haue resumed the whole cause into mine owne handes and determination, and that I haue discharged them thereof.

The Archbyshop perceiuyng the kynges benignitie so much to hym wardes, had much adoe to forbeare teares. Well, sayd the kyng, goe your wayes my Lord, and do as I haue bydden you. My Lord humblyng hym selfe with thankes, tooke hys leaue of the kynges highnes for that night.

On the morrow about ix. of the clocke before noone : the Counsaile sent a Gentleman husher for the Archbyshop, who when he came to the Counsaile chamber dore, could not be let in, but of purpose (as it semed) was compelled there to waite among the pages, lackeys, and seruyngmen all alone. Doct. Buttes the kynges Phisicion resortyng that way, and espying how my Lord of Canterbury was handled, went to the kynges hyghnes and sayd : My Lord of Cant.

if it please your grace, is well promoted: for now he is become a lackey or a seruyngman, for yonder he standeth this halfe houre without the Counsaile Chamber doore amongest them.   It is not so, quoth the kyng, I trow, nor the Counsaile hath not so litle discretion as to vse the Metropolitane of the Realme in that sort, specially beyng one of their owne number: but let them alone (sayd the king) and we shall here more soone.

Anone the Archbyshop was called into the Counsaile Chamber: to whom was alledged, as before is rehearsed.   The Archbyshop aunswered in lyke sort as the kyng had aduised hym: and in the end when he perceiued that no maner of persuasion or intreaty could serue, he deliuered to them the kynges ryng, reuokyng his cause into the kynges handes.   The whole Counsaile beyng thereat some-what amased: the Earle of Bedford with a loude voyce confirmyng his wordes with a solemne oth, said: When you first began this matter, my Lordes, I told you what would come of it.   Do you thinke that the kyng wil suffer this mans finger to ake? much more (I warrant you) wil he defend his life against babbling varlets.   You do but comber your selues to heare tales and fables agaynst him. And so incontinently vpon the recept of the kynges token, they all rose and caryed to the kyng his ryng, surrenderyng that matter as the order and vse was, into his owne handes.

When they were all come into the kynges presence, his hyghnes with a seuere countinance, sayd vnto them: Ah my Lordes, I thought I had wiser men of my Counsaile then now I finde you. What discretion was this in you, thus to make the Primate of the Realme & one of you in office, to wayte at the Counsaile Chamber dore amongest seruyngmen?   You might haue considered that he was a Counseller as well as you, and you had no such Commission of me so to handle him.   I was content that you should try him as a Counseller, and not as a meane subiect.   But now I well perceiue that thinges be done agaynst him malitiously, & if some of you might haue had your mindes, you would haue tried hym to the vtter-most.   But I do you all to witte, and protest, that if a Prince may be beholdyng vnto his subiect, and so (solemly laying his hand vpon his brest) sayd: by the faith I owe to God, I take this man here my Lord of Canterbury, to be of all other a most fayethfull subiect vnto vs, and one to whom we are much beholdyng, giuyng hym great commendacions otherwise.   And with that one or ij. of the chiefest of the Counsaile, makyng their excuse, declared, that in requestyng his induraunce, it was rather ment for his triall and his purgation agaynst the common fame and sclaunder of the world, then for any malice conceiued agaynst him.   Well, well my Lordes quoth the kyng, take him & well vse hym, as he is worthy to be, and make no more ado.   And with that euery man caught him by the hand and made fayre wether of altogethers, which might easely be done with that man.

APPENDIX B.

NOTE ON THE METRE OF *HENRY VIII.*[1]

1. Blank Verse.

The normal verse consists of ten syllables alternately stressed and unstressed, beginning with an unstressed syllable, without rhyme (hence known as ' blank verse '), and with a sense pause at the end of the line: *e.g.*

> A thou'sand pounds' a year' for pure' respect'! (ii. 3. 95).

As the line contains five feet each of two syllables, and each stressed on the second syllable, it is commonly called an 'iambic pentameter'.

2. Normal Variations.

A succession of such lines, however, would be monotonous in the extreme. Accordingly there are several variations in the rhythm.

(i) *Stress inversion.* The normal order of *non-stress* and *stress* may be inverted. *E.g.*, in the various feet:

> (1) Sto'ps on | a sud' | den, looks' | upon' | the ground' (iii. 2. 114).
> (2) The wild' | sea' of | my con' | science, I' | did steer' (ii. 4. 200).
> (3) To pray' | for her'? | What', is | she cry' | ing out'? (v. 1. 67).
> (4) A thou' | sand pound' | a year', | an'nual | support' (ii. 3. 64).
> (5) Against' | your sac' | red per' | son, in | God's' name (ii. 4. 41).

There are sometimes two inversions in the same line: *e.g.*

> (1, 3) Af'ter | all this', | how' did | he bear' | himself'? (ii. 1. 30).

This inversion occurs most frequently after a pause, and hence is commonest in the first, third, and fourth feet. It is seldom found in the second. It is very rare in the fifth foot, where it usually has a halting effect. Two inversions rarely come together.

(ii) *Stress variation.* The stresses may vary in degree; a weak or intermediate stress (`) may be substituted for a strong stress.

> I knew | him, and` | I know | him; so` | I leave him (ii. 2. 53).

The weak stress is particularly common in the fifth foot: *e.g.*

> Corruption wins not more than hon | esty` (iii. 2. 444).

There are, in fact, comparatively few lines with the normal five strong stresses. But there are certain limits to the variations; *e.g.* there are never more than two weak-stressed feet in a line, and two

---

[1] This note has been largely suggested by the "Outline of Shakespeare's Prosody" in Professor Herford's *Richard II.*

weak-stressed feet rarely come toget᾽ ꞓr.   Frequently the absence of
a strong stress is made up for by (*a*) two weak stresses, as

> He bores' | me' with' | some tric᷾ ': he's gone to the king (i. 1. 128).

or (*b*) an additional stress in a neighbouring foot, as

> Hath' a | sharp' edge'; | it 's long and 't may be said (i. 1. 110).

(iii) *Addition of unstressed syllables.*   An unstressed syllable is
frequently added.   It may be introduced in any foot, which then
corresponds to an anapaest instead of an iambus.

> (1) I have been | to you a true and humble wife (ii. 4. 23).
> (2) That man | i' the world | who shall report he has (ii. 4. 134).
> (3) With many child | ren by you: | if in the course (ii. 4. 37).
> (4) The foulness is the pun | ishment.   I | presume (iii. 2. 183).
> (5) Will bring me off again.   What 's this? | To the Pope! (iii. 2. 220).

Occasionally there are two such feet in the same line.

> (3, 5) To his | own por | tion ! and what | expense | by the hour (iii. 2. 108).

As a general rule these extra syllables, when introduced *within*
the line, come at the cæsura (see below, v.), though in Shakespeare's later plays they are found commonly in any foot.
   Extra-metrical.   But this unstressed syllable is most commonly
introduced at the end of the line, where it is extra-metrical : *e.g.*

> Say, Wolsey, that once trod the ways of glo | ry,
> And sounded all the depths and shoals of hon | our,
> Found thee a way, out of his wreck, to rise | in (iii. 2. 435-7).

This is known as a *double* or *feminine ending.*   It is comparatively
rare in Shakespeare's early plays, but it becomes more and more
common, till in the *Tempest* it occurs once in every three lines.   It is
used more frequently by some of his contemporaries, and in Fletcher's
verse it even tends to become the normal form.   In *Henry VIII.*
there are, roughly, six double endings in every thirteen lines.
   Two extra unstressed syllables are occasionally found at the end
of a line : *e.g.*

> Ta'en of your many virtues, the king's maj | esty (ii. 3. 60).

But no sharp division can be made between a line such as this and a
six-stressed line or alexandrine (3. i.); and it is sometimes best to consider the first of the two extra syllables as slurred.   See 4. ii. *α β.*
   Lines containing proper names are frequently extra-syllabled : *e.g.*

> Flying for succour to his servant Banister (ii. 1. 109).
> Henry the Seventh succeeding truly pitying (ii. 1. 112).

Such examples are particularly common in the English Histories.
Cf. v. 3. 159.
   It should be noted that in *Henry VIII.* the unstressed syllable

added at the end of the line is frequently a complete word, and occasionally an emphatic word.

> Go, give 'em welcome ; you can speak the French | tongue (i. 4. 57).
> And ye shall find me thankful. Lead the way, | lords (v. 5. 72).

Such extra-metrical monosyllables occur in the parts usually assigned to Fletcher.

(iv) *Omission of unstressed syllables.* On the other hand an unstressed syllable is sometimes, though rarely, omitted.

> Was in | his coun | tenance. | —You | he bade (iii. 2. 81).

Such omissions generally take place after a marked pause, and hence (*a*) occur commonly, like stress inversion, in the first, third, and fourth feet, and (*b*) are most frequently caused by a change of speaker : *e.g.*

> *Buck.* And keep it from | the earth |
> *Nor.*   —Sure | ly sir (i. 1. 56).

(v) *Pauses.* The normal verse has a sense pause at the end of the line, and a slighter pause (cæsura) within it. These are clearly marked in early blank verse (*e.g. Gorboduc*), where the cæsura falls commonly after the second foot. The varied position of the cæsura, and the omission of the pause at the end of the line, constitute, in Shakespeare's later plays, his commonest departure from the normal type. The lines in which the sense is, in Milton's words, "variously drawn out from one verse into another" are called *run-on* or *unstopt* lines, and form what is known as *enjambement* or *overflow*.

The 'unstopt' line, like the double ending, was gradually used more and more by Shakespeare. In *Love's Labour's Lost*, a typical early play, it occurs once in every eighteen lines, while in the *Tempest, Cymbeline*, and the *Winter's Tale*, it occurs on an average twice in every five. In *Henry VIII.* the proportion is slightly less ; but this is accounted for by the joint authorship of Fletcher. In those parts which are assigned to Shakespeare, the proportion is about the same as in his late plays.

(vi) *Light and weak endings.* The extreme form of the 'unstopt' line is that which contains a *light* or *weak* ending. These have the distinctive mark of consisting always of monosyllables. Thus—

> Turn me away, and let the foul'st contempt
> Shut door upon me (ii. 4. 42)

is merely an instance of an *unstopt line.* But there is a *light ending* in

> A loyal and obedient subject is
> Therein illustrated (iii. 2. 180);

and a *weak ending* in

> To the good of your most sacred person and
> The profit of the state (iii. 2. 173).

The difference between *light* and *weak* endings is that "the voice can to a small extent dwell" on the former; while the latter so "precipitate the reader forward" that he is "forced to run them, in pronunciation no less than in sense, into the closest connection with the opening words of the succeeding line". Hence *light* endings consist of the *auxiliaries*, *personal pronouns*, &c., and *weak* endings of *prepositions*, *conjunctions*, &c.

Light and *weak* endings are nowhere more common in Shakespeare than in the parts of *Henry VIII.* usually assigned to him. Some of his earlier plays do not contain a single instance of them.

3. Less-usual Variations.

(i) *Addition of stressed syllables.*   Lines are occasionally found with six-stressed syllables (*i.e.* with an additional foot); *e.g.*

> This pausingly ensued: Neither the king nor's heirs (i. 2. 168).

The pause is usually found after the third foot; but it is also found after the fourth (i. 2. 26) and after the fifth (ii. 3. 2, 7; iii. 2. 144). In the following line there are two additional feet:

> Your enemies are many, and not small; their practices (v. 1. 128).

In most six-stressed lines (commonly called *Alexandrines*) the pause is very marked.

(ii) *Omission of stressed syllables.*   Lines with only four stressed syllables are much rarer; *e.g.*

> There's more in't than fair visage.   Bullen! (iii. 2. 88).

The omission of the stress likewise may generally be accounted for by a marked pause.   Hence it occurs most commonly at a break in the dialogue; *e.g.*

> *Wol.* State-statues only.
> *King*   Things done well (i. 2. 88).

Indeed, a marked pause is the source of most metrical irregularities.

(iii) *Short* or *broken lines* occur most frequently at the beginning or end of a speech; but they are sometimes found in the middle of a speech, marking a change of subject or idea.   An excellent example of this is Wolsey's "And prithee lead me in" (iii. 4. 450).   With the exception of those at the end of a speech, they generally consist of commands, exclamations, addresses, &c.; see ii. 3. 81, iii. 2. 76, v. 4. 66, v. 5. 63.

The broken speech-ending is a characteristic of the later plays.

4. Apparent Variations.

Many apparent irregularities are due to the difference in pronunciation in Shakespeare's time and now.

(i) *Accentual.*   The accent has changed in many words; *e.g.* Shakespeare always has *aspéct* (iii. 2. 369) and *advértise* (ii. 4. 178).

Certain words have not a fixed pronunciation in Shakespeare.

It is often only by the position of the word in the verse that we can decide on which syllable the accent falls. Thus we have *cómpell'd* (ii. 3. 87) and *compéll'd* (i. 2. 34); *confídence* (i. 2. 167) and *cónfidence*; *cónfessòr* (i. 1. 218, i. 2. 149) and *conféssor* (i. 4. 15, ii. 1. 21); and *cómplete* (i. 2. 118) and *compléte* (ii. 2. 49). Schmidt points out that *cómplete* precedes a noun accented on the first syllable, while *compléte* is always in the predicate; see note on i. 2. 118. A very striking example of the same accentual change is found in v. 1. 132:—

> Might *córrupt* minds procure knaves as *corrúpt*.

It will be noted that the pronunciation which now survives is generally that which represents most closely the Latin quantity. The *English* accentuation of these Romance words tended in Shakespeare's time to make the stress fall on the first syllable; but the influence of Latin has frequently in Modern English restored the accent to its original place.

(ii) *Syllabic.*

(*a*) A vowel may be lost before a consonant at the beginning of a word; *e.g.* *'mong* for *among*; *an't* for *an it*; *'s* for *is* (i. 2. 209, &c.), for *his* (i. 2. 205), for *us* (iv. 2. 81). This happens especially with prefixes and unemphatic monosyllables.

The same omission takes place also within a word ('syncope'):

(*a*) *In the inflexion*, as in the past tense and participle, and in the superlative, *e.g.* *sharp'st* (ii. 4. 44), *daring'st* (ii. 4. 215), *willing'st* (iii. 1. 49). These shortened forms become more and more common in Shakespeare.

(β) *In the second last syllable*, of words of more than two syllables accented on the first; *e.g.* *mínister*[1] (i. 1. 108), but *mínistèr* (i. 1. 86); perhaps also *majesty* (ii. 3. 60), though this is an instance in which the vowel may be treated either as mute or as forming an extra syllable. See 2. iii.

(*b*) Two vowels coming together may coalesce, whether in the same word or in adjacent words; *e.g.* *virtuous* (ii. 2. 131); *to approve* (ii. 3. 74); *to endure* (iii. 2. 389).

There is no definite pronunciation of the terminations *-ion*, *-ian*, &c. Thus we find *moti-on* (ii. 4. 233) and *commotion* (iii. 2. 112), *affecti-ons* (iii. 1. 129) and *affection* (iii. 2. 35), *Christi-an* (v. 3. 178) and *Christian* (ii. 2. 129), *consci-ence* (ii. 2. 73) and *conscience* (iii. 2. 123). Cf. *separation* (ii. 1. 148), *meditations* (ii. 2. 64), *distraction* (iii. 1. 112), and *informations* (v. 3. 110).

(*c*) The liquids (*l, m, n*, and *r*) may have the function of either a consonant or a vowel; hence called 'vowel-likes'.

(α) By the former function they may cause the loss of a syllable: *e.g.* *sovereign* (ii. 4. 140); *general* (i. 1. 92); *indifferent* (ii. 4. 17); *inventory* (iii. 2. 137); *cardinal* (i. 1. 99), but *card-i-nal* (ii. 4. 68);

---

[1] The mark (.) under a vowel means that it is mute.

business (ii. 4. 149), but, contrary to present usage, *bus-i-ness* (iii. 1. 19).

(β) By the latter function they may make a new syllable: *e.g.* *entrance*, sometimes spelt *enterance*; *through*, sometimes spelt *thorough*.

(γ) The liquid or 'vowel-like' *r* frequently resolves a preceding long-vowel or diphthong into two syllables. Thus *hours* in v. 1. 2 and *hire* in ii. 3. 36 are dissyllabic. Cf. *prayers*, uncontracted in ii. 1. 77, but contracted in iii. 2. 177.

(*d*) Sometimes a consonant (usually *th* or *v*) coming between two vowels is omitted, the vowels contracting: as in *whether*, *other*, *even* (adv.), *over*, *ever*, &c. Similarly *heaven* is generally a monosyllable (*e.g.* v. 5. 67). Cf. *ta'en* for *taken* (v. 1. 119) and *toward* (ii. 4. 165).

5. Rhyme.

Shakespeare tended to use rhyme less and less. There is little of it in *Henry VIII.*, and the few instances which are not accidental (such as i. 1. 5, 6 and iii. 2. 105, 106) are in the parts ascribed to Fletcher, and occur only at the close of a scene (i. 2, iii. 1, iii. 2, v. 3, and v. 5). There it is intended to make, by its epigrammatic force, an effective ending.

6. Prose.

There is little prose, likewise, in *Henry VIII.* It is used in the porter-scene (v. 4), where it marks the change to the comic spirit and is more in keeping with the unceremonious character of the speakers, and in the matter-of-fact summonses in the trial-scene (ii. 4). The few lines of prose in v. 3 seem to be corrupt.

7. The Verse Tests.

It has been noted above that *Henry VIII.*, taken as a whole, diverges from some of the metrical characteristics of Shakespeare's late plays. But certain scenes show these characteristics unmistakeably, viz.: Act i. scenes 1 and 2, Act ii. scenes 2 and 4, Act iii. scene 2 lines 1–203, and Act v. scene 1; and the general divergence is accounted for by the different versification of the remaining parts. These accordingly are said not to be by Shakespeare. On æsthetic as well as metrical considerations, they are usually ascribed to Fletcher (see Introduction, iii). The following table shows the metrical characteristics of the portions belonging, apparently, to the two authors; it embodies the results of investigations made by Mr. Fleay, Dr. Furnivall, and Professor Ingram.

	Shakespeare.	Fletcher.	
Double-endings	1 in 3	1 in 1·7	} proportion.
'Unstopt' lines	1 in 2·03	1 in 3·79	
Light endings	45	7	}
Weak endings	37	1	
Rhymed lines	6 (*accidental*)	10	} number.
Alexandrines	23	8	}

We may now compare the *Winter's Tale*, probably Shakespeare's last complete play, with the parts of *Henry VIII.* which he is supposed to have written.

	Winter's Tale.	*Henry VIII.*
Double-endings	1 in 3·2	1 in 3
'Unstopt' lines	1 in 2·12	1 in 2·03
Light endings	1 in 32	1 in 25·46
Weak endings.	1 in 42·44	1 in 31.

It would accordingly appear that the Shakespearian parts of *Henry VIII.* are of a later date than the *Winter's Tale* (1611).

GLOSSARY.

advised (i. 1. 139), deliberate. Cf. E.E. use of *advice*=judgment; O.F. *avis*, Late Lat. *advisum*; originally "the way in which a matter is looked at, opinion, judgment" (Murray).

allow'd (i. 2. 83), approved. O.F. *alouer*, representing both Lat. *allaudare*, 'praise', and *allocare*, 'place'. Hence the two senses (which often blend) of 'approving' and 'granting', the former being more common in M.E. and E.E., the latter in Mod. E.

an (iii. 1. 16; iii. 2. 375; v. 1. 11), if. Spelt *and* in the Folios, and generally in E.E. Skeat connects it with Scand. *enda*, but it is probably an independent usage of the co-ordinate.

arch (iii. 2. 102), pre-eminent. Gk. ἀϱχι, through Lat. and O.F. *Arch*, 'cunning'—the usual meaning of the word now without a hyphen—is apparently the same word.

attach (i. 1. 217; i. 2. 210), arrest; (i. 1. 95), seize. O.F. *atachier*, probably from a root cognate with *tack*; thus lit. 'to tack to'. "The ... sense of 'arrest, seize' arose in A.F. and Eng. as an elliptical expression for '*attach* by some tie to the control or jurisdiction of a court', *i.e.* so that it shall have a *hold* on the party. A man might thus be *attached* or 'nailed'...by his body,...by his goods and chattels,...by sureties for his appear-

ance. In the first two cases the *attachment* consisted in arrest and detention" (Murray).

attainder (ii. 1. 41), 'the legal consequences of judgment of death or outlawry', viz. forfeiture of estate, corruption of blood (*i.e.* inability to inherit or bequeath), extinction of civil rights. O.F. *ateindre*, 'to attain', used substantively, also 'to strike, condemn', L. *attingere*, 'to touch upon'; subsequently warped in meaning by association with F. *teindre*, L. *tingere, tinguere*, 'to stain', and hence defined by lawyers as "the stain or corruption of blood of a criminal capitally condemned" (Murray).

avaunt (ii. 3. 10), begone, used substantively. F. *avant*, forward! Lat. *ab ante*.

avoid (v. 1. 86), quit, leave. Cf. *Coriolanus*, iv. 5. 25, "pray you, avoid the house". M.E. *avoiden*, Anglo-F. *avoider*, Lat. *ex+viduare*, to empty.

baiting (v. 4. 72), drinking heavily. M.E. *beyten*, 'to feed'; hence 'to take refreshment', &c. Scand. *beita*, causal of *bita*, to bite.

beholding (i. 4. 41; iv. 1. 21; v. 3. 156; v. 5. 70), obliged, beholden. A corruption of M.E. *beholden*, part. of *beholden*, O.E. *behealdan*, 'to hold, behold'. "The general acceptance of 'beholding' may have been due to a notion that it meant 'looking (*e.g.* with respect or dependence)', or to association with the idea of 'holding of' or 'from' a feudal superior" (Murray). The special sense of 'obliged' is found only in the participle.

beshrew (ii. 3. 24), a gentle imprecation. M.E. *beshrewen*, to corrupt; *shrewe*, bad. Cf. *shrewd*, infra.

bevy (i. 4. 4), company of ladies. Derivation and early use unknown. "Bevie, a beavie of ladyes, is spoken figuratively for a company, or troupe: the terme is taken of Larkes. For they say a Bevie of Larkes, even as a Covey of Partridge, or an eye of Pheasaunts" (Gloss. by "E. K." on "this bevie of Ladies bright" in Spenser's *Shepheards Calender*, April, l. 118).

bombards (v. 4. 72), large leather vessels for liquor. See note.

bores (i. 1. 128), cheats, deceives. Probably connected with *bourd*, to mock, O.F. *bourder*, 'to lie'. See note.

bound (i. 2. 112), beholden, under obligations. Shortened from *bounden*, past part. of *bind*.

burden (iii. 2. 384); **burthen** (ii. 3. 43). O.E. *byrþen*. The form with *d* began to appear early in the twelfth century. In E.E. the form with *th* is still the commoner.

camlet (v. 4. 80). See note. F. *camelot*, the form of the word in Sir T. Browne's *Vulg. Errors* (Skeat). Anglo-French statutes of Edward IV. have *chamelett*, and the spelling with *cham-* was the prevalent one in English till after the Restoration. The ultimate origin is obscure. It is frequently said to be so called from being originally made of camel's hair; but it is doubtful if it was ever made of this (Murray).

can (iv. 2. 173). O.E. *cunnan*. "The O. Teut. sense was 'to know, know how, be mentally or intellectually able', whence 'to be able generally, be physically able, have the power'" (Murray). Cf. the phrase, *I can no more*, with French "je ne puis plus".

capable (v. 3. 11), susceptible. Through O.F. from Lat. *capabilis*, *capere*, to catch.

chafed (i. 1. 123), enraged; lit. 'heated'. M.E. *chaufen*, O.F. *chaufer*, ultimately from Lat. *calefacere*, to make warm.

chattels (iii. 2. 343). O.F. *chatel*, Lat. *capitale*, principal, goods, &c. *Chatel* was the form adopted in legal Anglo-French, but the actual form adopted in English was *catel*, later *cattell*, *cattle* (see note iii. 2. 343). In the sixteenth century this was gradually restricted to 'live stock', while *chatel* began to be used generally for 'articles of property' (Murray).

cheer (v. 1. 142). M.E. *chere*, O.F. *chiere*, *chere*, Late L. *cara*, face. Hence 'mien, demeanour, courage', &c.

cherubins (i. 1. 23). "*Cherubin, cherubins*, are the original English forms, as still in French. But, in the process of biblical translation, *cherubin* has been supplanted by *cherub*; and *cherubins* has been 'improved' successively to *cherubims, cherubim*; while, concurrently, *cherub* has been popularly fitted with a new plural, *cherubs*" (Murray). Shakespeare has the singular form *cherub* in *Hamlet*, iv. 3. 50, and the plural *cherubim* in *Macbeth*, i. 7. 22.

cheveril (ii. 3. 32), elastic. M.E. *chevrelle*, O.F. *chevrele*, a kid, a diminutive of *chèvre*, Lat. *capra*, a she-goat. The meaning of elasticity is derived from the pliant nature of kid leather. See note.

chine (v. 4. 23), 'joint of beef', strictly 'backbone of an animal'. O.F. *eschine* (Mod.F. *échine*).

clinquant (i. 1. 19), glittering. F. *clinquant*, tinsel; now used only as a subst., but originally the part. of *clinquer* (obs.), to tinkle, and then an adj., as in *or clinquant*, "glittering gold". In Eng. it is used both as an adj. and subst.: cf. Addison, *Spectator*, No. 5, "I must entirely agree with Monsieur Boileau, that one verse in Virgil is worth all the *clincant* or tinsel of Tasso".

commend (ii. 3. 61; v. 1. 17), deliver: the usual sense in E.E. Through O.F. from Lat. *commendare* (from *mandare*), (1) to deliver, entrust, (2) to praise.

conceit (ii. 3. 74), opinion. Probably formed from *conceive* on the analogy of *deceit*, *deceive*, there being apparently no corresponding O. F. word. It never occurs in Shakespeare in the sense of 'high opinion of one's self'.

convented (v. 1. 52), summoned. From p. part. of Lat. *convenire*; a cognate of *convene*, which comes, through French, from the infinitive. Cf. *prevent*.

covent (iv. 2. 19), convent. M.E. *couvent*=O.F. *convent*, Lat. *conventum*. The latinized spelling *convent* was introduced c. 1550, and by c. 1650 had superseded the M.E. form, which survives in *Covent Garden*. The reverse process has taken place in F., in which the old form *convent* has been replaced by *couvent*.

dare (iii. 2. 282), daze. Now obsolete, and not known before c. 1200. M.E. *darien*, 'to gaze stupidly, to crouch'; whence this transitive sense of 'to daze, fascinate'. The word has no connection with the preterito-present verb *dare*, *durst*.

derived (ii. 4. 32), brought, drawn upon. Cf. *All's Well*, v. 3. 265, "things which would derive me ill will to speak of". O.F. *deriver*, Lat. *derivare*, *de* + *rivus*, a stream. Hence literally 'to make to flow from...to'.

eagerly (iv. 2. 24), sharply. M.E. *egre*, O.F. *aigre*, Lat. *acrem* (*acer*).

encounter (iv. 1. 4), meeting. O.F. *encontre*, ultimately from Lat. *in* + *contra*.

envy (ii. 1. 85, &c.), malice. See iii. 2. 237–243. O.F. *envie*, Lat. *invidia*. Used in E.E. both in this sense and in its modern acceptation.

equal (ii. 2. 106; iii. 4. 18), just, impartial. Cf. Lat. *aequus*. "As the form of the L. *aequus* does not permit it to be directly anglicized without the addition of a suffix, the Eng. *equal* represents the senses of that word as well as those of its derivative *aequalis*" (Murray).

estate (ii. 2. 68; v. 1. 74), state —which is merely a shortened form. O.F. *estat*, Lat. *statum* (acc. of *status*), condition.

exhalation (iii. 2. 226), meteor. See note. Lat. *exhalationem*, *exhalare*—*ex* + *halare*, to breathe.

fell (v. 1. 49), dire, terrible. Probably connected with *felon*.

file (i. 1. 75), list. Through O.F. from Lat. *filum*, a thread.

fire-drake (v. 4. 37), meteor. See note.

flaw'd (i. 1. 95), broken, cracked. From M.E. *flawe*, 'a flake, detached piece'; hence 'a fragment'; hence 'a breach, crack'.

fret (iii. 2. 105), eat, wear away. O.E. strong verb *fretan*, consume, contracted from O.Teut. *fra* +

etan, to eat. It is weak in E.E., but a strong p.part. survives in *fretten*, the Quarto reading of *Merchant of Venice*, iv. 1. 77.

gall'd (iii. 2. 207), wounded. From the subst. *gall*, a sore, O.E. *gealla*, a sore on a horse; perhaps connected with *gall*, venom, and influenced by O.F. *galler*, to rub, scratch (Bradley).

glad (ii. 4. 196; v. 1. 71), gladden: the regular form in Shakespeare. The suffix *en* is modern.

gloss (v. 3. 71), comment, explanation. M.E. *glose*, O.F. *glose*. The F. form has remained the same; but in the 16th c. the E. form, under the influence of Lat., changed to *glosse*. L. *glossa*, Gk. γλῶσσα, word.

gossip (v. 5. 12), sponsor; a form of *god-sib*, 'related to God'. M.E. *gossib* is an intermediate form. *Sib*, 'akin', survives in Scots. Shakespeare uses *gossip* also in the later sense of 'crony'.

gripe (vb. ii. 2. 134; sb. v. 3. 100). O.E. *gripan*. This is the common old form, and that regularly used by Shakespeare, but is now replaced, in general usage, by the late form *grip*.

have-at-him (ii. 2. 83). See note.

head (ii. 1. 108), armed force. See note.

holidame (v. 1. 116); 'by my h.', an oath. A corruption of *halidom* (which occurs in *Two Gentlemen of Verona*, iv. 2. 136). O.E. *haligdom*, holiness; *halig*, holy + *dom*. "The substitution of *-dam*, *-dame* in the suffix was apparently due to popular etymology, the word being taken to denote Our Lady" (Murray). Rowe reads, "holy Dame".

husband (iii. 2. 142), economist. Cf. *Taming of the Shrew*, v. 1. 71, "while I play the good husband at home, my son and my servant spend all at the university". This sense survives in the verb, *e.g.* 'to husband one's resources'. The original sense of the word is 'master of a house'. Scand. *hus*, a house, and *buandi*, pres. part. of *bua*, to inhabit, dwell.

incensed (v. 1. 43), incited. See note.

item (iii. 2. 320), likewise. Direct from Lat. Its presence in the enumeration of details (as in iii. 2. 320) gave rise to its modern substantival use as 'a separate particle'.

lighted (i. 1. 9), alighted. O.E. has both forms *lihtan* and *alihtan*, but the latter seems to occur only once.

Limbo Patrum (v. 4. 55, 56), prison. *Limbus Patrum*, according to mediæval theology, was the place bordering on hell where the souls of the saints who lived before Christ remained till his descent into hell. "The word *limbo* came to be used as a nominative all the more readily, because the Italian word is *limbo*, derived (not from the ablative, but) from the acc. *limbum* of the same Lat. word. Hence Milton's '*limbo* large and broad'; P.L., iii. 495" (Skeat).

lo (i. 1. 113, 202), usually said to mean 'look': cf. *Winter's Tale*, i. 2. 106, 'Why, lo you now, I have spoke to the purpose twice'. But Skeat points out that the O.E. *la*, lo! and *locian*, to look, have nothing in common but the initial letter. 'The fact is rather that *la* is a natural interjection to call attention.'

long (i. 2. 32; ii. 3. 48), 'belong'—which is the more common form in Shakespeare. M.E. has both forms *longen* and *belongen*, the latter being apparently merely an intensive. O.E. has only the simple *langian*, *longian*.

main (ii. 2. 39; iii. 2. 215), chief, principal; (iii. 1. 93; iv. 1. 31), general. O.F. *maine*, *magne*, great, Lat. *magnus*.

manage (v. 3. 24), government of a horse. Direct from O.F. *manege*; ultimately from Lat. *manus*, hand. See note.

marry (i. 1. 97; i. 3. 38), an exclamation derived from the oath 'by the Virgin *Mary*'.

mincing (ii. 3. 31), affectation; a figurative use from *mince*, to cut small.

mo (ii. 3. 97); **moe** (iii. 2. 5), more. M.E. *ma*, *mo*; O.E. *ma* (adverb), which was used as a neuter subst. followed by a partitive genitive, *i.e.* more of something; hence in E.E. *mo* came to be used plurally as the comparative of *many*. On the other hand, *more*, O.E. *mara* (adj.), 'greater', was used adverbially as the comparative of *much*.

model (iv. 2. 132). See note. O.F. *modelle*, from dim. of Lat. *modus*, a measure.

modest (v. 3. 69), moderate. F. *modeste*, Lat. *modestus*, measurable, *modus*, a measure. Cf. **modesty**, iv. 2. 74.

moiety (i. 2. 12), half: occasionally in Shakespeare for merely 'a part'. F. *moitié*, Lat. *medietatem*.

motley (Prologue). M.E. *mottelee*, O.F. *mattelé*, 'curdled', hence 'spotted', 'variegated'. *Motley* is used by Shakespeare also as a substantive, (1) as the dress of the fool, *e.g.* "Motley's the only wear", *As You Like It*, ii. 7. 34; and (2) as the fool himself, *e.g.* "And made myself a motley to the view", *Sonnets*, cx. 2.

naughty (v. 1. 138), wicked; as commonly in Shakespeare. Literally 'of naught'; O.E. *na*, no, and *whit*, thing. Hence 'worthless', 'good for nothing', 'wicked'. The sense 'mischievous' is modern.

peck (v. 4. 81), pitch; a variant of the older form *pick*, which occurs in *Coriolanus*, i. 1. 204, "as high As I could pick my lance". *Pitch* is a weakened form of *pick*, to throw (obsolete); cf. *dike* and *ditch*, &c.

perk'd up (ii. 3. 21), dressed up, made trim. Cf. *Shepheards Calender*, ii. 8, "Perke as a peacock". "The adj. was perhaps only dialectal, but the verb was common in M.E. and E.E., *e.g. Mary Magd.* (Satan speaks), 'Was I, pryns, pyrked, prykkyd in pryde'" (Herford). Connected with *perk*.

precipice (v. 1. 139). The First Folio reads *precipit*, probably an early form. There were apparently two forms in O.F., *precipite* (given by Cotgrave) and *precipice*. Lat. *praecipitium*, *praeceps*, headlong, *prae* + *caput*.

premises (ii. 1. 63), conditions, suppositions. O.F. *premtisse*, from p. part. of *praemitto*: literally 'that which is sent before'. The more correct form is *premisses*, which is adopted in the Cambridge Edition.

present (i. 2. 211), immediate. Cf. **presently** (iii. 2. 78, 229, &c.), immediately: the usual sense in E.E.

rinsing (i. 1. 167). See note. Through O.F. *rinser*, from Scand. *hreinsa*, from which *renching*, a Northern cognate, comes directly.

sennet (ii. 4, stage-direction), a particular set of notes on the trumpet or cornet, announcing the entry or exit of a procession. The word does not appear in the text of Shakespeare.

shrewd (v. 3. 176), ill-natured. M.E. *schrewed*, accursed, p.p. of *schrewen*, to curse, *schrewe*, bad, malicious. The sense 'astute' is modern.

simony (iv. 2. 36), trafficking in ecclesiastical appointments. F. *simonie*, Low Lat. *simonia*, from *Simon* Magus, who, as related in *Acts*, viii. 18–20, wished to purchase the gift of the Holy Ghost with money.

sooth (ii. 3. 30), truth. M.E. *soth*; O.E. *soð*, originally an adj., later also a subst. = 'the true thing'. Used as both adj. and subst. in E.E.

spinster (i. 2. 33), spinner; as always in Shakespeare. The suffix *-ster* (O.E. *-estre*) was originally a feminine termination, but was used later, independently of gender, to form trade-names; e.g. *spinster*, *webster*, *brewster*, &c., some of which now survive as proper names.

state (i. 4, stage-direction), a canopy; (i. 2, stage-direction), a canopied chair, a chair of state.

suggests (i. 1. 164), incites. M.E. *suggesten*, from p. part. of Lat. *suggerere*, lit. 'to carry or lay under', *sub* + *gerere*. Generally used in a bad sense in E.E. Cf. **suggestion** (iv. 2. 35), underhand methods.

tainted (iv. 2. 14), disgraced. O.F. *teint*, Lat. *tingere*, *tinguere*, to stain.

tell (i. 2. 43; ii. 1. 91), count. O.E. *tellan*, to narrate, count.

tender (ii. 4. 116), have regard for, value. Formed without change from adj.; see Abbott, § 290. F. *tendre*, Lat. *tener-um*.

throughly(v.1.110),thoroughly.

trade (v. 1. 36), beaten track. Cf. Surrey's *Aeneid*, "A common trade, to pass through Priam's house". Ultimately from O.E. *tredan*, to tread, but not an old form. The M.E. subst. is *trede*, a footmark. The meaning 'track' is intermediate between this and the modern usage of the word.

trow (i. 1. 184), believe, know. M.E. *trowen*, O.E. *treowian*, to have trust in, *treowa*, trust.

vouch (i. 1. 157), attestation. Connected through O.F. with Lat. *vox*, voice, and therefore distinct from *vow*, which comes ultimately from Lat. *votum*.

wit (iii. 1. 72), understanding. O.E. *wit*, knowledge, *witan*, to know.

worship (i. 1. 39), noble rank, nobility. M.E. *worschip*, *worþssipe*, O.E. *weorðscipe*, honour. Practically a contraction of *worthship*, the *th* being lost in the fourteenth century.

wot (iii. 2. 122), know. M.E. *wot*, O.E. *wat*, 1st and 3rd pers. sing. present of *witan*. Shakespeare uses *wot* in the 1st and 3rd pers. sing. and in the three persons of the plural.

INDEX OF WORDS.

(Other words will be found in the Glossary.)

GENERAL INDEX.

SHAKESPEARE'S STAGE IN ITS BEARING UPON HIS DRAMA.

§ 1. The structure and arrangements of the Elizabethan theatre are still under discussion, and many points of detail remain unsettled. The last twenty years have produced a very extensive and highly technical literature on the subject, chiefly in England, America, and Germany. It is based especially on the new evidence derived from (1) the original stage directions, (2) contemporary illustrations and descriptions. The following summary gives the conclusions which at present appear most reasonable, neglecting much speculative matter of great interest.

§ 2. When Shakespeare arrived in London, soon after 1585, theatrical exhibitions were given there in (1) public theatres, (2) private theatres, (3) the halls of the royal palaces, and of the Inns of Court.

Of the 'public' theatres there were at least three: The Theater, the Curtain, both in Shoreditch, and Newington Butts on the Bankside or Southwark shore. About 1587, the Rose, also on the Bankside, was added. All these were occasionally used by Shakespeare's company before 1599, when their headquarters became the newly built Globe, likewise on the Bankside. Of the 'private' theatres the principal, and the oldest, was the Blackfriars, on the site of the present *Times* office. It was also the property of the company in which Shakespeare acquired a share, but being let out during practically his whole career, does not count in the present connexion. At court, on the other hand, his company played repeatedly. But his plays were written for the 'public' theatre, and this alone had any influence upon his stage-craft.

§ 3. The 'public' theatre differed from the other two types chiefly in being (1) dependent on daylight, (2) open overhead, and (3) partially seatless; and from the court-stages also, in (4) not using painted scenes. While they, again, had the rectangular form, the typical 'public' theatre was a round or octagonal edifice, modelled partly on the inn-yards where companies of players had been accustomed to perform, prior to the inhibition of 1574, on movable stages; partly on the arenas used for bear-baiting and cock-fighting;—sports still carried on in the 'theatres', and in part dictating their arrangements.

The circular inner area, known thence as the 'cock-pit', or 'pit', had accordingly no seats; admission to it cost one penny (6d. in modern money), and the throng of standing spectators were known as the 'groundlings'. More expensive places (up to 2s. 6d.) with seats, were provided in tiers of galleries which ran round the area, one above the other, as in modern theatres; the uppermost being covered with a thatched roof.

§ 4. The **Stage** (using the term to describe the entire scenic apparatus of the theatre) included (1) the *outer stage*, a rectangular platform (as much as 42 feet wide in the largest examples) projecting into the circular area, from the back wall, and thus surrounded by 'groundlings' on three sides. Above it were a thatched roof and hangings, but no side or front curtains. In the floor was a trap-door by which ghosts and others ascended or descended. At the back were (2) two projecting wings, each with a door opening obliquely on to the stage, the *recess* between them, of uncertain shape and extent, forming a kind of

inner stage. Above this was (3) an upper room or rooms, which included
the actors' 'tiring-house', with a window or windows opening on to
(4) a *balcony* or gallery, from which was hung (5) a *curtain*, by means
of which the inner recess could be concealed or disclosed.

§ 5. The most important divergence of this type of structure from that
of our theatres is in the relation between the outer stage and the audi-
torium. In the modern theatre the play is treated as a picture, framed
in the proscenium arch, seen by the audience like any other picture from
the front only, and shut off from their view at any desired moment by
letting fall the curtain. An immediate consequence of this was that a
scene (or act) could terminate only in one of two ways. Either the
persons concerned in it walked, or were carried, off the stage; or a
change of place and circumstances was *supposed* without their leaving it.
Both these methods were used. The first was necessary only at the
close of the play. For this reason an Elizabethan play rarely ends on
a *climax*, such as the close of Ibsen's *Ghosts*; the overpowering effect of
which would be gravely diminished if, instead of the curtain falling upon
Osvald's helpless cry for "the sun", he and his mother had to walk off
the stage. Marlowe's *Faustus* ends with a real climax, because the
catastrophe *ipso facto* leaves the stage clear. But the close of even the
most overwhelming final scenes of Shakespeare is relatively quiet, or
even, as in *Macbeth*, a little tame. The concluding lines often provide
a motive for the (compulsory) clearing of the stage.

In the *Tragedies*, the dead body of the hero has usually to be borne ceremoniously
away, followed by the rest; so Aufidius in *Coriolanus*: "Help, three o' the chiefest
soldiers; I'll be one". Similarly in *Hamlet* and *King Lear*. In *Othello*, Desdemona's
bed was apparently in the curtained recess, and at the close the curtains were drawn
upon the two bodies, instead of their being as usual borne away.
The close of the *Histories* often resembles the dispersing of an informal council
after a declaration of policy by the principal person; thus *Richard II.* closes with
Bolingbroke's announcement of the penance he proposes to pay for Richard's death;
Henry IV. with his orders for the campaign against Northumberland and Glendower,
King John with Falconbridge's great assertion of English patriotism.
In the *Comedies*, the leading persons will often withdraw to explain to one another
at leisure what the audience already knows (*Winter's Tale, Tempest, Merchant of
Venice*), or to carry out the wedding rites (*As You Like It, Midsummer-Night's
Dream*); or they strike up a measure and thus (as in *Much Ado*) naturally dance off
the stage. Sometimes the chief persons have withdrawn before the close, leaving some
minor character—Puck (*Midsummer-Night's Dream*) or the Clown (*Twelfth Night*)
—to wind up the whole with a snatch of song, and then retire himself.

§ 6. But the most important result of the exposed stage was that it
placed strict limits upon dramatic illusion, and thus compelled the resort,
for most purposes, to conventions resting on symbolism, suggestion, or
make-believe. It was only in dress that anything like simulation could
be attempted; and here the Elizabethan companies, as is well known,
were lavish in the extreme. Painted scenes, on the other hand, even
had they been available, would have been idle or worse, when perhaps
a third of the audience would see, behind the actors, not the scenes but
the people in the opposite gallery, or the gallants seated on the stage.
Especially where complex and crowded actions were introduced, the
most beggarly symbolic suggestion was cheerfully accepted. Jonson, m

the spirit of classicist realism, would have tabooed all such intractable matter; and he scoffed, in his famous Prologue, at the "three rusty swords" whose clashing had to do duty for "York and Lancaster's long jars". Shakespeare's realism was never of this literal kind, but in bring-ing Agincourt upon the stage of the newly built Globe in the following year (1599) he showed himself so far sensitive to criticisms of this type that he expressly appealed to the audience's imagination—"eke out our imperfections with your thoughts"—consenting, moreover, to assist them by the splendid descriptive passages interposed between the Acts.

It is probable that the Elizabethan popular audience did not need any such appeal. It had no experience of elaborate 'realism' on the stage; the rude movable stages on which the earliest dramas had been played compelled an ideal treatment of *space* and a symbolic treatment of *pro-perties*; and this tradition, though slowly giving way, was still para-mount throughout Shakespeare's career. Thus every audience accepted as a matter of course (1) the representation of *distant* things or places simultaneously on the stage. Sidney, in 1580, had ridiculed the Romantic plays of his time with "Asia of one side and Africa of the other", indicated by labels. But Shakespeare in 1593-4 could still represent the tents of Richard III. and Richmond within a few yards of one another, and the Ghosts speaking alternately to each. Every audience accepted (2) the presence on the stage, in full view of the audience, of accessories irrelevant to the scene in course of performance. A property requisite for one set of scenes, but out of place in another, could be simply ignored while the latter were in progress; just as the modern audience sees, but never reckons into the scenery, the footlights and the prompter's box. Large, movable objects, such as beds or chairs, were no doubt often brought in when needed; but no one was disturbed if they remained during an intervening scene in which they were out of place. And "properties either difficult to move, like a well, or so small as to be unobtrusive, were habitually left on the stage as long as they were wanted, whatever scenes intervened" (Reynolds).

Thus in Jonson's *The Case is Altered* (an early play, not yet reflecting his charac-teristic technique), Jaques, in III. 2, hides his gold in the earth and covers it with a heap of dung to avoid suspicion. In IV. 4, he removes the dung to assure himself that the gold is still there. The intervening scenes represent rooms in Ferneze's palace, and Juniper's shop; but the heap of dung doubtless remained on the stage all the time. Similarly in Peele's *David and Bethsabe*, the spring in which Bethsabe bathes; and in his *Old Wives' Tale*, a 'study' and 'a cross', which belong to un-connected parts of the action.

It follows from this that the *supposed locality of a scene could be changed* without any change in the properties on the stage, or even of the persons. What happened was merely that some properties which previously had no dramatic relevance, suddenly acquired it, and *vice versa*; that a tree, for instance, hitherto only a stage property out of use, became a *tree* and signified probably, a wood. The change of scene may take place without any break in the dialogue, and be only marked by the occurrence of allusions of a different tenor.

Thus in *Doctor Faustus*, at v. 1106 f., Faustus is in "a fair and pleasant green", on his way from the Emperor's Court to Wittenberg; at v. 1143 f., he is back in his house there. In *Romeo and Juliet*, I. 4. 5, Romeo and his friends are at first in the street; at I. 4, 114, according to the Folio, "they march about the stage and serving-men come forth with their napkins"; in other words, we are now in Capulet's hall, and Capulet presently enters meeting his guests. This is conventionalized in modern editions.

§ 7. **The Inner Stage.**—An audience for which the limitations of the actual stage meant so little, might be expected to dispense readily with the concessions to realism implied in providing an actual inner chamber for scenes performed 'within', and an actual gallery for those performed 'aloft'. And the importance and number of the former class of scenes has, in fact, been greatly exaggerated.

Applying modern usages to the semi-mediæval Elizabethan stage, Brandl (*Einleitung* to his revised edition of Schlegel's translation) and Brodmeier (Dissertation on the stage-conditions of the Elizabethan drama), put forward the theory of the 'alternative' scene; according to which the inner and the outer stage were used 'alternately', a recurring scene, with elaborate properties, being arranged in the former, and merely curtained off while intervening scenes were played on the outer, or main stage. But while this theory is plausible, as applied to some of Shakespeare's plays (e.g. the intricate transitions between rooms at Belmont and piazzas at Venice, in the *Merchant*), it breaks down in others (e.g. *Cymbeline*, II. 2, 3; *Richard II.*, I. 3, 4), and especially in many plays by other dramatists.

It is probable that the use of the 'inner stage' was in general restricted to two classes of scene: (1) where persons 'within' formed an integral though subordinate part of a scene of which the main issue was decided on the outer stage; as with the play-scene in *Hamlet*, or where Ferdinand and Miranda are discovered playing chess in *The Tempest*; (2) where a scene, though engaging the whole interest, is supposed to occur in an inner chamber. Thus Desdemona's chamber, Prospero's cell, Timon's cave, Lear's hovel, the Capulet's tomb.

§ 8. **The Balcony.**—There is less doubt about the use of the balcony or gallery. This was in fact an extremely favourite resource, and its existence in part explains the abundance of serenade, rope-ladder, and other upper-story scenes in Elizabethan drama.

From the balcony, or the window above it, Juliet discoursed with Romeo, and Sylvia with Proteus (*Two Gentlemen of Verona*, IV. 2); Richard III. addressed the London citizens, and the citizen of Angers the rival Kings. From the window the Pedant in *Taming of the Shrew*, V. 1, hails Petruchio and Grumio below; and Squire Tub, in Jonson's *Tale of a Tub*, I. 1, puts out his head in answer to the summons of Parson Hugh. But whole scenes were also, it is probable, occasionally enacted in this upper room. This is the most natural interpretation of the scenes in Juliet's chamber (IV. 3, 5). On the other hand, though the Senators in *Titus Andronicus*, I. 1, " go up into the 'Senate House'", it is probable that the debate later in the scene, on the main stage, is intended to be in the Senate-house by the convention described in § 6.

For further reference the following among others may be mentioned:—

G. F. Reynolds, *Some Principles of Elizabethan Staging* (*Modern Philology*, II. III.); A. Brandl, *Introduction* to his edition of Schlegel's translation of Shakespeare; V. E. Albright, *The Shakesperian Stage* (New York); W. Archer, *The Elizabethan Stage* (*Quarterly Review*, 1908); W. J. Lawrence, *The Elizabethan Playhouse and other Studies* (1st and 2nd series); D. Figgis, *Shakespeare, a study*.

From one or other of these, many of the above examples have been taken.

C. H. H.